Stolen Youth

M000205163

12/6/05
To my friend
Rose Jane Lepski

Stolen Youth

FIVE WOMEN'S SURVIVAL
IN THE HOLOCAUST

ISABELLE CHOKO ∞ FRANCES IRWIN
LOTTI KAHANA-AUFLEGER
MARGIT RAAB KALINA ∞ JANE LIPSKI

YAD VASHEM AND
THE HOLOCAUST SURVIVORS' MEMOIRS PROJECT
New York • Jerusalem

Copyright © 2005 by Isabelle Choko, Frances Irwin and Jane Lipski (each for her own memoir), and by Tova Bar-Touv for the memoir of her mother, Lotti Kahana-Aufleger, and Vera Kalina Levine for the memoir of her mother, Margit Raab Kalina.

All rights reserved, including the right to reproduce this book or portions thereof in any form.

This book is published by Yad Vashem, the Holocaust Martyrs' and Heroes' Remembrance Authority, c/o American Society for Yad Vashem, 500 Fifth Avenue, 42nd floor, New York, New York 10110-4299, and P.O.B. 3477, Jerusalem 91034, Israel

www.yadvashem.org

and

The Holocaust Survivors' Memoirs Project

in association with the World Federation of Bergen-Belsen Associations, Inc.

The Holocaust Survivors' Memoirs Project, an initiative of Nobel Peace Prize laureate Elie Wiesel, was launched through a generous grant from Random House Inc., New York, New York.

Cover photos and all other photographs courtesy of the authors or their families.

Printed in Jerusalem, Israel.

Series Editor
David Silberklang

Managing Editor
Daniella Zaidman-Mauer

Project Coordinator
Gloria Golan

Editorial Board
Menachem Z. Rosensaft, Chairman

Yehuda Bauer
Melvin Jules Bukiet
Sam E. Bloch
Nathan Cohen
Eva Fogelman
Alfred Gottschalk
Israel Gutman
Bella Gutterman
Hagit Lavsky

Dan Michman
David M. Posner
Romana Strochlitz Primus
Thane Rosenbaum
Jean Bloch Rosensaft
Robert Rozett
Avner Shalev
Elan Steinberg

CONTENTS

FOREWORD

By *David Silberklang*

Five young women who had their lives uprooted and thrown into disarray by World War II and the Holocaust tell their stories here. These women were all young—four were in their teens when the war broke out, and one was a young mother in her twenties. Three are from Poland, one from Czechoslovakia, and one from Romania. If we were to trace their paths during the Holocaust on a map, we would find that their paths crossed at certain times, although they did not know this. Three of the women who tell their personal stories in this book went through Auschwitz-Birkenau; two were liberated from Bergen-Belsen. Of these last two, one went to Sweden after the war to recuperate from her illnesses, whereas the other turned down such an opportunity at the last minute.

From the camp in which she was incarcerated in Transnistria, Lotti Kahana-Aufleger watched other Jewish prisoners being taken across the Bug River, where they were killed. Somewhat north of there, most of Margit Raab Kalina's friends and acquaintances were murdered in the death camp of Bełżec, not far from the same river. Kalina begins her story with her family's flight from her home in Czechoslovakia, whereas Jane Lipski's underground activities in Będzin took her into Slovakia.

In all the stories told in this book, family plays a central role, especially parent-child relationships. Isabelle Choko* devotedly stayed with her mother until her mother died in Bergen-Belsen, whereas Frances Irwin fled her town at her father's behest as the Jewish community was about to be liquidated. Yet, her parents and her family were always on her mind, especially her father's last

---

* I would like to take this opportunity to acknowledge the editorial assistance lent by Shana Penn in preparing the manuscripts by Isabelle Choko, Lotti Kahana-Aufleger and Jane Lipski.

words to her. Margit Raab Kalina lost both her parents early in the war, yet she was a keen observer of family throughout, as reflected in her observations regarding parents and children during roundups and deportations. Lotti Kahana-Aufleger's entire story revolves around her family—her little daughter, her husband, and her parents. Indeed, her determination to do everything to save her family helped to keep her going even during the most dangerous moments. Jane Lipski lost her family in Będzin, but found a new one in her husband, whom she met and married in Slovakia. Yet, he was made to disappear by the Soviet authorities before she gave birth to her son in a Soviet prison. She, too, was driven by the determination to do all she could to save her little boy.

These five stories provide insights into what it meant to be a young Jewish woman enduring the worst during the Holocaust. Certainly, other Jews regardless of gender shared much of what these women describe. At the same time, issues that were specifically feminine are addressed in these memoirs— whether the beginnings of awareness of young men in one memoir, or marrying and bearing a son in another. Reading personal accounts from five different female viewpoints in one book is a rare and enlightening experience. Each story enriches our reading of the others.

In their converging, crisscrossing, and then diverging paths during the Holocaust and after, all unbeknownst to the authors, the personal accounts presented in these pages afford us a window into youth, womanhood, family, parent-child relations, and more, during the Holocaust. All of this makes *Stolen Youth* a memorable reading experience.

M Y F I R S T L I F E

by *Isabelle Choko-Sztrauch-Galewska*
Translated from the French by Irene Rothenberg

DEDICATION

This memoir is dedicated to my husband, children, grandchildren, and great-grandchildren. I ask their forgiveness if ever there were times, in the years since the war ended, that I seemed hard, insensitive.

I also wish to dedicate my story to all the young people in the world. Let them be vigilant. May they never allow hate, cruelty or rejection of others to intrude upon their lives.

ACKNOWLEDGEMENTS

I would like to thank the Holocaust Survivors' Memoirs Project and Yad Vashem for having selected my memoir for publication, and Elie Wiesel for initiating the project. My thanks, as well, to Henry Bulawko, who encouraged me to write about my experiences. I am also deeply grateful to my daughter-in-law, Irene Cinq-Mars, for the revision of the text, and my beloved son Marc for his editorial guidance. And finally, a special thanks to Irene Rothenberg, my lifetime friend, for translating the manuscript into English.

TABLE OF CONTENTS

FOREWORD

All the events reported here are true. All the persons in this account really existed and were truly part of my life. Some of the people mentioned, most notably my school friends, are still alive. While I may have inadvertently modified the chronology and condensed some of the history, what I portray here are the experiences that branded me most personally.

These pages were written bit by bit over a period of forty years. Only recently did I succeed in putting them together. Usually, I kept the past triple-locked in my deepest subconscious, but there were times when I would be inundated by memories and discovered that I had to write them down in order to free myself of them. I realized I could no longer live with the past. Still, I empathize with those people who cannot fathom that the Holocaust took place. For even I—if I had not suffered constant pain in my right arm, scars in my ankles, a hole in my thigh—if I had not seen dear Sister Suzanne Spender years later in Paris—even I would have trouble believing in the reality of my own nightmarish experience.

CHAPTER 1

Childhood In Łódź, Poland: Winter, 1938-39

I wake up—outside, everything is white. Snow has covered all the rooftops and windowsills. I jump out of bed and run to my parents' room to snuggle in my mother's arms. My parents' bed, made of gold-embossed rosewood, seems enormous to me. Sunday is not like other days, because my parents and I can spend the entire day together without interruptions from their jobs or my school work. I savor the morning. Mother's gray eyes look at me with love. Her hands, with their long, delicate fingers, touch me tenderly. At last we have time to smile at one another and talk.

It is Sunday, and in the afternoon, we'll go to the cinema. During the week, everyone is busy. Mother and Father work in their *sklad apteczny*, a kind of drug store that handles both medications and beauty products. I go to school and also take private lessons, where I learn French, rhythmic dance and most recently, piano and swimming. On Sundays, we go to the movies to see Charlie Chaplin, Harold Lloyd or Shirley Temple. I am considered too young to see the films that feature my favorite actors, Clark Gable and Tyrone Power. Instead, I collect their photographs and especially their movie posters, which make me dream.

At the time, I was ten years old, and though my name was Izabela, everyone called me Izia. "And how is Izia?" my parents' friends would ask when we'd meet them on the way to the cinema. Concerned that we'd get to the movies on time, such chit-chat irritated me. "How is Izia?" They could see that I was well. And the question—"How is Mrs. Galewska?"—annoyed me to no end, because our surname was Sztrauch; Galewska was my mother's maiden name. I'd tug on my mother's sleeve until we'd finally move on.

After the movies we usually hailed a carriage to take us to visit Babcia, my maternal grandmother, who lived with her youngest son, Henryk, in an apartment that had a telephone. A telephone was an absolute rarity in Polish households of the day. She and Henryk lived on the other side of Piotrkowska Street, the main artery that ran through Łódź. The city was known for its large textile industry, and Uncle Henryk owned a company that dyed fabrics.

Babcia was accustomed to being cared for by her children, especially by my mother, the studious and entrepreneurial eldest daughter. Mother had earned her diplomas by attending night school in order to work during the day and contribute to the household income. Her earnings helped support the education of her two younger sisters, who completed their studies without the added burden of holding down a job as my mother had done.

Education was highly valued in my mother's family, but antisemitic policies in Poland in the 1930s made it difficult for Jewish students to receive more than a grammar school education. A quota system restricted the number of Jews in secondary schools and universities. Only the four or five top scholars in each discipline were granted admission to Polish universities, so it should be no surprise that the Jewish students excelled in all their chosen fields. Luckily, all three sisters were able to overcome these barriers and earn their diplomas. The family's pride in their accomplishments helped me understand why my mother saw to it that I receive an excellent education, at least before the war began before we lost all control of our destinies.

The three sisters each went into business for themselves and set up their own companies. There was one pharmacy and two *składy apteczne*. The majority of their customers were women. My mother and her sisters christened all three companies with their maiden name, Galewska. That decision was an example of good marketing, ahead of its time, because the name and the three businesses became very well known in Łódź.

On Sundays in the late afternoon, most of the rest of the family would join us at Babcia's for tea and cookies—Uncle Leon, his wife Zosia, his son Mietek, Aunt Bela, her husband Zygmunt Friede, his daughter Danusia, bachelor Uncle Henry, and Aunt Pola and her husband Natas Kowalew, who occasionally left their baby son, Marek, at home. At the end of the meal, Babcia always served a kind of dry cookie that she had baked, but I would only eat the raisins, which I liked to dig out of the middle of each cookie. As the oldest grandchild on my mother's side, I was usually the center of attention. After we ate, the adults would ask me to recite a poem or dance, and I enjoyed performing for them, even if I may have played the little clown.

I loved fruit and especially chocolate. Though Mother always placed a high value on nutritious food and instructed the nanny to provide me a healthy, diverse diet, it was Father who supervised my departure to school each day—he was more of a morning person than Mother, who worked late nights—and he usually served me a delicious if not exactly balanced breakfast of warm milk, a piece of chocolate, and an orange, which was a real luxury in Poland. In the afternoons I was to have a snack and used to buy myself a seven-layer, chocolate torte cake called a Napoleonka, which was a kind of "work of art". But in general, I did not like sweets and would have preferred sausages and cold cuts from "Dyszkin," a local food specialty store, where the whole family used to shop.

As a general rule, my parents did not like me to visit them at the pharmacy. But I loved to go and more than once I forced my way inside. The smells from the pharmaceutical and beauty products filled my nostrils. The colorful glass jars and their fancy labels—"Guerlain", "Bourgeois", "Soir de Paris", "Bébé Cadum", a mysterious "Olla gum"—delighted me. My uncle Leon worked at the pharmacy as my mother's partner. I remember asking why he was a partner and the only one representing his family when both my parents worked in the business. Why didn't his wife work there too? Why did she instead stay at home with her son, while I was left alone? No one ever gave me an answer. I have to admit that the question did not really bother me much.

I adored the private school I attended. This may sound silly, but I was always happy to see my teachers and classmates. Most of the students were Jewish, though it was not a religious school. It was founded in the early 1930s by two young women, Mrs. Seligman and Mrs. Lebenhaft. Apparently, there was a third woman, too—a Mrs. Rusakowa, whom I do not remember. The school was simply named "Nasza Szkola" (Our School), but there was nothing simple about its avant garde vision and scholastic goals. The school's curriculum and philosophy were innovative and rigorous. It offered classes in history and religion, civic life, published a school newspaper and was coeducational, which was exceptional for the times. In the semester before the war broke out, there was talk of introducing sex education into the curriculum. The school also established a community service program that enabled students to help the needy. Every day, we were obliged to bring a piece of buttered bread to school to give to children from poverty-stricken families. Any student who forgot to bring their portion would be sent home. Through this program, I had my first contact with poor children and it was unnerving. As an only child from a well-to-do family, I could not comprehend that some children suffered from material want or that not all children were as coddled as I.

I had round cheeks, the color of peaches. It seemed that people liked to pinch them. In fact, some people gave in to this urge, but I did not appreciate the gesture, and the expression on my face did not encourage them to start again. Sometimes I'd hear people say, "She'll be pretty."

For me, the four years of school were very happy ones. We children used to meet one another after class. We also met the teachers after school and often spent our vacations together. Miss Schechter, all blonde and full of fun, was our physical education teacher, and Miss Czernianka, our homeroom teacher, was responsible for our class. I was in great shape, physically and morally. All around me, everything was an excuse for a party. I was invited to thirty birthday parties a year, and that is just from my schoolmates. Almost all the children fit in with the whole class. I was seven years old when my parents enrolled me. That was the mandatory age to enter the "big school."

"Nasza Szkola" would have lived up to any industrial country's educational standards, even though the standard of living in Poland was generally much lower than that of France. Nearly all the students were avid readers, which meant the bookstore next-door made a fortune from us, because books were the preferred gifts for birthdays and other holidays. I had long put aside my last doll, Shirley Temple, in exchange for books like *Uncle Tom's Cabin*. I cried and cried when I learned that slavery had really existed. I could not understand how human beings could harm other human beings like that. Rarely would you find me without a book in hand. I even kept an illustrated French dictionary on my night table. On my tenth birthday, Mother and Father gave me a pink lacquered desk and promised me a matching bookcase for my growing personal library. Alas! I never got a pink bookcase.

The young woman who took care of me frequently confided in me about her worries and her heartaches. I'd advise her and console her. This may sound funny considering my lack of experience, but she never laughed; she listened attentively to me.

My dressmaker lived in the courtyard of our apartment building. The owners of a cow that gave milk to several families also lived in the courtyard. I had a big problem. My parents would not let me play in the courtyard. I did not have much spare time, but occasionally, it would have been great fun to play there with the other children.

My mother was an anxious woman, especially with respect to me. On the rare occasions that I fell ill—maybe three or four times in ten years—she'd cry by my bedside and call in our doctor, who would invariably reassure her, "You didn't need to ask me to come. You cared perfectly for your daughter." I'd lay comfortably nestled in my bed, drinking tea and reading the French dictionary, which was my favorite bedside companion.

My mother worried that she and Father were relatively old to be the parents of a ten-year-old; this caused my mother considerable anxiety. She feared that she and Father might not live long enough to support my future studies. I once overheard them discuss a British insurance company, which had a branch in Łódź, and I was sure they had taken out a policy for me. I was to collect the money from the policy either once I became of age or in order to further my studies. But after the Nazis occupied the country, all such documents quickly "flew away."

I spent that last, innocent winter with several of my classmates skiing in Rabka, a well-known Polish winter sport resort. Mrs. Seligson, whom I helped, was very satisfied with my participation and decided that soon I would be "*do tanca i do rozanca*" (good for dancing and marrying). One was my friend Marysia, a laryngologist's daughter who lived in my building. We used to walk together to school because she was smaller and less independent than me. She always gave me her complete support in case, for example, there was a vote at school. Marysia sat with me in the classroom's back row, where the best students were placed in order to leave room in the front for those who might be slow learners and need more attention. Irka, Jozio or Romek also sat in the back with us. In the front you'd always find Rysio, the eternal hooligan and another Marysia, who never stopped fooling around.

Irka was the daughter of a very well known physician. She and I always competed for first place. Her slenderness matched her lively and quick spirit, whereas my roundness matched my slower thinking. Always busy with thirty-six other things, I had an annoying habit of doing my homework on the way to school. Effortless ease made me careless. So frequently I left the first place awards to Irka. After school, Irka's governess, "Fraulein", used to take us to Narutowicza Park. Irka did not like to eat; no food gave her pleasure. I'll never forget the trouble she had swallowing a banana. My friend, the girl with brunette hair and black eyes that gleamed like hazelnuts, tall, thin and so quick, took hours to swallow a mouthful of banana.

The end of the school year approached. Every year we organized a show. As usual, we prepared a show. Irka and I, dressed in tuxedos, high hats, patent leather shoes, and canes in hand, were to dance the Lambert Walk. I had a lot of experience dancing. In addition to the rhythmic dance lessons, my youngest uncle Natas taught me the waltz when I was three. Irka and I prepared our number to perfection. Of course, the parents were all delighted to admire their children. That year, the show closed after rehearsals because the war had started.

Of the approximately forty children in my class, only six survived the war—three girls and three boys. That was a huge percentage if you consider that the majority of Polish Jews died. Marysia was one of them. For the entire duration of the war, from 1939 to 1945, she and her parents remained in Łódź, were among 600 people in charge of cleaning up the ghetto and then among approximately 1,000 who hid until the Soviets arrived in January 1945. Romek, Jozio and Irka also survived. Romek and Jozio were both separated from their mothers and deported, but each managed to survive the war. Irka and her parents were saved by Chiune Sugihara, the famous Japanese consul general in Kaunas, Lithuania who, in the summer of 1940, arranged exit visas for hundreds of Jewish families to immigrate to Japan. The fifth of my surviving classmates was Marjan, who fled to Russia with his parents, where they survived despite extremely adverse conditions. The sixth survivor was me.

Back in Łódź after my skiing holiday in Rabka, I resumed my normal routine.

Mother spent time with me whenever she could. On some afternoons, she'd take me to the ice skating rink, her feet freezing while she waited for me. Unfortunately, she did not know how to skate. My great joy was to dash around on the ice, feeling the wind that pinched my cheeks and clouded my eyes with tears. The speed was pure rapture.

Shortly after I returned to Łódź that winter, before the war broke out, I learned that my younger cousin, Danusia, who had reddish blond hair and freckles, would be coming to live in our house for a few days. This news did not delight me, mainly because it meant that I would have to give her my bed. My family took the rules of hospitality very seriously. Guests were always given a warm welcome and absolute priority over the hosts' comfort. The Easter holidays were approaching, a time when my father's whole family usually came together—Babcia II (my paternal grandmother), Aunt Frania, Aunt Eva, her husband, and Aunt Mania and her husband. Two uncles were absent that year—Zygmunt, who lived in Paris, and Mietek, who lived in Warsaw. Aunt Frania invited us all to a traditional meal.

Babcia II, who had lived in Łódź for twenty years, owned a small photography studio where she taught me to retouch photographs. I learned how to create contrasts and sharpness of line. That was my first artistic activity. She lived alone after the death of my *dziadek* (grandfather). He had died after he was forced to leave the family estate in the area of Kielce near Radom. It was toward the end of World War I, 1917 or 1918. My grandfather had been renowned in the region for his goodness and generosity. I knew him only from his portrait. His face spoke to me; his expression and his eyes were so eloquent. The estate had been requisitioned by the Cossacks toward the end of the First World War. In the photographs my father showed me, it seemed very large. There were horse stables, numerous buildings, about forty dogs, a carriage and wheat fields that stretched far and wide. Father told me stories such as when he fell from a horse, and how much his aunts loved the dogs. Every year an enormous feast was held at harvest time. The most beautiful girl was chosen who, coifed in a crown of flowers, walked at the head of the procession. Though my father's birth is registered in the town of Szydlow, not far from the estate, he and his brothers and sisters rarely left the property.

They were even tutored privately at home. His family had long lived on this property.

When I was growing up, we did not spend much time with Father's family, mainly because Mother was more interested in her own family. Later, during the war, she would confide that she regretted not being sufficiently attentive to his family.

My father was a gentle man, with light blue eyes and dark brown hair. Until I was eight years old, I did not know that he had long suffered from an illness related to his nervous system. In 1937, he took advantage of special conditions connected with the International Exposition in Paris to travel there to consult a specialist named Dr. Levastine. I wanted to go with him but my parents would not let me go. It was one of only two times that I met with a categorical refusal from my mother and father, who usually acceded to all my needs. After Father's visit, I decided that one day I wanted to help him and others whose chronic illnesses were difficult to heal. I thought about becoming a physician like my friend Marysia's father. But I changed my mind when I remembered that his profession constantly called him away from his family and I knew I did not want those kinds of interruptions. Instead I got the idea to become a researcher in medical chemistry and develop remedies for illnesses. This ambition emerged after I had decided to become a dancer.

Father, who was very attached to family and friends, adored me. Only once did I experience the limits of his patience. I must have been a terrible nuisance because he took off his belt and shook it at me. On the day that this scene occurred, the terrible feelings were quickly dissipated by the joyful news that my Uncle Henryk had become engaged to marry. A confirmed bachelor, he had met a young, charming, blonde woman and would soon put an end to his celibacy, as our family members delightedly remarked at the time. The wedding ceremony was to be held in beautiful Krakow, the ancient royal city and the country's medieval capital. Finally I was given a chance to travel. I was thrilled to be invited to the wedding and remember most vividly the grand hotel in which we stayed. It made a great impression on me.

On our arrival, the hotel's huge lobby was crowded with people. A group of French men and women were among the hotel guests. Mother encouraged me to listen to their conversations to see how well I could understand them. When I realized that the only words I could comprehend were "thank you, good morning, and goodbye" I felt terribly ashamed. I did not wish to disappoint my parents, who had been investing in a career or graduate studies in France for their young daughter. Suddenly the future seemed ominous. I feared I would never fulfill my parents' dream for me. By the time I did make their dream a reality, however, they had long been gone, victims of Nazi Germany's Final Solution.

After the Easter gathering, my busy days expanded to include after-school lessons in piano, swimming and rhythmic dance. Mother would take me to the swimming pool two evenings each week. We had to go by train because the pool was outside the city. Although the water frightened me a bit, I soon gained confidence, thanks to my teacher's instruction.

Music lessons were quite a different story. I chose to study the piano after my attempts to play the violin proved disastrous. For even though I was drawn to the violin and its emotional range, it was easier to master the piano. My ear was keen but my singing was off-key. Piano lessons lasted only one year.

The dance class, which I attended twice a week, conditioned my body. It was pleasurable to feel my physical self growing gracefully and my step becoming supple. After class, my friends and I would stand at the window and watch a group of women practice their routines. We'd roar with laughter at how clumsy they appeared, especially in contrast to us. It was an unforgettable spectacle.

I was already being tutored in French by "Mademoiselle," the daughter of a Russian general. "Mademoiselle," who claimed to have spoken French since her early childhood, had allure. She wore her white hair curled tightly with a black hat perched on top of her head. She always wrapped herself in a gray knit shawl, which she'd roll and unroll incessantly. A huge safety pin held the ensemble together, and a black umbrella completed the dramatic picture. "Why do you carry an umbrella everyday?" I used to ask her. "Because it might rain," she'd reply without hesitation. That was certainly indisputable. Then the lesson would begin, and if my homework was done well, we'd end the session with a game of "66," a popular card game in France, according to "Mademoiselle." By the time I moved to France, however, I never met a single person who had heard of the card game.

After "Mademoiselle" left, I used to wait for the moment when my mother would sit down at her dressing table to "freshen up" before my father's return from work. She'd pat a bit of powder and "Guerlain" perfume on her nape. The toiletries rested in a lovely wooden box, painted with garlands and figurines. For the most part, Mother spent little time in front of the mirror. She wore her brown hair in a short, simple bob, and her only real vanity lay in wearing a whalebone corset, which I sometimes helped her to lace. It seemed to be so much work and slavery, just to affect a tiny waist that she did not really have.

Mother actually showed far more interest in my appearance than in her own. She taught me to apply Nivea cream to my face every day to protect my complexion, and she arranged for a dressmaker to sew my clothes according to the latest fashion. Despite the indulgences, I still had responsibilities. I had to diligently pursue my studies and extra-curricular activities, help out in the kitchen and make my bed on weekends. I was also expected to keep my commitments, keep my word and always tell the truth. And I was to practice modesty, because I'd been taught that it was for others to notice my good qualities. This would sometimes work against me in my future professional life, because I am not sure that anyone would have noticed my undisputable capabilities, had I not also been a pleasant looking woman.

Moral and spiritual values clearly dominated my family's thinking more than emphasis on material matters like physical appearance. Our celebrated stars were scholars, scientists, writers, and musicians; but not movie stars, who we regarded as frivolous phoneys.

I can still recall the day that a woman enrolled her daughter in "Our School." The new student was older than the rest of us and quite different from all the other students, for she was almost entirely deaf and dumb. She was able to read lips but could only mouth indistinct sounds. Some children made horrible fun of her. Before this circle grew bigger, I intervened by asking the teacher if the new student could sit next to me in class. We became friends and learned to communicate. I am sorry to say I don't recall her name. It remains in the mists. However, her smile, though a bit twisted, delighted me, and I remember it vividly.

One evening, the doorbell rang and, to my surprise, standing in our doorway was my friend and her mother, who presented me with a pot of flowers. I was so moved by the gesture and their words of appreciation of my friendship that I did not know where to hide. My sensitivity to her was genuine and natural. After all, my parents and teachers had taught me to be caring and considerate of others. They taught me that there is good in every human being and that virtue and sincerity will always be rewarded. The black period through which I lived subsequently led me to reconsider whether virtue is always rewarded. In order to survive in spite of every obstacle and every evil, I had to find an explanation for why this evil was happening. The conditions of the war and genocide were so unique that men had forgotten the fundamental humanity of life, and still, life went on—with evil and humanity, both.

It was not until summer vacation in 1939 that I began to sense a bizarre change in the atmosphere in Łódź.[1] Before the war, I had heard that antisemitism was on the rise in our city, partly as a result of spreading Nazi propaganda. I knew my origins were Jewish. My family occasionally visited the local synagogue, lit the Sabbath candles every Friday evening, and ate traditional meals during Jewish holidays. On the whole, however, we led assimilated lives and the differences between Jews and Catholics completely escaped me. Although I knew that Jews went to synagogue and Catholics to church, we all learned the same Polish language, history, and literature at school. To me, the only obvious difference, other than the separate places of worship, was in language options. Some Jews spoke Yiddish, the everyday language, and Hebrew, the language of prayer. My parents spoke Yiddish whenever they wanted to keep a secret from me—and it sounded Greek to me. Otherwise, my family spoke Polish. Everyone I knew spoke Polish, Jews and non-Jews alike.

Despite the uneasy changes underfoot, I played with my friends and even learned to flirt with boys. All of us girls and boys used to meet at Lucynka's home, where we exchanged our first secret glances and first kisses in the shelter of the big living room sofa. That summer of '39, I went to sleep-away summer

---

1   The city had a large Jewish population — in fact, the second largest Jewish community in Europe, second to Warsaw. Prior to World War II approximately 233,000 Jews lived there, making up one-third of its entire urban population. Jewish settlement dated back to the 18th century. By the early 20th century, the city had become a major industrial center—known as the "Manchester of Poland"—and Jews were prominently involved as textile workers, industrialists, merchants, tradesmen and retailers. In addition, Łódź Jews were proud of their cultural life. The famous pianist Arthur Rubinstein was born there, as were the poets Julian Tuwim, Itzhak Katzenelson and David Frischman. A diverse educational network supported Orthodox and Reformed religious schools, a Yiddish school and a Jewish school for girls.

camp as usual. Every year about forty children gathered in Kolumna, a small village near Łódź, for fun and recreation. I always came with a large suitcase filled with clothing because Mother had decided that I should have the wardrobe of a princess at my disposal. This included one green suit with a pink collar and assorted hats, a blue dress trimmed with velvet ribbons, and so forth. My parents spent too much money on me. I was having a wonderful time that year. I loved to play in the fields of sunflowers that spread out like a yellow carpet as far as the eye could see. I was, of course, oblivious to the fact that this would be the last time I'd be able to roam carefree and happily in sun-drenched fields.

It was the end of August, while waiting in the boarding house of the summer camp for my parents to pick me up, that I first heard people say, "There's going to be a war." I recalled my mother's stories of the war of 1914-1918. She had gone to school during those years accompanied by the whistle of bullets. Her family never had much to eat other than potatoes. Recalling my mother's childhood experience of war, I began to worry.

When my parents finally arrived at the summer camp, they seemed terribly disturbed and preoccupied beyond recognition. Accustomed to being the center of their attention, I was dumbfounded that they showed no joy at seeing me. On the train to Łódź, my mother whispered, "We shouldn't unpack the suitcases." But in order to emigrate, one needed money and a visa, and the will to abandon Babcia and the family. So we stayed. All around us everything had changed. Daily radio reports told of the impending war. We were instructed to carry gas masks and put together air raid shelters. Everywhere, people were talking about the war, and preparing for it. We lived each day in a frenzy, preparing for the imminent assault. We made "gas masks" out of rectangles of gauze and sewed cloth attachments that could be secured over one's mouth and nose. I doubt these homemade masks could have saved us in the event of a real toxic gas attack.

One night my parents woke me hastily, helped me get dressed, grabbed two suitcases they had prepared in advance, and held my hand as they led me down to the street. We encountered indescribable chaos. Throngs of men, women and children were rushing in the same direction. "The Germans are coming," I heard my parents say. News had spread quickly through the community that able-bodied men should escape to the Soviet Union, or else, they'd be sent to labor camps in Germany. We did not understand until much later that this rumor was actually part of a plan by the Germans to trick the men into journeying on the eastward-bound roads. Those roads were subsequently blown up. The Germans had a Machiavellian plan quickly to eliminate the potential for male-organized resistance. Their follow-up plan was to weaken the population through hard physical labor, humiliation, and cruelty. At the same time, they spread propaganda to reassure the persecuted Jewish population that we'd survive and be safe if we worked and obeyed orders. These developments unfolded gradually over time.

My parents wanted to warn the rest of the family. We set out for Aunt Bela's home first, struggling against the current of fleeing, frightened people. Because her house belonged to *Volksdeutschen* (Poles of German origin) in a non-Jewish neighborhood, the commotion had passed by her neighborhood and her whole family. As a matter of fact, they were still sleeping peacefully when we arrived to alert them. Bela's husband Zygmunt immediately set out on the road toward Russia. He would be the only member of his family to survive. My father was too ill to consider fleeing. Instead, he, my mother, Aunt Bela, her daughter Danusia and I all hurried to Babcia's house, where the family held a long meeting and concluded that Aunt Pola's husband, Natas Kowalew, should also leave, but that Babcia and the rest of us would stay put.

CHAPTER 2

War And Defeat

N azi Germany invaded Poland on September 1 and its armies marched into Łódź a week later. When the bombings began, everybody was supposed to go down to the shelters, but Mother decreed that we would be just as safe staying at home. When the planes flew overhead, she instructed us to lie down next to the dining room wall, which she said would be adequate protection. She was right—the raids did not last long, and the city did not suffer much damage.

After a few days, we were informed that the Germans were entering Łódź. I considered taking a place at the window to watch the bullets fly, but the battle was already over. Poland had capitulated by the end of September. There were many local sympathizers who welcomed the Germans with smiles and flowers.

For me, the darkest pages of my life will now be inscribed. The German authorities drove many Jews out of Łódź to other parts of its occupied territories.[2] Without wasting time, the Germans began to enforce the antisemitic laws, putting prohibitions on travel, public transportation and access to all aspects of public life. We were robbed of our citizenship. No formal registration was necessary because all Jews in Poland were automatically registered with the

---

2   Between September and May of the next year, an estimated 70,000 Jews had left our city.

entry "Religion: Jewish". The wearing of two stars became compulsory, one in the front and one on the back. That way, even from the back you could recognize a Jew. The requisition of Jewish enterprises, and the unimpeded confiscation of private property belonging to Jews, became an everyday occurrence. Jews were forbidden to cross Piotrkowska Street, the main artery dividing the city. In this way Jewish families, everybody actually, found themselves separated, isolated, and without any possible communication with the outside world. The infernal machine to crush the Jews was set in motion.

During one of the first days of the war, my mother asked Pani Mania (Mrs. Mania), a Catholic who had worked in our pharmacy for many years, to take me across Piotrkowska Street to visit Babcia. Despite Mrs. Mania's pleading, I refused to remove my stars for this trip, so she walked a little ahead of me. Before I had taken two steps on Piotrkowska Street, a German soldier who had been directing traffic called out, "Wo gehst du?" (Where are you going?) Having already begun to learn German, I understood him perfectly well, but I stood as if paralyzed. Mrs. Mania scurried ahead, and I lost sight of her. "Komm mit mir" (Come with me), the soldier ordered. He seemed poised to approach me, but I just stood there staring at him, dumb and immobile. Finally, worn down, he shouted, "Gehst weg" (Go away), and I dashed for home. That day, I must have beaten the 400-meter record. I arrived at home completely out of breath and told my misfortune. Thereafter, my mother never again entrusted me to anyone else's care.

My parents tried to maintain a semblance of normal life. I resumed my extra-curricular activities, including French lessons, though they did not last long. One morning, loud knocks shook our front door during a French lesson. Mademoiselle turned green and hastily gathered up her books and notebooks, but I stopped her, having decided to continue the lesson. Two men wearing civilian clothes burst into the room. Hardly looking at us, they calmly searched the apartment for items of interest to them, then left with their arms full of our belongings. They did not get their hands on my chocolate bar, which was in my backpack, so I felt I now knew where to tell my mother to hide her valuables before the next raid occurred. This incident had terrified Mademoiselle and put an end to my French lessons.

One afternoon my parents took me to the pharmacy, where I looked on in astonishment as Mother, with tears in her eyes, handed the store keys to two men I had never seen before. A few words were exchanged, and then we turned and left the pharmacy behind forever. My mother and father squeezed my hands hard as we walked home in total silence. The fruit of over twenty years' labor had been relinquished to strangers who had only to hold out their hands for the keys to a Jewish business. That business was my mother's creation, a part of her being. She was utterly despondent but had little time to lament. After a second German raid of our apartment, the door of my parents' bedroom was officially sealed. Apparently, the beautiful rosewood replicas of a bedroom set in Wawel Castle in Krakow had appealed to the Germans, so my parents had to put a new bed in the living room. No matter, for in February of 1940, a new law ordered all Jews to leave their homes and move into a ghetto.

CHAPTER 3

Diamonds For Bread: The Łódź Ghetto

The Łódź ghetto was the first major ghetto that the Germans established in Poland. About 200,000 people were forced to live there. They came from Łódź or were deported there from other parts of the country. The ghetto was set up in Baluty, the most miserable, shabby quarter on the city's outskirts that flanked a cemetery. Surely, the antisemites were delighted that the Jews had been assigned to such a decrepit place, as if it was predestined for us. The Catholic Poles were also badly treated, subject to deprivations, and destined for forced labor.

In those days, the great majority of Catholic Poles not only did not help the Jews, but also denounced them and turned them in to the Germans. Even the Jews who succeeded in hiding or escaping were usually recaptured as a result of denunciations. They were often denounced by people who had been their friends, neighbors, customers or doctors. The betrayals were horrible. The difference with other countries is striking. Some like Denmark refused to compile lists of Jews. In others like France, despite the Vichy government, many people often helped Jews. Only Poland had the unhappy privilege to collaborate so intensively with the Germans to exterminate the Jews. Almost nowhere did survivors account for such a small percentage of the former community. Before the war I always felt Polish. I identified with my nation. Yes, I had dreams of one day going to France, but my country was Poland. Today, I would not say as much. Poland is just the country of my firstbirth.

The borders of the ghetto were demarcated by barbed wire. Armed soldiers with dogs were positioned at each guard post. Each resident was allotted approximately five square meters of habitable space. Seeking the best possible situation under the terrible new circumstances, my mother found a house at 22 Zawisza Street, and the whole family along with several friends moved into it. Babcia, Aunt Bela, Danusia, Aunt Pola and her two-year-old son Marek settled together in one large room. In the time to come, I would often take care of Marek. My father, my mother and I moved into a room no more than fifteen square meters that faced north and was always cold and dark. The only consolation was that it looked out onto a garden. There was one bed for my parents and another smaller bed for me, as well as a cupboard, a table, a coal stove and a board that supported a burner, all of which we had loaded onto a cart and transported to the ghetto.

The rest of our possessions stayed behind in our apartment: the sofa, the sideboard, tables and chairs, even my cherished pink desk. My parents' beautiful bedroom, which had remained sealed, was never mentioned again. The only consolation was that there would not have been room for more furniture in our pathetic hovel. I forgot to mention that in the big cupboard next to my bed, Mother stored items she had been able to take home before the pharmacy was confiscated. What an irony! We did not have the basic necessities, but we had beauty products. Of course, the flasks and bottles were earmarked for barter in exchange for food and coal, but it turned out that nobody wanted the shampoo. I washed my hair with French shampoo during my four years in the ghetto and it stayed beautiful and shining. Bartering was a crucial survival skill in the ghetto. I knew that there were women who bartered their diamonds for bread. Depending on its size, a diamond was worth three, five, ten loaves of bread. Today, whenever I see a diamond, I envision superimposed above it a large farm bowl dusted with white flour. A diamond, beautiful as it may be, will never be worth more than a loaf of bread in my eyes.

Before we left our old apartment for good, two persons came to see my parents. Pani Mania, to whom my Mother entrusted many things and in particular my Shirley Temple doll. Then came a gentleman in peasant clothing, whose identity I do not recall. He carried away crystal pieces, various other precious objects as well as my Mother's diamond. Mother thought that after the war, we'd be able to retrieve these things, sell them and start a new life. But that was a foolish hope. I would never see any of them again. Oh, excuse me—in 1949, Mrs. Mania returned one item to me—not the Shirley Temple doll that my husband had vigorously insisted on and that I had asked for, but rather a little heart-shaped pendant of no monetary value that held photographs of my parents. That was all I ever got back, though I must confess that I made no special effort to recover the other objects. After the living people had been taken away from me, somehow, the things…

Life in the Litzmannstadt (Łódź) ghetto began to organize itself. The Germans established a *Judenrat*, "Jewish Council," to carry out its orders. They named Chaim Rumkowski, "der Älteste der Juden" (the eldest of the Jews), as *Judenrat* president. At the time, I strongly criticized this man, because at age 64 he married a young woman, and I thought it was an indecent act, given our collective circumstances. What's more, Rumkowski and his people were part of an elite circle of privileged Jews who seemed to lack nothing. What an absurdity that inside the ghetto, there were people who not only had heat and enough food to satisfy their hunger, but could even claim champagne and silk stockings. Their privilege revolted me. However, I later learned that Mr. Rumkowski was not the worst of the leaders who enjoyed similar circumstances. He and his entourage did manage to set up a hospital, a school, a library and a concert hall.[3]

The ghetto also maintained a prison, court system, and police force, which was probably useful, though the police were chosen from among the biggest and usually illiterate bullies. Still, they seemed to enforce a rudimentary order. At the end, it was they who were designated to clean out the ghetto. Several families were to accompany them, for instance those of some physicians. About 200 persons in all, I think. They actually stayed behind and some of them got rich by picking up anything of value after all the inhabitants of the ghetto left. Hidden afterward, they managed to be there when the Soviet Red Army arrived and liberated them.

---

3   The *Judenrat* also organized numerous departments. The health department, though it lacked the needed resources to control the spread of disease and starvation, set up public kitchens in factories and schools to feed workers and students. In the beginning, an agriculture department designated garden plots in residential neighborhoods. An education department oversaw 45 primary religious and secular schools, two high schools and a vocational school. Yeshivas were clandestinely established, as were an orphanage and a summer camp for youth.

After we arrived, my mother immediately enrolled me in the ghetto school. My father continued to work every day at demanding physical labor, despite the extreme fatigue caused by his illness and exacerbated by worry and deprivation. Mother, through her connections, found a job in a food store. Although food products were very strictly rationed, the employees of these stores enjoyed certain advantages, and from time to time a jar of jam, some flour or potatoes would be distributed. Those were life-saving treasures, since our usual rations barely kept us alive.

In the ghetto, I learned how to cook—rather uniquely, I admit. To make a cake, simply combine a bowl of coffee grounds (*Ersatz*, of course) with a soup spoon each of flour and sugar and form the resulting mixture into pancakes to be fried with a bit of fat, if it's available. Nobody ever asked me to cook these recipies after war was over. The main meal often consisted exclusively of potato pancakes; meat or fish appeared at our table only rarely. When we had no more potatoes, we grilled potato peels in a frying pan. We hardly ever ate whole potatoes, because you get more volume when you grate them and mix them with a bit of flour. Because real bread was rare, my biggest treat, even today, remains a piece of bread.

On April 30, 1940, the gates of the ghetto were shut, sentry boxes erected, and barbed wire surrounded us. We were locked in. Nobody could leave or enter without authorization. Our household plotted how to cope with the newest restrictions. We provided one another with emotional support, often by socializing together in the bigger of our two rooms in the evenings. Two talented boys lived with us—one a mimic, who made us laugh, and the other an excellent singer, whose music uplifted our spirits. Although generally we had no contact with the outside world and rarely heard any news, occasionally, one of these boys would bring us information. It was rumored that a sender-receiver post was hidden somewhere in our building, but I did not know where, which, for security reasons, was probably for the best. Possession of such a device was punishable by death.

CHAPTER 4

The Awakening Of Adolescence

I had to go back to school, but this time it was not to my beloved "Our School". At the ghetto school we had to study the German language. I quickly discovered that I was allergic to this subject and, as a result, received my first poor grades. School, in general, interested me less and less. Father's illness, our deprivations, daily survival and unpredictable events of all kinds distracted me from my studies. Only the Hebrew lessons sparked my interest. I loved learning the ancient language and feeling its links to Jewish history. Learning Hebrew also strengthened my defenses against the contempt I encountered from other Jews because I did not speak Yiddish. For example, if I was standing in line in front of a food store and someone would ask me a question in Yiddish that I could not understand, the level of disapproval bordered on insult—"What a little princess," they seemed to imply, "she only speaks Polish." In turn, I'd respond disdainfully, "You can't speak Hebrew, and I can, and that's the first language of the Jews." Still, I should have known Yiddish, which has its own irreplaceable history, literature and expressions, some of which is now part of everyday conversation in New York City. I have since learned the basics of that language to the point that I cannot be cheated.

At the time, my reticence to study Yiddish was partly related to the fact that it resembled German, which was the detested subject in my daily studies. Fortunately, the German taught at school bore little resemblance to the vulgar German that the occupying soldiers spoke. In school, we learned Goethe's poem

"Röslein, röslein, röslein rot, röslein auf der Heiden" ("Little rose, little rose, little red rose in the fields"). Goethe's beautiful verses etched themselves deeply into my memory. Rereading that poem today, I think I understand why—because it's about a budding rose that a bad boy broke, and I could have been comparing my life to that rose. The soldiers' German, in contrast, seemed to consist of "Schnell, schnell!" (Quick, quick!) and "Los verfluchte Jude!" (Get out, you damned Jew!). Throughout the war I only heard German expressions meant to hurry us along or to insult us.

Despite the hardships of daily life, I continued to see my friends, and I even fell in love with a young man who looked like a god. His blue eyes sparkled like the sea on a sunlit day. Muscular though not tall, his blond, angelic looks made all the women, young and old, swoon. I was at an age when I had only begun to flirt with boys, and I was devastated when he made it clear that he preferred tall, blond Sarenka, whose plumpness evoked a life of privilege. I was tall and thin, with an angular face and big blue eyes that usually expressed hope or sadness or anguish. How could I rival a gay and laughing young girl? In any case, in our circle we had decided that we must wait until we were eighteen before having a real lover, though eventually we revised that idea, because we realized we might never reach eighteen.

Time passed. My mother took me to concerts in the ghetto to distract if not console me. I remember hearing a real orchestra perform beautiful classical music and thinking about the absurdity of our situation. I also borrowed a lot of books from the library and used them to transport myself into a world that might be sad at times but was never as tragic as my daily life.

One day, a boy older than me with brown hair and gray eyes joined our class. He kicked up a terrible fuss and kept yelling, "I'm not Jewish, I don't want to stay here, I'm German!" This boy had been sent to the ghetto after it was discovered that his grandmother was Jewish. Considering the songs and military marches he taught us, it seemed quite plausible that he was not only German but a member of the "Hitler Jugend" (Hitler Youth), though I had no way to verify this. Soon after his arrival, other newcomers appeared in the ghetto. After the Germans attacked the Soviet Union on June 22, 1941, all Soviet citizens were considered to be enemies, and local Jews of Russian nationality were interned in the ghetto, too.

A Russian woman named Anka came to live in our house with her son, Fredek, and her daughter, Lusia, aged eighteen and twenty-one respectively. As soon as my mother learned that Fredek spoke French, he acquired me as a pupil, and Mother once again nursed her old dream that I would continue my studies in Paris. I would finally get there in 1946 but only after enduring many, many hardships. Just then, the Germans noticed that the ghetto children were going to school and in one fell swoop, shut down the classrooms. Children, including me, now had to work. Concerts were also banned. The library could offer only certain works considered neither "decadent" nor hostile to Naziism.

As always, Mother reconnoitered. I began working in a hat factory, where I plaited straw hats. Because Łódź had been a key industrial center before the war, the ghetto became a major work site with around 70 factories that contributed significantly to war production.[4] We Jewish residents were used as forced labor to produce textiles like uniforms for the German army. At the hat factory, I was paid by the piece and became adept. Later I joined a group of hat makers who taught me to form hats. We were paid in what was called "monkey money" or Litzmannstadt (Łódź) marks. This kind of money circulated only inside the ghetto and we could not buy much with it. After I gained more experience, I was promoted to take charge of distributing supplies, such as needles and threads, fabric, and sewing machines, from the factory supply store to the hatmakers. In addition to that job, I took care of my little cousin, Marek, a beautiful little blond boy who laughed all the time and whom I loved very much. His mother, Aunt Pola, was able to bring us cod liver oil from a pharmacy where she worked. It tasted awful, but apparently contained vitamins that we needed badly. My 18-year-old cousin Sabine opened a day care center—well, not a real center, since that was forbidden, but she took care of little children and did so admirably. Sabine suggested that I supplement my income by giving rhythmic dance lessons to the children. I discovered how much I enjoyed those kids.

One day Sabine took me to see her ailing parents and I'll never forget what I saw. Sabine's parents lay in a big bed in a cold, dark room. Suspended above

---

4   The *Judenrat* hoped that the ghetto's productivity would serve to prevent deportations and destruction of the ghetto itself. Though the Łódź ghetto factories produced goods for Nazi Germany, and the ghetto outlasted most others, its ultimate fate would be liquidation.

them were several open umbrellas, which were intended to prevent water from running down from the ceiling directly onto the bed. The bedridden couple, deathly pale and emaciated, could barely move. Neither Sabine nor her younger brother Gutek was able to help their parents. Sabine's father had been a career soldier, but just before the war had gotten very fat. Not very tall, he weighed more than 100 kilos. In the ghetto, he lost more than half of it and hunger literally made him mad. In his madness, he was said to have eaten his own fingers. I hope that was not true.

There were very few young and able-bodied men in the Łódź ghetto, which was populated mostly by women, old men and children. After that famous night when the men fled Łódź at the start of the war, we had to search far and wide to find a doctor for the ghetto inhabitants. Everybody worked—children from the age of twelve and adults until a very advanced age. We had to work because the Germans did not tolerate unproductive people. They made systematic raids of the ghetto, quarter by quarter, to take away children, the sick, and the old. We were constantly barraged with propaganda designed to reassure us that people were being sent to labor camps, where, supposedly, they'd be treated better.

When Babcia was taken ill and died in the ghetto, I went to the cemetery for the first time in my life. When Babcia II had died, before we had all gone to the ghetto, I was considered too young to go to her funeral. Despite my protestations, I had been left at home. Now, I was no longer too young to witness death. Another page of my life was over.

Death was everywhere.[5] Epidemics of typhoid fever, dysentery and tuberculosis could not be contained. One day I awoke burning with fever, which my mother diagnosed as diphtheria. Because a lot of warmth is needed to cure that disease, my parents carried me into the big room, the only one still heated. Nobody could come near me since diphtheria is contagious and thus very serious. After a few weeks I recovered and life began again. I hardly saw any of my old school friends, however. Marysia and her parents lived in a heated apartment and received supplementary food rations. The one time I visited them, I did not feel at ease and never returned. Anyway, I had other worries. The

---

5   Around 43,000 people died in the ghetto of starvation and disease.

Germans continued to "visit" the ghetto and systematically took away people who could not work. One morning I woke up all yellow, even the whites of my eyes had turned yellow. Mother announced that it was jaundice, neither serious nor contagious, but definitely spectacular. It was the kind of spectacle, she declared, that the Germans must not get wind of or they might send me away. She planned to take me into hiding. We escaped the house through interior courtyards that interconnected and allowed for flight in case of danger. We hid inside the ghetto in various neighborhoods. In the evenings, when the Germans left our neighborhood, we returned to our place. Soon enough, my jaundice left as it had come.

Some time passed without major incidents until Aunt Bela was struck by a lung infection. What else could we expect given the conditions in which we lived? If Bela continued to be hungry and cold, even medication would not heal her. Her illness was followed by my contacting another, more serious fever. The doctor listened to my breathing, took my hand and said quickly, as if to get rid of a burden, "It's typhoid." I had never heard of this illness and the name did not scare me. I actually smiled. The doctor sighed.

Mother knew that without medication and proper nourishment, typhoid is fatal, but she did not breathe a word to me. The doctor prescribed a strict diet. For two days, I could only drink pure coffee and pure cocoa. Then some biscuits, rice, potatoes, and later an egg. He wrote each item on a piece of paper, but I could not see how my mother would manage to get such products. None of us had seen any of the prescribed "medications" in nearly two years. The doctor promised to come back every day until the crisis passed. I grew more ill. My mind would not function. I could not read. Mother went out and came back with coffee and cocoa—a miraculous feat. One day, she even brought me an egg. Father's family gave me their Red Cross package, which his brother had sent from Paris, though I learned this only after the war. For several years, the Germans had allowed such packages, which were transported by the Red Cross, to enter the ghetto. By the fall of 1942, even these were prohibited. Though we followed the doctor's instructions to the letter, I still felt ill and the fever did not abate. My mother had no medicines to help me. The French shampoo was of no help at all. But I went through the disease's crisis and afterward felt a real improvement. The fever dropped and I wanted to get out of bed. Life seemed possible again. I wanted to take a walk outdoors and to eat a hearty meal. Seized by a sudden hunger one morning, in my parents' absence, I ate a big piece of raw turnip. This was absolutely taboo and could have triggered a relapse. Fortunately, nothing happened, and I improved rapidly. I went back to work. The days of waiting continued. Waiting for news of the world, our only hope. France, the lighthouse of the universe, had already capitulated long ago in June 1940, though the British and the Soviets fought on.

The next crisis arose. Father grew more ill every day. He received a Red Cross package containing medicines, but they did not help him for long. He was wasting away before our eyes. His skin became yellowish, his blue eyes glazed over, and his thinness frightened me. The meager food supplements that my mother was able to scrounge together were not sufficient. We were all very hungry and cold. That winter was particularly harsh and our flat had no heat, like most in the ghetto. Every day we broke the ice in the bucket in order to wash and heat up the (ersatz) tea. One day, I came home from work to find my mother bending over my bedridden father. He was in a coma, and she immediately sent me to the pharmacy to get injections. Totally crazy, I ran through the ghetto and was lucky enough to find the injections, which could not heal him but could keep him alive. My father improved a little, but that night I heard my parents whispering, "She's old enough, strong enough, and intelligent. She'll be all right." I wanted to cry, but fatigue and sleep had won out. The next evening, my father passed away. Mother suffered terribly. She reproached herself for not having treated him with greater kindness. What more could she have done? I consoled her and we remained in each other's arms for a long time.

It was the end of February 1942, and everything went on as before, except that now, only Mother slept in the big bed. I had cried when the war began, but my father's death left me without tears. I spent the whole night after my father died reading. I did not have a father anymore, I was cold, I was hungry. I hid in my books and continued to do so. I devoured everything written by winners of the Nobel Prize for literature. I read to escape this too horrible world. I had learned that while a piece of bread lasts only a few hours, books could provide the long-lasting consolation and nourishment I needed in order not to lose hope.

A new distraction presented itself. Boys became more and more interested in me. But they did not dare approach me because I was so young. I began to associate with big boys of eighteen to twenty-one. I distanced myself a little from my Mother, preferring to go out with my pals. In a boutique next to our house a man worked who thought he was Don Juan. It's true that he was tall and dark. He had a beautiful face with matte skin, big black eyes. He flirted with all the girls that attracted him. He would offer a jar of jam in exchange for a kiss and it worked. He held the well-known jar of jam in his hand. His kiss was followed immediately by a slap in the face; my hand flew all by itself. The jar fell to the ground. The astonishment on his face was incredible: a girl who resisted him and resisted a jar of jam. My little shrunken stomach saved my honor, since hunger did not make me suffer too much. I felt it, but it was not too cruel.

After the Americans entered the war, a frenzy took hold of Uncle Natas. Convinced that the Americans were so strong that they were to land soon and end the war, he determined that we all should learn English. He himself gave lessons to anyone who showed interest—accelerated courses, since we had to hurry. I was part of this group, but alas, we realized soon enough that the Americans were not going to rescue us all that quickly.[6]

Another year passed, and we heard that the Russian front was advancing. I moved around in a circle of people much older than I was. We behaved as if the world was going to end tomorrow. The boys had begun preparations to wage battle against the Germans. They did not want to include me because of my tender age, though I was nearly fifteen.

In early May 1943, the tragic news arrived that the Warsaw ghetto had fallen with very few survivors. The young men who were active in the Łódź ghetto resistance decided their strategy would be different—much less heroic, but leaving a greater number of people the chance to survive. I wanted to fight, even though I knew the Łódź ghetto did not interest anybody.

How many fighters could we have commanded? What weapons might we have acquired? I confess that I had no idea. I only knew that the annihilation of the Warsaw ghetto thwarted all our plans. Very soon new German propaganda

---

6   The year 1942 marked the end of the ghetto's autonomy. Tens of thousands were deported, but the Judenrat
continued to function. The Germans took command of all internal functions. A series of mass deportations in September sent nearly 20,000 Łódź Jews to the death camp at Chelmno. Those of us who remained were forced to work in ever increasing numbers of factories.

posters appeared on the ghetto walls: "You are to report to the railroad station in order to leave for work in Germany. You'll travel as a family and you'll be safe." My mother's first reaction was—"We're going to hide"—because of course we believed less and less in German propaganda.

My mother wanted us to stay where we were. She showed me the place to hide—a cellar with a very complicated access through a staircase that led to a closet in a dark corridor. The corridor was in a house that had several entrances. How will we get food and water? I asked. Who will help us? Finally, giving in to my fears, we decided to hide closer to our house, in a pile of coal. Every morning, truckloads of German soldiers disembarked, swept through district after district, and herded everybody onto trucks. We came out of our hiding place in the evenings after the trains had left the station. We were so black and stiff that my mother decided to change our hideout to a place under the floor in the house's main room. Three of us crawled into that hole, and a neighbor replaced the carpet and the table to conceal the trap door. A few hours later the sound of boots shook the floor. We heard the Germans banging the floor with their gun butts to find the hollow spaces, where people might be hiding. Soon the soldiers pulled us from our hiding place and shoved us outside with their gun butts, shouting, "Raus, raus" ("Outside, outside"). Once on the street, we were pushed into a tram and taken to the station where hundreds of people already waited on the platform. A cattle train arrived and we were crammed in.

Installed, so to speak, in the middle of that crowd, my mother found acquaintances. Not everybody could sit on the floor at the same time, so we organized a kind of relay system for sitting and for pulling oneself up to the skylight that was the only access to fresh air. The few men present tried to help the women and children. Everybody took care of the very old and the very young though there were few of them. The selections that had taken place in the ghetto had already taken their toll on us. I was tall and looked much older than my 15 years. That may have saved me in earlier selections, and would do so again.

As time passed, the air in the train compartment became scarcer and scarcer. I sat huddled in a corner with my legs curled painfully beneath me. My mother sat by my side, tightly clutching my backpack, our only piece of luggage. I found out later that she had packed my school report cards along with the few other mementos that remained. Why? The report cards could be useful if there was a school at our next destination, she said. She was not giving up the last shreds of hope. But at that moment, the bare essentials were absent: air, water and food.

CHAPTER 5

Auschwitz-Birkenau

F inally, the train stopped. We heard voices, and then the door slid open. Soldiers pushed us out onto a platform, shouting the usual *"raus!"* and distributed water. They gave us only a few minutes' respite before the train left again. Interminable hours passed before the train reached its final destination. We were exhausted. We were unloaded beside railroad tracks. Where were we? Walking alongside my mother, I noticed a band of haggard beings with shaved heads who were dressed in odd clothes with big blue stripes. They were "marching past" inside a barbed-wire enclosure. The guards reassured us that, as rumor had it, "Those are crazies locked up in that camp."

We continued walking along the rails and passed a group of men who were busy cleaning and repairing them. Suddenly one of them approached me and murmured quietly, "Watch out, little girl! At the end of the train there is a selection. To the left LIFE, to the right DEATH. So with all your strength dash to the left." "And my mother?" I asked in anguish. The man looked at her, shook his head without a word and quickly walked away. I realized suddenly that I was the only one who knew what fate lay ahead. How could I pass the word without shouting and without stirring up a panic. The only solution I found was to murmur incessantly, like one possessed, "Go to the left, go to the left." I walked quickly so that as many people as possible would hear me. I pulled my mother along with me without stopping. After a while, my voice became a sob, which I tried to control so that my words remained audible. I hoped no one would take me for a crazy woman.

The crowd carried us along, and we soon arrived before the "jury." Two men and one woman stopped me, looked me over and pushed me to the left. They hesitated visibly when it was my mother's turn. Luckily the stream of humans suddenly grew denser, and I was able to dash in and grab my mother's hand. We ran for our lives to the left. Actually, there were two selections. One to choose those able to work and the other to separate the females from the males. I prefer not to think of the boys separated from their mothers or especially of the mothers who lost their children.

We arrived at a large square, at the far end of which water sparkled like a mirage. Everybody rushed toward the water basins, and I had my first shocking encounter with a crowd. I tried to reach the treasure but I was not up to it. Shoved and trampled, I gave up trying to get my turn and watched from afar as the precious liquid flowed onto the ground. There was so much pressure from the crowd that no one was able even to wet his lips. The lesson I learned from this incident remained etched in my memory and dictated my conduct in all future such circumstances: Never follow the movements of a crowd. Don't struggle in its midst.

After this incident we were led to an enormous barracks. At the door, I stood immobilized before the unreal vision that presented itself—a group of completely naked women with shaved heads and haggard eyes. The two soldiers in the center of this group seemed to belong to another world. They ordered me to undress. One pointed at me and said to his cohort, "Look at those beautiful breasts." It was the last remark about my physical appearance that I would hear for a long time to come. At the precise moment my head was shaved, I ceased to exist as a human being

I certainly no longer needed French shampoo. Still naked, shoved along by dozens of others, Mother and I found ourselves participating in a mass shower. At the exit, each woman was given a shirt, pants, a striped dress, a star and a pair of clogs. We were outfitted to play the "madwomen." After this metamorphosis, I had trouble recognizing my mother, who I noticed had aged quickly and prematurely. Her face was a web of wrinkles and her hair had turned gray in the ghetto; now in the camp, she no longer had hair. I had grown up a lot in recent months and knew I looked older than my age—at least eighteen or nineteen. I preferred not to have to look at myself. No danger of that, however, since the "set designers" had forgotten to install mirrors and I did not have the spare time to worry about how horrible I might look. Instead, I watched as our luggage and clothing were confiscated and with them, all the mementos from our previous existence, all the mementos from the other world.

Later, reassembled outside, we spent the night on the ground. We put our bodies very close together, one on top of the other, for warmth. Under the stars, we were able to doze a little. The next day, after we were divided into various units, we learned that we were in a concentration camp called Auschwitz-Birkenau. It was August 1944, and luckily the days were mild, though the nights were cold. Every day new convoys arrived. As the front advanced, more Jews, gypsies, and resistance fighters were herded into Auschwitz-Birkenau. The tattooing department was so overworked that we were no longer "entitled" to have the "nice blue numbers" engraved on our forearms. We found that the older prisoners were stingy with information. Everybody tried to hoard whatever secrets might improve his everyday existence. We learned there were "kommandos" (work groups) that could leave and work outside the camp. That position was coveted by every prisoner, because it was almost impossible to get any supplemental food on the premises. The daily rations were just enough to keep the prisoners from dying of starvation.

Leaving the barracks after getting up that first morning in Auschwitz-Birkenau, I saw a group of people about a hundred meters away. Going closer, I noticed two men carrying hampers of cabbage. Hands reached out, grabbed leaves, some snatched the leaves away, others who stood on the periphery tried to get closer. The scramble became a free-for-all. Faithful to my convictions, I observed the desperate mob scene from afar. Finally, the cabbage leaves flew into the air and nobody could catch them. I took it as proof that my way of thinking was correct and I should not change it.

At six in the morning, we had to appear for roll call, which was taken daily in order to verify the number of prisoners. A hallucinatory ensemble of gaunt, emaciated and sick human beings lined up for that interminable roll call. Later that day my mother searched for acquaintances, desperate to get information and find a way out. Free to move around the blocks of barracks, I encountered in the very center of our camp an enormous sort of barbed wire cage with a barracks installed in the middle. Suddenly the barracks door opened and "kapos" (prisoner supervisors) began pushing out deformed, skeletal beings who dragged themselves forward, some still standing, others on all fours, some creeping along, unable to pull themselves upright. I could distinguish no human characteristic among these living dead who obeyed who-knows-what fate. Who were they? Where did they come from? Were they men or women? Why were they in this state? I would never know, but my whole being went out to them. Could they be helped? There were no holes in the wire. I remained helpless and paralyzed by the shock.

Later, I described this scene to my mother, but even she had no explanation for the tragedy. We entered our barracks and took our places on the floor. Various rumors were making the rounds: The "kapos" were recruited from among the deportees. The red-headed harpy who constantly walked around with whip in hand was a survivor who escaped from an oven (that is, a gas chamber) and went completely crazy. There was talk of ovens and gas chambers, and I assumed that that must have been what the man on the railroad track had been talking about, too. But I could not conceive that it could really be true. I took refuge in my own world and rigorously preserved my detachment.

I heard other rumors that some women were subjected to medical experiments by German doctors. I later learned that my cousin Sabine was one of the victims. During the years that we spent together in Paris after the war, we never alluded to our respective tragedies. The pain was still too sharp.

CHAPTER 6

Kommando Life In Celle

The next day we were inducted into the life of the barracks. Sustained by the energy of despair, Mother pursued her habit of reconnoitering. She learned that we were in a transitional block and were going to leave soon for a camp near Hanover, Germany. It was a work camp, not a concentration camp, but that detail in no way changed our living conditions. This time the trip in the cattle train was shorter. We got off in a forest some distance from the village of Celle, not far from Hanover. We walked to a clearing where some wooden barracks stood. The SS Commandant was there waiting for us. About forty women were assigned to each room, and my mother and I entered our new universe together. There were bunk beds, but beds all the same that were furnished with a straw mattress and a cover. A stove in the middle of the room provided real luxury. My mother took a bottom bunk and I climbed on top. At last, I felt I could isolate myself from the crowd that had engulfed me for such a long time.

Our barracks were crowded with Jewish women from Poland, Germany, Czechoslovakia, and Romania. The young women from Germany seemed to keep to themselves. They probably thought me too young to include me in their group. Until today, I still don't know if it was political or some other consideration. We noticed another prison camp nearby, where men, women and children were dressed in civilian clothes. They had come from Holland and seemed to receive better treatment than we did. They never tried to communicate with us. Starting on the day after our arrival, after enduring the endless roll call, we went to work.

Our work group was assigned to the public works firm "Hochtief" (very deep). We quickly coined the phrase "hochtief begraben" (buried very deep). At six o'clock in the morning, we of the striped clothing began marching. The road seemed long, but I marched it every day, morning and evening. The road passed through a village, and to my great amazement, I saw that some people still led normal lives in real houses surrounded by real gardens where happy children played. As we passed, the children threw stones and taunted, "Jude, Jude" ("Jew, Jew"). I concede that unquestionably we were no longer of the same world, were not even the same creatures, but I would not even have thrown stones at a mangy dog. Those children must have been specifically conditioned to act that way.

We were supervised by soldiers of the Wehrmacht, the regular German army, who escorted us from the time we left the camp in the morning until we returned in the evening. When we arrived at the work site our first morning on the job, the foreman ordered us to dig a huge, deep hole that would serve as the foundation for a shelter. At first, we were able to throw the earth to one side, but as the hole grew deeper, the earth had to be thrown higher and eventually the top of the pile reached over our heads. Our shovels had to be full, we couldn't cheat or stop, except for the single soup break of the day. Even today, when I have severe pains in my right arm, elbow, or shoulder, I recall those first days on the work crew.

The camp's SS Commandant paid us a visit almost every day, staggering his arrival times so he could play a perverse game of hide-and-seek, observing everyone before they were aware of his presence to verify that his orders were being properly executed. One day, weary from throwing the soil up more than 1.5 meters (I'm only 1.56 meters tall), I stopped to rest. The soldier who was watching us yelled for all to keep working, and at that moment the SS Commandant emerged from behind a bush. "Wer arbeitet nicht?" (Who is not working?) His words lashed out like the crack of a whip. The silence was absolute, nobody moved. None of us had ever denounced anyone before. I was taught to believe that even the meanest people can be responsive to truth and have something good in them. But I also knew that without an answer to his question, the SS Commandant would punish everybody, and in the evening, instead of going back into the barracks, we would remain standing outside for several hours. After a whole day's work that ordeal would be unbearable.

The SS Commandant stood near me. With a determined look I stepped forward, stared him in the eye and said, "It's me." I didn't have time to complete the second word before a terrible blow from his fist sent me flying. When I opened my eyes, I was lying on the ground. A fire was burning inside my head. I could barely move. Somehow I lifted myself up and tried to remain standing, grateful that my mother wasn't there to witness the scene. The soup provided a needed respite. Solidarity ran deep in the work camp. All the women surrounded me, bringing a little water or holding my head to relieve the pain. Even the old Wehrmacht soldier came over to me. He held out his canteen full of soup and said, "Ess doch" (Eat). Then he added in a consoling tone, "You'll see, soon you'll be free and you'll ride in a car."

I have always assumed that the arrival just then of a private car was what triggered his choice of words. This soldier had known for some time that we were not prostitutes or criminals, as he had been told, but women whose only crime was their Jewish origin. He no longer despised us, but, like everyone else in the camp, he was scared to death of the SS Commandant. And so, because orders were orders, I had to work the rest of that day. After a few days the swelling in my head subsided and I looked human again. Certainly, my courageous behavior brought me closer to the others in the work team. From that day on we talked together more often, and if I did not bond closer with any of those companions, it was due largely to my mother's presence in the camp. I spent my only free moments—the evenings just before fatigue carried me off, as well as Sundays—with Mother.

In the camp, I completely stopped menstruating. This occurred, I heard others say, because unbeknownst to us, we were administered some kind of medication. In any case, the taste of the soup that we were served twice a day was not altered by the medication.

One day, prisoners dressed in civilian clothes arrived, who were going to work with our crew. Listening to their conversation, I realized that they were French. Learning that I could speak a little French, my co-workers begged me to talk to the new arrivals, though that was technically forbidden. I decided to do it and asked, while looking elsewhere, "What time is it?" A dozen heads turned abruptly to locate the feminine voice. When they did so, they looked away, and each in turn questioned me quietly in order not to attract the guard's attention. Thereafter, I got news every morning from a man in a beret who would approach me while carrying a beam or an iron bar, pass by very closely, and give me the news of the day: the Russians are advancing, the British are fighting hard, the Americans have already landed in France. But France was far away, and what brought us the greatest joy was when we could actually hear the bombings. They meant that the Allies were active and close by, and we took secret pleasure in seeing the fear on the faces of our "courageous" Germans. Within seconds they were all in their shelters. And, free as the air while the bombing lasted, we prisoners were bursting with joy. It had been such a long time since I laughed. Once, a soldier left behind outside heard our outburst and fell into a mad rage, but the planes came and he quickly joined his comrades.

One day while we were working beside a garage, it rained so hard that we went inside. One of the French prisoners took out a package of biscuits to divide among us, and almost all the girls rushed for them. I was one of the two or three who did not move. Then a tall, blond prisoner offered me an apple, but a faster hand then mine snatched it from him. Quite firmly, he retrieved the apple and handed it to me. Apple in hand, I decided to share it with my hungry companion, for I had retained the unbelievable advantage of never really suffering from hunger. I had neither stomach aches nor the intestinal discomfort that drove others crazy. My stomach must have shrunk to measure.

Since I no longer had books, I withdrew into my own dream world, which was interrupted one day by the arrival of Italian prisoners. There were not many of them, but the Germans despised them more than all the other, non-Jewish prisoners and mistreated them terribly. I learned later that the Italians were, in fact, not prisoners but allies of the Germans. Strange allies.

After the meeting with the French prisoner who gave us food, my behavior changed. I began to feel the need to hide my shaved head and tie up my dress, which was much too large and hung around my legs most dismally. I ripped a piece from the bottom of my pale pink shirt to tie around my head like a turban and another piece to roll into a belt. Mother helped me since I had no mirror. I am decked out in a pink turban and matching belt. Other women, too, were trying to "look human" again. My tall, skinny friend Anna also adopted a turban, and everyday she placed a doily on the board from which she ate her little piece of bread or her tin can of soup. I don't know how she managed to hold on to that doily, but I knew several women who had managed to conceal valuables—a souvenir menu, or a photograph, or a powder compact, or a pendant.

Mother suffered terribly from fatigue, hunger and her worries about me. I was in constant pain. The combination of the stiff clogs, long marches to work and being on my feet all day had caused festering sores on my ankles. Mother made bandages for me out of toilet paper, but the wounds would not heal. Then it began to get very cold. My delicate feet could not withstand walking in the hard wooden clogs.

The work site was sometimes closed due to severe weather. Even then, the SS Commandant was always full of ideas for putting us to work. One day, he sent everyone, including Mother, to work in a salt mine. For the first time, I escaped work and stayed behind alone in the barracks because of the pain in my ankles. Suddenly, for we had been living without a calendar for a long time, I was struck by the cruel realization that it was my sixteenth birthday, September 18, 1944, and I had been locked up for more than four years. I, who thought I had lost all my tears, burst out crying and could not stop. I looked out the single window in the barracks at the rain and the dark sky and the violence of my sobs redoubled. I prayed for my father to look down and see me clearly from wherever he was. I had decided once and for all that if the Lord could allow such atrocities, either He was not good or He did not exist. But my own father had existed and was so sweet. He loved me so much that I felt he should be able to help me or have me come to him. I was so weary that I had no hope left. Everything was so horrible, so sad, and I—in what condition am I at sixteen years old?

The whole afternoon passed like this. Eventually, my laments were interrupted by the return of the work crew. Mother informed me that the salt miners had refused to admit women into their universe. That decision temporarily saved many of us from strenuous work that we might not have survived, given our physical condition, our lack of proper food and the atmosphere inside a salt mine. Our daily nourishment consisted of a small piece of bread and ersatz coffee in the morning, soup at lunch and a hot, grayish liquid in the evening.

A few days later we were back on the old work site as usual. My job was to put iron bars into a forming machine. They were meant to serve as reinforcement to the shelter under construction. With the winter settling in, I suffered more from cold than hunger. I remember thinking that the alert sirens seemed louder that day, or else my sensitivity to them had increased. For once, we were ordered to go into the shelter. Waiting quietly there for the end of the alert, I noticed a commotion at the top of the stairs when a co-worker whispered in my ear, "Go quickly, the tall blond is asking for you." I ran up the steps four at a time and told the guard I had an urgent need. Standing alone in front of the shelter, I saw "the tall blond" a few steps away. He showed me a package, then moved quickly toward a machine, opened its cover, hid the package inside and left. Two seconds later I retrieved the package and hid it beneath my dress, tightening the belt around it. For the first time, I do not regret its fullness.

I returned to the shelter and waited impatiently for my mother to return, for she was now usually with a different work group. It was only back in the baracks that I opened my dress and could admire the contents of the package—a letter, a big piece of bread, an egg, an apple and a piece of chocolate. I had not seen the color of chocolate in four years. It was nothing short of a miracle. Mother took possession of everything but the letter, and divided the riches into rations. I dove into the letter. Fortunately, I read French better than I spoke it and had no trouble deciphering the words of "the tall blond." His name was Hans Johansson, he wrote, a French national of Swedish origin who had lived primarily in Paris. Now, a prisoner of war, his job as a chauffeur gave him access to small wonders such as those he had just provided. He wrote that he loved me and enclosed a few sheets of blank paper and a pencil so I could send him notes. He promised that, within the limits of possibility, he would try to procure whatever I requested. My brief list was finished quickly. Besides food, which was vital, what I most wanted were a mirror, a toothbrush, a jacket and gloves. Hans Johansson was my angel from heaven.

Every day, whether the wind blew or the rain fell, "the tall blond" appeared in his truck or came by bike to bring me a bundle of hope. His fidelity was unwavering. Each time the procedure was the same: he found an auspicious place to hide the package, I would take a walk and when I felt that no one was watching me, I would run to retrieve the package. Either no one ever saw me or the soldier on guard just looked away. This daily physical and psychological support saved my life, because it gave me strength to survive all that came next. It armed me for the final tragic trials. We wrote each other every day. I described my life in Poland, he told me about the work he had done in Paris. I remember that he felt he was unworthy of me, as if my bourgeois background made me superior to him. Under the circumstances, his sentiment was rather tragi-comic. Unfortunately, I never saw him again after the war.

The weather was brutally cold. It was difficult to work. Before I received the coat that Hans got for me, the foreman of a neighboring work site gave me his. Perhaps he was moved by my shivering. I wrapped myself in it immediately. It gave me a feeling of warmth and comfort. The soldier guarding us took notice and subjected me to a harsh inquisition. Where did you find it? Who gave it to you? I insisted repeatedly that I didn't know the man who had given it to me. Luckily I was dealing with a Wehrmacht soldier who grew tired of the interrogation and left me and the coat alone. I ran to the toilet and hid it under my dress to shield it from prying eyes. Later, I gave my mother the coat that Hans had brought me. Looking back, it seems that I only thought of myself in those days. Total egoism.

The foreman at our work site was a rigid disciplinarian. He did not beat us (I saw him beat a woman only once), but he demanded that we work every instant. The older foreman, who unfortunately was not in charge of us, seemed more indulgent. He employed a young Russian woman, dressed in civvies, to do the housekeeping in his office. When she became ill, he chose me to take her place. To work in a warm place and without being watched or harassed was pure luck. Satisfied with my work, the old man gave me a candy at the end of the day. No doubt he could not imagine the quality or the quantity of our daily food rations. For a few days, at least, I was happy and kept warm in front of a fireplace. Unfortunately for me, the Russian woman got well and I returned to the work site.

On days when the cold kept us from the work site, we were put before a frozen, snow-covered mound of coal and told to pick out the pieces. Though my hands felt frozen, I put my precious gloves aside to keep them dry. But soon I could not stand it and put them back on. That evening, I discovered that my toes were frostbitten and I had painful chilblains; wounds on my ankles and chilblains on my toes (thank goodness, no one could see them). After evening roll call, I literally fell into bed. Perhaps it was fortunate that I did not have the strength to think about the pain.

Despite the winter weather, the man in the beret continued to bring news of the front. He ended each report by saying, "Hang in there," for though the Germans were being beaten everywhere, we had no idea what they were holding in store for us. It was at that point that some recently arrived Hungarian women were assigned to our work group. They were all filled with anguish, which is difficult to describe. They were cast into this hell directly from a quasi-normal life and they seemed to simply snap. This group of women cried for hours, hiding in the toilets as if the soldiers would not be able to find them there. As a result, we were under permanent surveillance. Since the toilets were our only refuge, where we could breathe a bit, this state of affairs punished all of us.

One woman from my group was not so lucky. During a lunch break, she chatted with a chauffeur. Their conversation was overheard by the SS Commandant, who was standing behind a nearby tree. He lunged in front of them and, with all his might, beat the woman. His blows rained all over her face, head and body. When he tired of his game, he walked off with an order to the soldiers to make sure his victim worked through the rest of the afternoon. That was the rule. In her condition, however, she could not stand upright. She was barely conscious. Our group propped her up and did her work in her stead. Each of us took turns holding her to appear as if she were working. The soldier who guarded us was not deceived but he closed his eyes to our efforts.

The most difficult work was still ahead of us. Soon we were assigned to lay railroad ties. Sixteen to twenty of us had to shoulder an iron rail and move in cadence to place it in the chosen spot. We realized that quickly lowering one's shoulder put an additional burden on the rest of the group, and throughout the job, not one woman faltered. Only one woman on our work crew ever died, and when she did, the Germans ordered us to be present at her burial. I didn't know her or how she died, but we marched behind the coffin as ordered. My mother walked next to me and, exhausted, she suddenly broke ranks. When a German overseer, a female officer whom we did not often see, shoved her back in place, I exploding in rage and, forgetting all caution, screamed, "Don't touch my mother!" The overseer, astonished, stopped for a moment but did not react further. I was incredibly lucky that day.

CHAPTER 7

Bergen-Belsen

T he winter went on relentlessly. The cold weather immobilized the work site. Then, in February 1945 orders came to evacuate our camp and transfer the prisoners to Bergen-Belsen. Telling us this, the SS Commandant added, "You'll wish to be back in this camp." We did not dare laugh. We could not imagine what could possibly be worse. Alas, he was right. One morning they loaded us onto trucks for the short trip to Bergen-Belsen, and I never saw the "tall blond" again. In our new barracks, everyone slept on the floor, but it was so crowded there was no room even to stretch out our legs to sleep. As we were not working, we never moved out of the camp, though others continued to move in. One day, after the customary roll call, a new group of women appeared in the barracks. Dressed in normal clothes, they sat on the floor staring at us with what we thought was hostility. When we learned that they were Ukrainians, we were scared to death, for we all knew Ukrainians were terrible antisemites. We huddled together in the corners, and stayed as far from this threat as possible until, after a short time, they were moved away, I don't know where. I admit that I did not investigate their fate.

Soon my ever-vigilant mother noticed a group of French women in nearby barracks. She told me to pay them a visit and try to communicate. Then she searched for familiar faces. I thought that she knew the whole world. She encountered a nurse of her acquaintance who offered me work in the infirmary in exchange for soup. I accepted instantly, since nourishment at Bergen-Belsen was non-existent and the "tall blond" was far away. Neither I nor my mother were aware of the inherent danger. I went to the infirmary every day to make the beds and shake out the blankets. These were full of the lice that had taken possession of the place. Lice transmit typhus, and I got infected with the terrible disease.

After the incubation period, it was my turn to get sick with typhus. I began playing my role in what seemed like the worst horror film; you can't imagine how horrible. I had a terrible fever that left me unconscious most of the time. When I awoke, I realized that I was covered with lice. The lice had transformed the blotches characteristic of typhus into sores. They literally gnawed at my flesh, swarming over my shoulders and pubis, their favorite breeding ground. How would I ever play Lolita? Mother tried to get rid of them, but it was a lost cause.

On the rare moments I'd emerge from a delirious sleep and open my eyes, I could see that horrifying spectacle. I wished for death. Mother was always there, offering something to drink, because I could not tolerate solids. Her constant presence day and night was my sole consolation. And then I lost total contact with reality. Days went by, my fever finally abated, I opened my eyes and my mother was still there, but she had become an old woman. Her hair had grown back almost white. Her beautiful hands were skin and bones, and her face was wrinkled and colorless. Though I was feeling a little better, I noticed that several corpses were being removed from the barracks every day. Mother's body soon began to bloat, but I didn't grasp the gravity of her condition. She had sacrificed what remained of her strength and showed utterly unimaginable courage to save my life. What had she felt, seeing her only daughter go through such an ordeal? Had she been able to hold on to any hope? I wished it with all my heart.

That night, Mother woke me hallucinating. "Izia," she called, "przyszykoj me kasze." ("Izia, fix me a kasha.") I calmed her and embraced her. "Tomorrow morning, Mother, tonight it's too late." In the morning, I woke, talked to my mother, but the body next to me lay inert. I shook her, I yelled, but nothing could bring my mother back to life. My mother was dead. I remained still for a moment and then I pressed very hard against me the only human being left to me in all the world. I could not accept the evidence. When men came to take away the body, I held on, determined to stay with my mother. Finally, very strong hands lifted me up and others took away the corpse. Sobbing, I lay immobile on the ground, unwilling ever to move again. I was ready to die too. The last thread binding me to life had snapped. Now all the people whom I had loved were all gone from this world. What use was it to go on living? The paroxysm of despair sapped me of the last strength I had recovered with great difficulty after healing from the typhus. Mother had died "an old woman" at age forty-five.

I don't know how long I lay prostrate, two or three days, maybe more. I no longer noticed the people around me, not even the two young women, more dead than alive, who slept on either side of me and tried in vain to attract my attention. For how long had they been talking to me? Finally their words reached my consciousness. "You are the only one who can get up, you have to help us. We can't move anymore, so you have to get up. We're hungry and thirsty, you're the only one who can go out." I could not believe what they were saying. What, I can get up? But I did not need anything since I was ready to die. Finally, I looked at them—the older one had respiratory troubles and heart failure; the other had an internal infection, a yellowish liquid oozed from her nose and ears. Obviously, they were telling the truth. Only their head and arms were still moving. And nobody was going to bring us food or drink. "Get us some soup and water," they beseeched me.

Suddenly I felt I had no right to abandon them without trying to help them. I decided to stand up but overestimated my strength. My long legs, gnarled from disuse, refused to obey. I was able to pivot back and forth until, after many efforts, I found myself on my knees and could advance on all fours to the door and crawl outside. My whole being was called upon to concentrate and I tried to stand up, which I finally succeeded to do. The fresh air renewed my strength enough that I was able to make my way, taking hesitating steps down an interminable road. I bent gingerly to pick up an empty tin can lying on the ground, knowing that getting up again would be a real challenge. I continued and saw a small group of women sitting around a large container. I approached and stretched out my tin can, then quickly swallowed the lukewarm liquid they poured into it. I stretched out the can again, explaining in an international gibberish that I also needed soup for my friends in the barracks.

I returned very slowly not spilling a drop of the precious liquid. The reception I received was ample reward for my efforts. I repeated the trip every day and slowly grew surer on my feet. But the soup must not have been rich enough in vitamins, for my strength abandoned me again. I lay on the floor with my two neighbors. We barely succeeded in exchanging a few words. They whispered to me, "When the world learns of this, nothing like it will ever happen again." Words to console the dying. The survivors would have the sad privilege of testifying to the contrary.

One night, I dreamt that all my teeth fell out. I picked them up and put them on a table. In the morning, I noticed that my teeth really were loose and did not dare touch them, though the food I ate hardly threatened to loosen them more. I was so afraid that my dream was going to become a reality. I dozed off from exhaustion. Luckily, my teeth waited for the British.

CHAPTER 8

Liberation

T he day the British Army arrived, on April 15, 1945, I heard, as if in a dream, "You are liberated, we're here." These words were repeated several times in English. The voice continued, "We can't come in right away because of the typhus epidemic in your camp, but we'll be there as soon as the disinfection is completed." Then men wearing masks and overalls came into the barracks and spread a cloud of white powder over us. The following day the door opened and a young soldier poked his head in. Before he withdrew it, I noticed that his face was drenched with tears. A few minutes passed, no doubt the soldier was warning his friends of what they would find inside. When the door opened again, several soldiers entered and searched for the living. We had stopped removing the corpses, and those of us still breathing lay among others who were beginning to decay. Before, the Germans forced the prisoners to remove the bodies and pile them up outside, one on top of the other, forming small mounds. Even though I could no longer get up, I could still move. A soldier whose helmet was different from the others came towards me, turned me over, then he cautiously turned me back. "Can I operate on you without anesthesia?" he asked. I understood him and nodded. What I could not have communicated was that he could have cut me into little pieces and I would not have felt anything. For years, I had practiced a kind of voluntary cerebral anesthesia, now it had become total. The army doctor, or so I deduced from his duties, removed the barracks door, mounted supports on either side of it and placed me delicately on the improvised operating table. Then I saw that there was a swelling the size of an orange on my right thigh. The doctor needed to intervene immediately. I've no recollection of feeling any pain. But the army doctor must have suffered for me, because he left for a while, and returned with a piece of chocolate to console me. I said "thank you," even though the chocolate tasted of ashes. I savored none of it. I did not care. I was surrounded by filth but it did not bother me. I was full of the smell of death. The reek of decomposing bodies overpowered all other smells. It haunted me for months.

Like many survivors, I suffered from diarrhea. The nourishment that the British provided was not effective, but I had no idea what would have suited us. I knew only that our bodily functions, especially our intestines, were completely upset. The British soldiers who liberated us had not expected to find a death camp at Bergen-Belsen. There were so many sick women. The British did not have the experience to cope with the living dead. The operation I underwent had not helped my condition and I remained on the edge of consciousness. No doubt sent by the army doctor, a man came and carried me in his arms to a small van that took me to an improvised hospital. There was no space available in any of the rooms, so they put me on a bed in a hallway. I was still alive, but neither my body nor my head would move. Only my eyes continued to see everything around me. They tried to feed me, but no food went down. My mouth felt nothing and my throat was completely closed. Even liquids could not pass through. They put me on intravenous. The many doctors that passed by my bedside called me "the girl with the blue eyes," because they were my only noticeable feature. The fever made my eyes gleam even more intensely.

Next thing, I got pleurisy. But this time I was surrounded with capable doctors who possesssed all the needed medicine. My condition improved a little, though I could see my body, which was mostly bones and sores, scarred over by typhus and now covered with eczema. I was still too weak to be conscious of my condition.

The British liberators had brought with them several French nuns (from Bac Street in Paris) and Polish nuns. I do not know how Sister Suzanne Spender learned that I understood a bit of French, but she came to me and offered a crucifix. I explained that, being Jewish, I could not wear it. She smiled and said, "You may keep it as a souvenir." I accepted immediately.

Sister Suzanne took wonderful care of me. She found me a place in a room, washed me, and made me eat. With the help of her strong arms, I took my first steps, wobbly as a newborn, and relearned how to walk. After a few days the goal was to walk as far as the scale, because I had to be weighed. Once I stood still on the pan, the needle stopped at 25 kilos. I looked again, but it would not change. The last time I had weighed myself, at the very beginning of the war, I recall that I weighed 40 kilos. I had not grown much since then but I was five years older. Five years of confinement, five years of martyrdom and there I was—not in great fettle but alive. Exhausted by the walk, I lay down again still guided by her helping hands. Sister Suzanne was ministering to me when a Polish nun came in. "Ty sie nie wstydzisz ze siostra Suzanne Ci myje nogi?" (Aren't you ashamed to have Sister Suzanne wash your feet?), she flung at me. I was shocked and would have preferred not to understand Polish. Obviously, Catholicism did not present the same countenance in Poland as it did in France. The behavior of these two nuns exemplified, though in a simplistic way, the two faces of the same Church. I felt I was suddenly back in the sad times of antisemitic persecution. She could see my condition clearly, how could she talk like that? Wasn't her vocation to help her fellow human beings? I never saw the Polish nun again, whose name I hadn't learned. It's just as well. Still she should have been kinder to me, since she was closer to me in language and culture. I hope that she forgot her vocation only when facing a little Jewish girl.

Though my condition continued to improve, when I finally looked in a mirror for the first time in months, I did not recognize myself. I could not believe that the image I saw in the mirror was me. A face of pallid color, sunken cheeks. I still looked more like a skeleton than a living human and had completely forgotten that my hair, barely grown back after being shaved, had fallen out as a result of the typhus. The last "gift" of this terrible illness. I eliminated mirrors from my universe.

Sister Suzanne advised me to accept an offer from the Swedish authorities to provide care in Sweden for a number of deportees. I decided to be part of it. Before I left for Sweden, Sister Suzanne asked me if I had any family abroad, and I told her that my father's brother, Zygmunt Sztrauch, had been living in Paris before the war. I had no details however, for the paper had long since disappeared on which my mother had written the addresses of our family and friends and the people to whom she had entrusted our valuables. I would leave Sister Suzanne with regrets.

Before departing, I tried again to learn the fate of my two neighbors from the barracks and was told that they did not make it. I am the only one who survived. I had not managed to save anybody but myself.

Bergen-Belsen was one of the rare camps where, at the end, industrial extermination had not been necessary. Hunger, thirst and sickness had achieved the same ends. My last image of Bergen-Belsen was of German women soldiers being given a hand up into a truck by a British soldier. The British, who had liberated us, had already been sent to the rear. There was fear, no doubt, of how they might react toward the "poor" Germans. The British soldiers who had replaced them, of course, could not know how it was.

I boarded a ship sailing for Sweden. It distressed me that the ship was German, but fortunately, the personnel, including my nurse, were all Swedish. When I told the male nurse about my love of Swedish literature—by authors such as Selma Lagerlöf and Björn Björnsen—he took particularly good care of me and we became friends.

But a new disaster occurred. I broke out all over in white pustules full of liquid especially on my forearms. The only doctor on board was a German who agreed to pierce and disinfect the sores. When he approached me with the scissors, I began to yell that no German would ever touch me again, and it took all my nurse's persuasive force to convince me to accept the man's treatment. Though the sores healed quickly, I was still too weak to walk. I requested books but could not read Swedish. One of the youngest survivors on board the ship, I also was one of the sickest.

The other young women on the boat came to visit me often. They were moved by my youth and my state. When I asked their names and one of them introduced herself as Hanka Sercarz, I exclaimed, "You are my cousin!" According to my father, all Sercarzes belonged to our family. Hanka and I decided to stay together. A few years older than I and in better health, Hanka looked after me until we arrived in Norköping, where a hospital had been set up to take care of us. Before it closed, I saw through the rear door of the ambulance that transported me from the ship to the hospital a fabulous vision of blue sky, trees and smiling faces and knew that I had been reborn.

EPILOGUE

My parents' hope was fulfilled.
I was alive. I was going to live with my uncle in France. "My Second Life" was about to begin. The past, the hell, I had to bury it. I double-locked it in my very depths.

I was leaving for Paris, which had been left intact. This was just confirmed to me. The City of Lights, where one could live like the king of France, was waiting for me. A second chance was given to me and I was ready to embrace it.

In "My Second Life," I have tried to keep my promises. I have given testimony so that the young and the not-so-young know what had happened. I survived the greatest catastrophe of the 20th century, during which millions of human beings were massacred: Jews, gypsies and others.

I am often asked whether I have forgiven and my answer is: "I could, but you must ask the opinion of my parents and of the others who were exterminated." I am also asked whether I hate those who hurt me so badly and I invariably answer: "Hate kills those who hate, love makes them live. So I prefer to love."

Above all, I found that the Germans assume the crimes of their fathers and that they try to make life easier for us, the survivors. I think that that is all we can ask of the culprits' children.

Hitler had lost. My belief in humanity had won.

MY SECOND LIFE

I heard that Sweden had supplied Germany with steel during the war and was now trying to redeem itself, but I only knew that the population welcomed us with open arms. Men working on a project outside the hospital noticed us through the panes, and, much to our amazement, sent us an enormous box of cakes, chocolate, fruit, etc. All the workmen in the building had chipped in to send these gifts, and we brandished the delicacies by the window to indicate our thanks. After that, we received many visitors, particularly women who asked many questions and shook their heads. One tall, rather heavy girl with luxuriant brown hair came back to see me a few times. Her name was Brigitt, and though she was my age, she seemed enormous in comparison. Eventually she invited me to her house. Now able to move around, though not on long walks, I happily accepted. This would be my first free outing since the war began. Brigitt came to get me in a car. We drove into the country for quite a while until we came to a large property where her parents were waiting for us. They took me on a tour of their farm, during which what seemed like hundreds of pink pigs suddenly rushed at me through an open door. Though they only jostled me, I'll admit that, as a city girl, I was a bit startled, but I went on to admire the rest of the farm. Back at the house, my hostess set a giant omelet of at least eight eggs and ham. She lay her hand gently on my threadlike arm and said the omelet was to help fatten me up. Back at the hospital I made a firm decision to gain weight quickly and eventually got quite fat. I never wanted to evoke pity again. The days passed quite fast between the treatments and the visitors, but every night I awoke from being chased by an enormous chariot filled with people in greasepaint. The cart pursues me relentlessly and I run from it as fast as I can across roads, bridges and valleys. Luckily it never reaches me, but I always woke up exhausted and uneasy.

After some deliberation, Brigitt's family offered to adopt me. I must have passed the test of the pink pigs. But first I was to go with other patients to the charming village of Lövsta-Bruk to finish convalescing. Just before my departure for Lövsta-Bruk, a telegram came informing me that Uncle Zygmunt and his family were alive and had just returned to Paris. Sister Suzanne had found them listed in the phone book and called them. (When I saw her not so very much later in Paris, Sister Suzanne fell onto her knees and prayed for a long while. I'm sure my metamorphosis from the living dead into a rounded young woman with abundant brown hair and a pink, smiling face must have seemed like a miracle.) My uncle also sent a money order with the telegram and I found myself thinking, What do I need? I have everything. I had been given two dresses, a coat, shoes, and some underwear. Hanka, who had just found an uncle in Belgium, talked it over with me and we decided to buy me a nightgown, which I really wanted, I did not know why. I had made inquiries and learned that the French had also suffered during the war and that the Jews were persecuted there as well. I decided to use more than half of the money to buy things still lacking in France—especially nylon stockings, chocolate, coffee, and soap—and send them to Paris. I wrote my uncle to tell him that I planned to finish my studies and take up research in chemistry and anticipated returning to school in Sweden to prepare for my baccalaureate exams. My uncle's response was a categorical "no." A seventeen-year-old girl could not stay alone, far from her family. And so, after convalescing in Lövsta-Bruk, I set out for France, fulfilling my mother's dream—and my own dream.

I realize that I may have painted a rather flattering portrait of myself in these pages, but after the war, few were left alive who could contradict me. Of my entire family, the only survivors were Zygmunt Friede (Aunt Bela's husband, who fled to Russia), Uncle Zygmunt and his family in Paris, and my cousin Sabine Mann, who had run the illicit child-care center in the ghetto. Sabine was very broken by the suffering she endured as a subject of the Nazi doctors' experiments and never regained the energy that had once characterized her. Only her natural goodness survived. She and I spent many years together in

Paris after the war, but did not allude to our respective tragedies. She never completely escaped from the Germans, and toward the end of her life suffered from constant anxiety that they would return for her.

I went to Bergen-Belsen on the 50th anniversary of the camp's liberation. The train rolled past forests, villages, houses surrounded by gardens where children played and I wondered how the people who lived accepted the abominations committed just outside their doors? What had induced their children to throw stones at us? The only situation that seems, to me, to be analogous is the age-old institution of slavery. On the island of Goree, there is an awe-inspiring museum, in a beautiful, big bourgeois house where, long ago, quiet families whose children played and laughed with joy lived upstairs above a basement crammed with black people destined to be shipped to the slave markets. The museum's pictures depicting the slaves' lives mirrored photographs I had seen of the concentration camp.

EPILOGUE TO MY SECOND LIFE

W hy this eyewitness account? I have already answered this question in the foreword to my book: to keep a promise I made to those who did not survive, and to bear witness by every possible means, to bear witness forever.

I must admit, however, that these were not the only incentives. There was another reason, which I alluded to in my story. Some inner force impelled me to write whenever I felt alone. I would jot down my memories and describe images that haunted me. When I had finished my story, I felt as though I had been set free, that a great weight I had been carrying for so long had finally been lifted from my soul.

My first life, like that of Anne Frank, ended in Bergen-Belsen. The tremendous difference was that she really died, whereas I had a second life after the war. Simone Weil, a well-known personality, was another survivor of Bergen-Belsen. Our destinies have been somewhat similar. We both lost our mothers in the camp; we both married and we both had three sons. The resemblance ends there. After the war, Simone Weil returned to her home. In spite of inconsolable losses, she returned to her country, her house, and her family. I had to face the unfamiliar in a complete void.

I was very fortunate, though. I was resurrected without being overly scarred either psychologically or physically. During the war, I was both "too young" and "old enough." That's what saved me. I was too young to understand the full impact of the disaster I was experiencing, and I was too young to have

69

responsibilities toward others. My actions had consequences only for me. Yet I was old enough to acquire a solid foundation for life through the education my parents gave me and the love with which they surrounded me. It was this inviolable wealth that allowed me to be reborn.

After the war, many survivors found themselves completely broken, crushed by the hardship, ill treatment and suffering they had endured. They were unable to resume a normal life. They lived with open wounds, unable to overcome their pain.

Luck was with me in "my second life." Even though my suffering had left a permanent scar, I was able to start a family, learn several trades, keep on living, and love.

I have been a chess champion of France. I have helped miners at Charbonnages de France find new jobs. I have been involved in the arts and, most importantly, I have had the opportunity to bear witness to my experiences with young people.

I have a husband, children, grandchildren, and—wonder of wonders—great-grandchildren. It took me a long time to realize what effect my experiences had had on my children, however. I thought I had protected them by practically never discussing my past and by making only rare allusions to the war. My oldest son was the first to really dispel this false impression. In response to my statement, "I didn't talk to you about the war very much," his immediate reply was, "Your silence was far more eloquent than your words."

It was only quite recently that I realized how much my grandchildren have been involved in my past. I have had more discussions with them on that topic than with my own children. I hope with all my heart that this burden will not weigh too heavily on their shoulders.

Their reactions have been very different depending on their personal circumstances. I think their reactions are directly related to what they have learned from their parents and at school. As one of my sons said recently: "The Jewish mother [that's me] is far too involved in her grandchildren's education."

I would, nevertheless, like to transmit a heritage to my grandchildren. My greatest legacy is, I believe, my ability to transform all difficulties—even the most tragic—into strengths rather than weaknesses, and my ability to glean from each situation a spark of hope that can ignite a bonfire of promise. I want to pass on my ability to attempt to remain dignified in all circumstances and to accept life's responsibilities, no matter how difficult they seem. I hope this legacy will be passed on for many generations and that my great-grandchildren—my pride and joy—will also be the beneficiaries of this heritage.

"REMEMBER TO BE A GOOD HUMAN BEING"

A MEMOIR OF LIFE AND THE HOLOCAUST

by Frances Irwin (Frymet Oksenhendler)
as told to Rachel Epstein

TABLE OF CONTENTS

INTRODUCTION

I was born and raised in Końskie, a town near Radom in the center of Poland. The town had a population of fifteen thousand, half of whom were Jews. More than half of the Jews were shopkeepers and were engaged in light industry, although there was also one Jewish doctor, which was unusual. What made the town special was our *shul* (synagogue), which had been built in honor of King Casimir the Great (Kazimierz Wielki), who allowed the first Jews into Poland in the fourteenth century. The *shul* was built of wood without the use of nails and it was like a historic landmark in that we were not allowed to fix or alter it, especially the inside. People came from all over the world to see that beautiful *shul*, and we lived four or five houses away from it.

Our family's location near the *shul* is significant because religion played an important part in our life. One of my first memories is getting up very early to say morning prayers because my father insisted on it. I said them at home, sometimes alone and sometimes with my older sister, with whom I went to school each morning. In the morning I went to public school from 8:00 a.m. to 1:00 p.m., and then to a Bais Yaacov [Orthodox] school for girls, where we learned until 5:00 p.m. After that I would come home and do homework from both schools, which made me very unhappy because I had no time to play. Most of the children around me were playing, but I had to rush home, eat lunch in a hurry and then run to Hebrew school, which was far away.

As much as I hated going to Hebrew school when I was a child, I am grateful now for my Jewish education because when I go to *shul* I can read Hebrew and I understand what the prayers are about. My father actually established the Bais Yaacov school in Końskie, which made him unusual because most religious people of that time did not believe it important to educate girls.

I remember being the youngest child at Bais Yaacov and standing on a chair to give a speech about *Tu B'Shevat*, Jewish Arbor Day that occurs usually in February. My father, as President of the school, was sitting on the dais, and I can still feel the hug and kiss he gave me and see his proud face as he lifted me off the chair when I was finished. I never forget things like that and because of these memories holidays are sad times for me. Usually people love it when the holidays come, but for me it is the opposite. My husband used to make me feel better on these holidays, but now that he is no longer here holidays are very sad.

Końskie was a shoemaking center and my father's business supplied the shoe factories with leather that had been prepared in Radom. He sold both wholesale and retail from a store as well as from a large warehouse behind the store. At a certain point I remember that the Poles opened leather stores to compete with the Jews but they really could not compete because they did not have the required knowledge and contacts. One Polish woman opened a shoe store, but she had to come to my father to buy leather and she would transact her business at midnight with my father going to her store so that she would not be seen going into a Jewish store.

My father, grandfather, and my brothers were *Hasidim,* followers of the *Gerrer* rabbi,[1] who was saved by going to Palestine when the Nazis came. But my father was more open-minded than the typical *Hasid*, as his belief in the importance of education for women demonstrates. He was exceptionally honest and wise and had a reputation for being able to solve problems, a reputation that extended even to the non-Jews in the town. For instance, the Mayor used to come to my father for advice, but he would come secretly so no one would see him asking a Jew for help. My father was not a rich man, but they called him "the richest man in town" for the good deeds that he did.

My mother was also exceptional; she was the most wonderful, charitable woman imaginable. She used to help all the poor people in the town and never thought of herself. I remember my father saying to her, "You must think of

---

1   Rabbinic dynasty from Góra Kalwaria (called Gur by the Jews).

yourself too." On Wednesdays she would go to the butcher and buy meat for her friends who could not afford to do their own shopping, choosing different friends to help each week, depending on what she could afford. Then she would buy meat for herself, for our family, on Thursdays. I never knew why she shopped in that order until I went to Israel after the war and met people from Końskie who had known my mother before Hitler came. One of those people was the butcher where she used to shop, and he remembered asking her one day why she shopped for the people she was helping before she shopped for herself. He said she told him, "When I take care of the poor people first, then I enjoy what I am buying for myself more."

My mother probably inherited this charitable behavior from her father; he used to help a man who supported himself as a burglar and regularly broke into my grandfather's factory. My grandfather would tell the manager to leave the door open on Friday so that the burglar would not have to violate the Sabbath by breaking the lock when he made his Friday evening "visit."

I remember my mother making cranberry jam every summer, which we ate all winter and into the following summer. The pots she used were bigger than I was. When she put the jam into jars she left a large portion in the pot and put the pot, along with spoons, out into the yard so that any children who wanted to could come to our house and eat what was left in the pot. Half of my class and the neighbor's children used to follow me home that day to taste the jam. They could hardly wait and would keep asking me when my mother was going to be making her special jam.

My mother also made cookies but I never ate them. I would accumulate them and give them to a friend who was very poor. One day my mother saw me going out with the cookies in a bag and became very angry when I told her what I was doing. She said, "Why didn't you tell me? I'll make a double recipe and you can bring hers to her on Friday." I think this habit of being a small eater helped me to survive in the camps and not die from hunger as many people did.

Our house revolved around the Jewish holidays, beginning, of course, with the Sabbath. Preparations began on Thursday when my mother did all the shopping and baking. Friday was the day for cooking, which brought forth the most wonderful aromas. Sometimes I think I can still feel that smell of Friday's chicken soup with its boiled chicken and thin round pieces of dough, and of

Saturday's roast goose that we would eat cold with the *cholent*[2] that was cooked by the baker.

We did not go to *Bais Yaacov* on Fridays and on late Friday afternoons we would wash and change into our festive Sabbath clothes. My mother, who was blond and wore a blond *sheitel*,[3] even changed her *sheitel* on Fridays. She would get dressed up and wear all her jewelry as if she were going to a wedding. My father and brothers would go to the *mikveh* [ritual bath], when they came home from the store and then go to *shul*. My father came home from *shul* with guests, people who had been there to pray but had no place to eat for the Sabbath. Because of the guests we never knew how many people to set the table for and we always added extra place settings for these people who my father would seat next to him at the enormous table.

The Sabbath atmosphere, with the *kiddush*[4] and the Hebrew songs and the table and the food is impossible to describe. It was as if God himself were in the house.

Passover was also a big celebration. The only time we would get new clothes was for Passover, when we were outfitted from top to bottom. I remember that my poor friend Malka, the one I brought the cookies to, never got new clothes for Passover. Once, when I was older and my mother bought me a new green salt and pepper tweed suit for Passover that she wanted me to wear to my grandmother's, I started to cry that Malka never got any new clothes. I asked my mother if I could lend Malka the suit for Passover and I would wear the dress from last year and then Malka will give it back. My mother agreed and when I gave the suit to Malka we were both crying. After Passover I said the suit didn't fit me any more because I did not like to eat and had gotten skinny, and I gave the suit to Malka to keep.

Because I was such a poor eater, my sister would follow me to school with food to try to make me eat. Once when she was doing this she got run over by a car and broke her leg. Since there were very few cars in our town she was not

---

2   Cholent, a traditional stew that is cooked slowly overnight and eaten on Saturday, consists of meat or chicken, potatoes and grains.
3   A wig worn by married Orthodox women, based on the Talmudic injunction that married women should not appear attractive to men other than their husbands.
4   Blessing on wine that is drunk before Sabbath and festival meals.

used to looking out for them, and this car was a military car, as I remember, filled with soldiers. My sister's breaking her leg was terrible, the worst time of my life...

Getting back to Passover, it was the most beautiful holiday. My father reading the *Haggadah*,[5] and the songs, and all of us participating. *Shavuot*[6] was also special as the whole house was full of fruit, vegetables and tree branches. On *Rosh Hashanah* and *Yom Kippur* you felt very holy. It was actually scary, that feeling of holiness. My father would stay in the *shul* from *Kol Nidre*[7] to the next day, praying and learning, and I was the one who brought him a pillow in case he wanted to make himself more comfortable on the chair. After that I was afraid to go home because of the holiness. I do not remember being afraid of people, but the holiness was scary. It felt as if even the air you were breathing was different and holy. *Sukkot*[8] was very beautiful. We had a wooden *sukkah* behind our house all year round and we took the top off for the holiday, and all the men, including my grandfather, ate in it during the entire holiday.

I had two brothers and two sisters. I vividly remember my oldest brother's wedding. My parents used a matchmaker to pick a wife for him and because she didn't have a mother, we organized his wedding. We invited the whole town and emptied out the house so there would be room for them, even for the poor people. The *huppah*[9] was on the street and the street was filled with hundreds of people holding candles.

After they were married my brother and his wife lived in rooms we had added to the back of our house with their own separate entrance through the backyard. This brother was president of Young *Aguda*, of the Agudas Yisrael ultra-Orthodox political party. Through Young *Aguda* he worked hard, rounding up sick people and taking them to vote, so that a Jew could be elected to the Polish Parliament. Finally he succeeded, and this person represented the *Aguda* in the parliament.

---

5   Story read before the Passover meal that recounts the Jews' slavery in Egypt and their exodus to the Promised Land.

6   Festival commemorating God giving the Torah to Moses on Mount Sinai; it is also an agricultural holiday.

7   The prayer recited at the start of the Yom Kippur service.

8   Eight-day festival commemorating the exodus from Egypt. The sukkah, a wooden booth reminiscent of the portable abodes that the Israelites lived in, is used for eating and sometimes sleeping during this holiday.

9   Wedding canopy held above the bridal couple during the ceremony.

My second oldest sister lived in Radom after she was married and I once went with my father to visit her there, just before Hitler invaded Poland. The only other time I left my town was when my mother took me to Kraków to register me for the seminary where I would study to become a Hebrew teacher. This school had been started by Sarah Schnirer who was an orthodox feminist, founder and head of all the *Bais Yaacov* schools. Feminism was rare then and she was well known in Poland both before and after the Holocaust.

Of course, antisemitism did not arrive in our town with Hitler. I remember once on the way to school seeing a Jewish man lying on the street bleeding to death. We were screaming and when the policeman heard our screams, he said, "Why did he walk on the street? If he hadn't walked here, he would have been alive!" That always struck me as terrible antisemitism, and, of course, I already mentioned how the people did not want to be seen buying from my father because he was Jewish.

I first heard about Hitler in 1936 when I was 14. The information came from Polish-born Jews who had been living in Germany and came back to Poland due to Hitler's rise to power. This was before *Kristallnacht* and the Jews who returned did not say that terrible things were happening to the Jews. We just knew he was not a good person but in our wildest dreams we could not imagine what was going to happen.

CHAPTER 1

Under Nazi Rule

W e did not even really know when the war began. We heard bombs exploding and everyone said it was maneuvers. But when we saw people taken to the hospital we knew it was more than maneuvers. We ran away to the woods just the way we were, not taking anything with us. At this point the Poles were also running away. We stayed in the woods for a few days and when it was quiet and there were no longer any houses burning we started to walk back to town. I remember my father putting something on his face, covering his beard so the Germans would not see it. I do not know why he understood that this was a good thing to do, but he did.

We came back to find our house just as we had left it. The next day the Germans said that all the men had to line up in the market square and would work for them. On September 12, 1939, the Germans arrested a large number of Jews because they supposedly killed a German. They were forced to dig a tremendous hole and then start running. The Germans started shooting at them and about forty of them were killed. My uncle was one of those who was buried alive, so we knew right away what the Germans were out for.

There were other signs as well. We had to bring all our gold and silver to the Germans, which we did, except for a few small things that we gave to the Mayor's wife, the woman who used to buy from us secretly, because my father liked the Mayor and wanted to help him.

The day after they ordered all the men to the square we made a hole in the wall so my father could hide in a spare room in the back. We put an armoire in front of the hole and my father hid there. From the day the Nazis came my father did not go outside. My father refused to shave his beard but my brother shaved his and was taken to a work camp. My other brother was in Warsaw and could not come home.

The Germans closed down my father's business but one day a Pole who used to buy leather from us brought some Germans to the warehouse and they piled all the leather we had onto trucks and shipped it back to Germany. We lived on the little money we had before the Germans came.

On the evening of the third day that the Germans were in the town we saw the outline of flames through the windows. The Germans had set our beautiful *shul* on fire! When the fire spread to the nearby houses they were afraid that the whole town would burn down and asked the Jews to put out the fire. We had no water in our house, so we had to go to the well and pump water. Everyone, including women and children, was part of the fire brigade chain.

While the fire was burning we felt as if we ourselves were on fire; it was the most terrible thing because that *shul* was like our heart. We worked all night and by morning the fire was out. My father had been in real danger because we lived so close to the *shul*, but he still refused to go out.

As soon as the Germans came to town they began to set up a ghetto. Since our house was already in the ghetto we had to take in other people from outside the ghetto. The house became terribly crowded and most of these people were sleeping on the floors, that is, when we could sleep. We would listen for the sound of German boots and were terrified that they would come to our house because we heard that they came to houses at night and took out people and shot them for no reason at all.

Because I spoke Polish without an accent I would sometimes leave the ghetto to go look for potatoes or any kind of food I could buy to smuggle back into the ghetto so we would have food for my brother's children, an older boy and a younger girl.

Then one day we saw all the Jews coming in from all the small villages around our city, and the houses in the ghetto were so crowded that they could not even lie down at night; they had to stand.[10]

The Jewish police would watch us and were terribly distressed that they could not help because the Germans totally controlled them and used them for their own purposes. If a policeman did not do what the Germans wanted, he was shot. We knew we could not expect anything from them, but they tried to help the Germans as little as they could.

We lived in the ghetto for a more than a year[11] and then one day the Judenrat (Jewish Council) ordered all the Jews into the market square to be resettled, telling us that any Jews left in the town would be shot. My father decided that I should run out of the ghetto and hide. I did not want to leave my family and my father and I argued about it for a whole day. My mother was crying and begging him not to send me away but he said, as if he knew what was happening, that I was the only one with a chance to survive because of my perfect, unaccented Polish, and he wanted someone in the family to survive. He told me to take good care of myself that winter, and in the spring, he predicted, the Germans would lose the war. He said it would last only one winter. His last words to me were: "Remember to be a good human being because only the person [who has been hurt] himself can forgive you, not God. So please remember that." Those words are always in my mind; every time I want to do something that is not right, or do not want to do something that I should do, what my father said comes back to me.

I felt terrible because I did not want to leave my family and I could not understand, or did not want to understand, why he chose me. But once it was decided that I would go by myself, we had to figure out how to do it. There was a 4:00 PM curfew in the town, which applied to Poles as well as Jews, but my father got the idea that I could leave by the sewers, and asked a Jewish policeman to be sure he closed the sewer cover after I went down.

I went to complain to my brother about what my father wanted me to do, and

10 Several waves of refugees arrived in the town — from Łódź in 1939-40; from Płock in February 1941, and from the nearby small towns and villages in summer-fall 1942.

11 The ghetto had been closed apparently in spring 1941, and the author is probably referring to this as the period from which she is counting "more than a year." The deportations to Treblinka were in November 1942.

I saw his children lying in bed crying with hunger and I said to myself, "I'm going to make my father happy and go, but I'll probably never survive because they'll find me and shoot me." My father made sure I had warm clothes and boots, which had been my sister's, and he gave me all the money he had. And I remember that when the family was preparing to go to the market square my mother asked my father what she should pack for the family and he said that all he needed was a clean shirt, *tallis*[12] and *tefillin,*[13] "in case I'm going to be able to *daven* [pray] once more."

When I got down to the sewer where the water was up to my knees, I heard voices and I was scared to death. But when a voice asked in Yiddish, "Who is it?" I was not afraid anymore and I answered, "It's me. I'm Jewish," because I realized they were afraid that I might be Polish. There were actually quite a lot of people in that sewer, all with the same idea of escaping.

At night we would go out searching for food. We knew there was a Polish cooperative farm nearby and we asked the same Jewish policeman who had helped me get into the sewer safely to help us make a hole in the wall so we could get into the egg storage area without cracking the lock. We were hiding in the cooperative farm when we saw all the Jews being taken out of town. We also heard people rummaging through the houses and shooting people who were hiding. The policeman came by the window where we were watching and threw us a box of hard candy and told us, "They're sending us all away. You're on your own."

We used that candy to stay alive because there was no more food. Every day each of us got one piece of candy and we used it to wet our mouths when they were dry. Even today when I take a candy in my mouth I never finish it; I take it out of my mouth, which is a habit left over from those days. At night it was essential to be quiet and one of us would serve as guard to make sure no one was snoring.

Suddenly we heard a noise. It was the Poles rummaging through the apartments where the Jews had lived and taking what the Germans had left. The Poles knew more about hiding things than the Germans and they soon

12 Prayer shawl worn by men during morning prayers.
13 Phylacteries, two small leather boxes containing prayers and worn on the weaker arm and forehead by men during morning weekday prayers.

discovered where the bricks had been removed to let us into the cooperative farm. We started to run and the Poles shouted to the Germans, "Juden." We scattered all over. I knew exactly where to go; I ran quite a distance to my friend's backyard, which had a big outhouse. I went into one of the toilets, locked it, and stayed there until it got dark. When I went out I did not know where to go or what to do, and I was terrified because I did not think there were any Jews left.

My first idea was to go to the Mayor's wife and ask her for help. On the way there I met my homeroom teacher from public school. She belonged to the Sokolnia, a very patriotic nationalistic Polish organization. She was an antisemite and I was afraid she was going to turn me in. She asked me if I had been resurrected like Jesus because I looked like I had come back from the grave. I told her that I was hiding and I had not eaten or combed my hair, which was in braids down to my knees. I was very surprised when she said, "Come with me," and she took me to her house and told me to wash up and comb my hair and gave me something to eat. She said she knew there were some Jews—the stronger ones—working on a big farm at the end of town. She told me I would be able to bribe a German to let me work there, which I somehow had the courage to do. I stayed there for about four days, and I think I was in the egg cooperative for about a week, although I am not at all sure of the lengths of time involved.

Then we heard rumors that even this farm was going to become *Judenrein*, and this time I did run to the Mayor's wife. By then I had become obsessed with the need to survive, and I told her that my father had chosen me to be the family member to outlive what was happening. We both knew I needed Polish papers. She got them from her husband's office and gave me a new name, Grubman, which could be either Polish or Jewish. I spent the night there and when her husband came home he told me there were some Jewish men working for the Germans, picking up scrap iron, and that maybe I could stay with them. The Mayor and his wife went out and I knew that if the Germans caught me there they would kill them, so I had to leave.

I left a note, filled my pockets with all the food I could find, and went to where the Jews were working. I stayed there for a few days and then the Germans started talking about sending the men away because they did not need the iron any more. The Jews were talking about going to Szydlowiec, a town not far from mine, where the Germans were concentrating the Jews as they made the small towns nearby *Judenrein*. At first I thought I would go there too but then I decided to go into the woods and join the partisans who were fighting Hitler.

I never found the partisans, so I was alone, hiding in the wheat fields at night and looking for blueberries in the woods during the day. This went on for a summer and half of the winter, and when they cut the wheat and it no longer covered me I slept in the woods. After the blueberries were gone I ate raw potatoes. The whole time I was terrified that a German or a Pole would find me.

One night I went to the train station and used my Polish papers to go to Szydlowiec. I was told to go to an old dilapidated leather factory that my father used to do business with and I stayed there for a while until somebody heard that I was from Końskie. He asked if I knew someone named Oksenhendler who he used to deal with. That was my family name and I became very excited. He told me that my brother-in-law was in Radom, that they had taken away my sister—the one I used to go to school with—and the children but not him because he was young and strong.

In Szydlowiec I met three girls, one of whom said she knew how to smuggle us into Radom and that it has to be on Sylvester Night (New Year's Eve). "All the Germans are drunk," she told us, "And they don't know what they are doing. I'll show you how to get into this little ghetto with a high fence, which you have to be prepared to jump."

We got on the train to Radom and sat there terrified. The train was dark because the Germans were afraid of being bombed, and they were all over singing songs about killing the Jews, bragging that this one killed so many and that one killed so many more.

The four of us smuggled ourselves into the Radom ghetto and then we all ran in different directions looking for people we knew. When I found my brother-in-law we were so emotional we could not talk for a while. We were just crying. Then we began reminiscing. He told me what happened to his family and I told him what happened to mine. We did not sleep at all that night; we just talked and cried.

He went to work early in the morning and I stayed in his tiny room without any food, just as he had told me to do. He returned with the news that the

Germans had caught two of the girls who had smuggled into the ghetto with me and that they had told the Judenrat that if the other two did not come forward they would take out ten Jews and shoot them. This was a nightmare.

I knew I could not go right away because it was after the curfew when Jews were not allowed on the street. Early in the morning my brother-in-law took me to the Judenrat. As the officer was calling the Gestapo to say they had me, the fourth girl walked in. Both of us knew we could not let innocent Jews die for us and we thought we would be shot as soon as we came forward. After we had been sitting at the Judenrat for about an hour, an SS man came and took us to the Gestapo office where the other two girls were already waiting.

The SS man said, "Now you're all together, tell us how the partisans communicate." Because of the partisans they were afraid to go into the woods. We told them the truth, which was that we knew that the partisans lived in the woods but we had no idea how they got ammunition. The Gestapo men did not believe us, and they called each of us to a different room to interrogate us individually. They spoke to me as if I were a little girl and promised that if I told them the secrets of the partisans they would send me to Palestine to live. They offered me anything they could think of, but I kept telling them, "I don't know their secrets because I don't belong to the partisans." I did not want them to know that I had come because of my brother-in-law because I thought that would put him in danger.

They tortured me by chaining me to the leg of a bed and putting food just out of my reach, which they said I could have if I told them what they wanted to know. They beat me too. Then they took me to another room and a different SS man came and started to beat me in the worst way, and then, finally, I said, "I'm Jewish and you can shoot me and it'll be over with." When one of the SS men heard this he said, "What? There's a Jew still alive? Let's shoot her and stuff her and put her in the museum."

The following day they put me in a truck by myself and said, "You're very lucky. They didn't shoot you. You're going to jail." I was terrified. I did not know anything about jail. It was a subject we never talked about at home, but somehow I had the idea that in jail I would be eaten alive by rats. I kept asking God why they did not shoot me and asking my father why he had made me leave and run away to be so scared of rats.

When we arrived at the jail, they put me in a room with the other three and we were all black and blue and swollen from the beatings and we all cried together. There *were* rats, but we were covered up and when we saw a rat we started to move and the rat ran away. We sat in jail without being beaten and without working but also with very little food, living mainly on the few scraps of bread brought to us by the Judenrat. The Judenrat also told us that the Germans were going to make the area *Judenrein* by taking the Jews to Treblinka, which we later learned was one of the killing camps.

One night a guard told us to get dressed and leave our cell. We were terrified because we had heard people being shot in the night and we thought this was about to happen to us. One of the guards said to me, "What's wrong with you people? Why are you crying? You're going to a place where you'll have a chance to live out your life." They put us on a truck with a lot of people, all Poles, no Jews, people who were killers and robbers and political anti-Germans.

CHAPTER 2

Two Years in the Hell of Auschwitz

We drove for I am not sure how long until we came to a place with the words *Arbeit Macht Frei* on the entrance gate. We said to each other, "Maybe the guard was right and we will have a chance to live and work here."

They told us that we were in Auschwitz, a name that meant nothing to us. But as we were going in we saw people coming back from work, five in a row, thin like skeletons and so weak they could hardly walk. And all the time classical music was playing over the loudspeaker. The combination of these broken people in rags and the classical music was unbelievable. All of a sudden we saw that these beaten-down people were trying to stand up straight and walk better and that an SS man was looking them over. Later we learned that the SS man was Mengele. None of this made any sense to us; we thought we were in a madhouse.

The ground was so limey it did not absorb water. It was almost like quicksand and it was hard to lift your feet out of the mud. Then we noticed the barbed wire. We did not know that it was electrified, but we saw that every few steps there was a booth with an SS man inside.

We started to cry and one of the SS men said, "Don't cry yet; you haven't seen everything yet." As we were being taken into a building one of the women asked me if I wanted to give her my boots—beautiful boots from home—before they were taken away. I was smart enough to say yes, which the others did not do because they thought they were going to get their clothes back. After they took our clothes, they gave us showers and took us outside naked. This was February or March in 1943. An SS man pointed out our bruises to the other people coming in and said, "This is what happens when you don't listen; you get beaten up like these girls."

They shaved our heads with a razor and two SS women were arguing about who would get my beautiful blond braids. The woman doing the shaving cut them off separately and gave one braid to each of the women.

They put numbers on our arms with a needle and added triangles to our numbers as they were doing to the Poles, and this time we did not tell them that we were Jewish. We were given a dress and wooden shoes—no underwear—and were taken to Block 14, which was filled with Poles who recognized, as the Germans did not, that we were Jews and were always threatening to tell the Germans.

When I started working and complained to another Jewish woman who also had a triangle, she told me I should ask to be transferred to her location, a Jewish block, and that I would not be putting myself into any additional danger because Jews who came like us and like the Poles from jails were called *karteimässig*, which meant they were not to be taken to the gas chambers.

We had not known about the gas chambers when we arrived, but we saw the black soot and fires coming out of the chimneys and smelled the fat and bodies burning, which smelled like meat burning. When we got to the block we asked right away, "What are those chimneys?" The other prisoners told us that they were for burning the people who have been gassed because it does not take as much room to store ashes as to store bodies.

It felt good to be among Jews and we started talking Yiddish, and people began telling us how Auschwitz worked. They told us that when a transport came Mengele made his selections, putting those he wanted to be in camp on one side and those to be gassed on the other side. And they told us about the ovens, the burning, and that Jews were chosen by the SS to work there, and that if they refused they were shot and someone else was picked to do the work. These people in the ovens were the *Sonderkommando* who took out the gassed people and examined them to remove any gold teeth for the Germans. This was the most terrible kind of work. They sometimes recognized family members.

There are no words to describe what these people must have felt but they had to do it because they wanted to survive.

I was sent to work with an *Aussenkommando*, which meant I was working outside the camp. The Germans were dynamiting the buildings around Auschwitz, partly because they did not want any witnesses to what they were doing and partly because they needed the space to build more barracks as more people were coming all the time. Our job was to pick out whatever the SS told us they wanted, things like pieces of iron or metal and unbroken bricks. We would put the iron and the bricks in separate wheelbarrows and wheel them over to freight cars where they were being sent back to Germany for the army. It was a terrible job.

The barracks we slept in had three levels of wooden shelves, each level for about fifteen people, covered with straw. We were so crowded we could not lie down, so we slept sitting up. If one person had to move because she was stiff, we all had to move with her. We were packed in like sardines, wearing the same dress we had worn all day and without any blankets. Body heat from our neighbors was what kept us warm. If it had been raining, we went to sleep in wet clothes that dried on us at night.

They woke us up at 4:00 in the morning and we took turns going to the kitchen to pick up iron kettles of black water they called "tea." We held our noses closed when we drank this liquid, because it smelled so bad, but nevertheless everyone drank it. I was so hungry that I did not turn down this stuff. I knew that if I did not drink it I would have nothing to drink all day.

The day began with the *Appell* (roll call). We stood outside in rows and they counted and recounted until it became light outside. They did not want to send us to work when it was still dark.

The worst time for my kind of work was in the winter because then the snow accumulated on our backs and shoulders and when we straightened up for even a few seconds, the SS saw the snowfall from our shoulders and knew that we had stopped and set the dogs on us. That happened to me once. I knew I had to stand up straight for a few seconds and they set the dogs on me with a big smile. (I ask myself often, "Am I dreaming?" "Did this really happen?"). People who were bitten on the neck bled to death, but I was lucky because the dog bit me on the thigh and somehow it healed. My dress was full of blood and when I got back to the camp I washed it off with black snow filthy from the chimneys where they were burning people.

They brought lunch in trucks to where we were working. Each of us had a metal bowl and spoon, which was the most important thing in our lives because if we lost it, or if we pushed or talked, we did not eat. We held it continually and even slept with it. We never let those things out of our sight. Can you imagine it? It was crazy. As we marched in rows of five to our work, we put the bowls and spoons down before we began working. At lunchtime we quietly retrieved our bowls because if we made any noise they hit us over the head really hard. Lunch was soup that was made from all the scraps from the SS dinner that should have gone into the garbage. It was mainly potato peels and hot water with an occasional bit of potato or piece of meat.

Before it got dark they took us back to camp where Beethoven's beautiful music was playing and Mengele was making his selections. Then we had the *Appell* again, just like in the morning. They would count us over and over again. We were so exhausted we were praying they would stop. Finally they did, gave us a piece of bread, and let us into the barracks.

People died during the night and rats and mice ate parts of their bodies. The rats also went after the living people but we could push them away. We were always being eaten by the enormous lice that lodged in the seams of our dresses. It would keep us up all night, picking at and killing lice, which is one reason we were so tired when they woke us up for the *Appell*.

In the morning we took out the dead bodies, which had to be counted. We would put them on the ground, a truck would collect them, and the bodies would be taken to the ovens. It was so horrible and yet we could not even cry; there were no more tears.

The air in Auschwitz was so terrible from the soot from the burning bodies that our saliva was black, and this burning was endless.

On our way to work we passed the *Sonderkommando*. These were Jews who had the job of taking the bodies from the gas chambers and putting them in the ovens to be burned. But before the bodies were burned these Jews had to remove any gold teeth. We would see them pulling the gold teeth out of the bodies and if they stopped for a minute they were shot and replaced by other people from the camp. I cannot imagine how they felt because sometimes they discovered that the bodies they were working on were members of their own family.

It is impossible to describe the inhuman conditions in Auschwitz. The hard labor without rest, the hours standing at the *Appell,* the lack of food, working to exhaustion, being beaten like mules, the rats and lice. Yet despite these inhuman conditions, the will to survive and to see Hitler defeated was strong.

We talked about getting out, being free, surviving. We would cry as we thought about our parents and families, hoping that they were alive somewhere, fighting to survive the way we were. We would pray together, making up prayers, asking God for certain things. Many people said to us, "What are you praying for? There is no God." But we answered, "There has to be a God because we're alive. We're still here."

We even managed to observe the holidays a little. We found out when it was Passover and did not eat our bread on the first day, but we could not survive without that bread so we ate it the following day, but that first day was a small reminder of Passover.

I thought especially of my brother's and sister's children. After seeing what went on in Auschwitz, I did not think they were still alive but I kept hoping. When we passed by the gas chambers I saw the way they were tearing children from their mother's arms and not even waiting to get them into the gas chambers before they killed them on the spot. We could hear the mothers screaming. I really already knew in my heart that they were not alive and I thought about them a lot.

Every time you saw another transport come in you prayed that when your family got to wherever they were going they were chosen to work. I was pretty sure my mother and father would not have been selected for work, but I was always hoping that work somehow was saving my sisters and brothers. Hoping to see our families when all this was over was what kept us alive; otherwise, there was no reason to want to live the way we lived in Auschwitz.

I remember a song that was written in Auschwitz and became popular there called *Niewolnicze Tango* (Slaves' Tango). It was about dreaming of surviving and coming out of Auschwitz and what it would feel like to be free. These are the words: "We dream of the smell of green fields, not of smoke, and that the whole world will get together and sing the freedom song, and each country will play its

own instrument, yet we're never going to forget the horrors of Auschwitz."
Nobody ever wrote about this song, which was in Polish, not in Yiddish.

I often wonder how I managed to live through Auschwitz. I know one reason
is that I had a friend who saved my life. She worked in the *Bekleidungskammer*,
which was where they took and sorted the belongings from the suitcases of
people who came to Auschwitz thinking they were going to be resettled
someplace where they could actually use the possessions from their old lives.
Her job was to sort through the clothes and open up seams to find the money
and jewelry that people had sewn into their clothes. This is something I knew
about as my mother's diamond had been hidden in the seam of my dress.

My friend's name was Roza Robota. She came from Ciechanów in Poland
and risked her life to bring me pieces of clothing to cover my feet because I kept
losing my wooden shoes and had to walk around barefoot because my feet were
very small and the shoes very big. Once your feet touched the limey soil in
Auschwitz you could get trapped, like in quicksand, and she saved me from that.

One day there was a big explosion in Auschwitz. The alarm went off and the
SS men were running all over. At first we hoped that this meant we were about
to be liberated; then we were afraid that they were going to empty the camp and
put us all in the gas chambers. We had the *Appell* early that day and they kept us
in the barracks.

The next day we found out that an oven had been blown up—it is still visible
in Auschwitz if you take a tour—and that four girls, including Roza Robota, had
been arrested. The other three were Regina Safirsztajn, Ala Gertner and Ester
Wajcblum. Ala, Regina and Ester worked in an ammunition factory not far from
Auschwitz and smuggled in a little bit of dynamite every day. They gave the
dynamite to Roza who left it in one spot near the *Sonderkommando* who picked it
up and accumulated it until they could blow up one oven. They reckoned that if
one oven was out of commission perhaps they would gas fewer people because
they would not be able to burn them. One German was killed and about a dozen
were wounded. The oven did not operate anymore, so maybe a few lives were
saved or were left to live a little longer. These women were extremely brave; they
knew that if they were caught they would not only be killed, but also tortured.
Even with the torturing, the four women never revealed any names because
there were no other arrests. They were hanged before the entire camp on

January 6, and I light memorial candles and say the *Kaddish* prayer in their memory every year on that day. Roza Robota was the most caring person who ever lived on this earth… and she had such a terrible death.

One day I had such a high fever that my tongue felt like black shoe leather and I could not move it from side to side. But even in those inhuman conditions people were so good to me. They tried to hold me up during the *Appell* when the SS woman was not watching. I am often asked why my experience during the war has not made me bitter, and my answer is that I learned about friendship in Auschwitz when people helped keep me warm by shielding me with their bodies, which was all they had. The day when I had the fever I bent down to pick up some black snow, so my mouth would not be so dry, and the SS man saw me do it and gave me such a terrible beating that I did not think I would survive.

But that same day something happened which made it possible for me to survive. When we were standing at the *Appell*, a high-ranking SS man came by and asked if any of us were seamstresses. Naturally everyone said they were, because we knew if we were going to do sewing it had to be an inside job with better conditions. And I was the one he chose. This was the biggest miracle that happened to me in Auschwitz because I could not take working outside one day longer. The sun burned through you, the rain drenched you, the wind dried you out, and in the winter you froze. Being chosen allowed me to survive Auschwitz. Every time that it was really very bad and I could not take anymore, something happened that made it seem as if an angel were watching over me and helping me to survive.

The next day I was put to work sewing on buttons by hand for German uniforms. Even now when I sew on a button it never falls off and my friends save their buttons for me to attach. As we worked we listened, and every time a bomber flew over us—we could tell the bombers because they made a heavier noise than other planes—we hoped that a bomb would hit the tracks so they could not bring in any more transports, but it never happened.

CHAPTER 3

From the Jaws of Death to a New Life

One morning, in January 1945, they took us out for the *Appell* and told us we were leaving Auschwitz. We had heard rumors that the Russians were approaching, and that was why we were being taken away. As we walked out we met the men, who had been separated from us by barbed wire, and we started to march together without knowing where we were going or what we were doing. There was deep snow on the ground and it was freezing cold. At night they put us in a barn and guarded us so we would not run away. This was the Death March, and many people died on the way. Others who could not walk were shot by the SS and left where they fell.

When I thought I could not walk any more and that this was the end, we came to a wagon loaded with knapsacks and blankets for the SS. A Pole name Juzek said, "Come on here," and picked me up and covered me with the blankets and knapsacks so I would not be seen. Then when the SS came for their stuff, I jumped down so they would not find me. That day of resting and not walking saved my life, again. The man who helped me was a political prisoner in Auschwitz, a communist or a Polish patriot. Those people were not gassed. If I could have remembered his last name I would have looked for him after the war.

I do not know how long we walked or even if they fed us—how can there be a blank like that?—but after a while they started pushing everyone who had been marching onto freight trains. But they could not fit us all onto the trains and I was one of about seventy people who were left as the trains pulled away. We thought we would be shot there and then, but an hour later we were put on a truck and we ended up in Mauthausen, in Austria. Mauthausen was like Auschwitz, a very large camp with gas chambers, but by the time we got there, according to a Jew who was there, the gas chambers had stopped operating. We realized we had a chance to survive, and what further added to our hope was when they put us into a room and locked the door we realized there were eighteen (a number whose name in Hebrew, *Chai*, means life when adding up their numerical value) of us there.

After a few days they transferred us to a women's camp in Lenzing, where it was so bad that the sleeping conditions—lice and mice and cold and rain—were just as bad as Auschwitz. However, without gas chambers the place had an entirely different feel to it. But we still had the horrible SS women who would beat us and shout at us and tell us, "Don't think you're going to survive because we'll make sure that before the war ends you'll be dead."

At noon they brought the soup that we used to get for lunch at the factory into the barracks where we were living. All of a sudden we heard a voice screaming in broken German, "Don't eat the food; the food is poisoned. You're going to die if you eat the food." He was a French kitchen worker and he had picked up some German and was warning us. Then the SS women started screaming at us and beating us and urging us to eat but somehow we held out and listened to the man. Those of us who wanted to eat were pushed away from the food by those who believed we would be poisoned and a real fight broke out.

We had heard shots before and then there were shots again. The SS women disappeared and we spent the whole night alone, crying and hungry, not knowing what was happening and afraid that the SS men would come in with their dogs and shoot us.

In the morning soldiers arrived in trucks and opened the doors and since we did not know what kind of soldiers they were we were very frightened. One soldier was a Jew whose parents came from Poland and he started to talk to us in broken Polish that we could hardly understand, but we soon realized he was saying, "Stop crying. You're free. There are no more Germans here. We're American soldiers and we'll help you and take care of you." The other soldiers were standing around crying like I had never seen—big men with guns in uniforms crying. And we were crying too. We told the Jewish soldier what the

Frenchman had said about the food in the kitchen being poisoned. He realized we were starving and he gave us all the food meant for the soldiers and he opened the cans and fed us. At the same time a different soldier fed the food from the kitchen to a cat and it died on the spot.

We stayed in the barracks and other soldiers who wanted to see us brought us food. We really could not go out because our clothes were so worn they kept tearing and we had no shoes.

One day some men came and started talking to us in Yiddish. They said they were from an organization called the Joint (American Jewish Joint Distribution Committee) in the United States and that they had packages for us. We thought angels had come down to earth to help us; we could not imagine that people as far away as America knew about us and about our situation and wanted to help. When we got the packages we were so emotional we could not even open them. We kept listening to them say, "The Jews in America will not forget you." One man told us that in a day or two they would take us to a decent place and asked us to be patient.

Once they left we opened the boxes and found that they were filled with big woolen scarves, crackers, candy, all kinds of food in packages, cigarettes, soap, toothpaste, and creams. These things were so precious because someone had given them to us. We slept holding the stuff; we did not want to let it out of our sight.

At last we had decent food to eat. They brought us soup and we realized it was made for us and that it was real soup, not made from leftovers from the SS. It was so thick that our spoons stood up in it. We said to ourselves, "It's not water, it's soup." I later found out it was split pea soup, which I had never had before. Unfortunately some people ate too much of it and got sick.

The people from Joint measured our feet and said they would bring us shoes and better clothes as soon as they could and would also move us to a better place.

They took some of us who were sick to an American field hospital. I was not sick but I was so skinny they were afraid if I moved around my bones would break. They put me in a body cast and I was fed so that I would have some meat on my bones. I also had no muscles. I do not remember how long I was there because every time I asked they answered me, "What, are you in a hurry? Take it easy; we're going to make you well." Reluctantly I let the nurses take the package that Joint had given me, which I only gave up because they gave me their word that they would return it. There were a few soldiers and a nurse who spoke Yiddish and they were the ones I spoke with.

When I got out of the cast I began moving around, slowly and holding on at first and then, gradually, walking on my own. When they released me they kept their word and returned my package. I was brought to where the other women were—the SS barracks in Kammer Schörfling, Austria. This was the most beautiful spot I have ever seen in my life, near the Attersee, with villas across the road where rich people lived. I wondered if perhaps the owners of the villas had been Jews whose homes had been taken from them.

Even the SS barracks was beautiful and I was given a beautiful skirt to wear. But I did not have any top to go with it so I unraveled the scarf they had given me and the soldiers got me crocheting needles and I crocheted a sweater with short sleeves because there was not enough wool for long sleeves. I brought that sweater with me to America and today it is in the Holocaust Museum in Washington. It was dark sand brown, like a manila envelope. We all got the same skirt but in different colors. Mine was black.

The Joint kept helping us, but not directly. They would bring things for us to the Central Committee in Salzburg,[14] which is the organization that took care of us. We had a representative that we elected who spoke for us to this committee. Soon men came to live in half of the barracks, and when a man became our representative we were able to get more things from the Central Committee.

But even with the man representing us we were not getting everything we needed. So a group of five of us went to Salzburg, and when we were standing in line for the bus a large group of SS women who had just come from visiting their husbands in a POW camp joined us. When we were at the head of the line the bus driver opened the back of the bus, which meant that these women got seats and we did not. One woman shouted as she got off, "If you think the Hitler regime is over, you are wrong. Another Hitler is coming... and you are

---

14 The survivors in the DP (Displaced Persons) camps elected a representative leadership, the Central Committee of Liberated Jews in the American Zone. The reference here is to the Salzburg office of this committee.

not going to live long." This has been ringing in my ears all these years. I cannot get it out of my head because antisemitism still exists.

While we were living there, people from the *Hagana*[15] came and asked us if we wanted to go to Palestine. They said they were going to take us out of the DP camps and smuggle us in. They said the arrangements would take a while and during this time we should take care of ourselves, get well, be patient, and that through the Central Committee they would let us know their progress.

We became friendly with the men who had come to the camp, and many of the women started dating them. One of the men, Reuben Ivanonovich, liked the way I kept talking about Jewishness and that we have to do things to help ourselves and have to go to Palestine because it is the only place for Jews, and when people would talk about going back to Poland I would talk them out of it. Reuben used to say he saw things in me he did not see in other women.

I started going out with Reuben and almost immediately the *Hagana* said we should come to Salzburg so they could begin the process for taking us to Palestine. I told Reuben of my plans and encouraged him to come, but he had two brothers in America and said that because of them he could not go with me. He accompanied me to Salzburg and stayed there while the *Hagana* started us on our journey to the Middle East.

At the border between Austria and Italy I became very sick and began coughing violently. One of the *Hagana* men approached me and said that my loud coughing could ruin it for the whole transport, and that I had to go back to Salzburg, get well, and join the next transport. In Salzburg I met Reuben again and he said, "You see, it is meant to be. Now you should really decide we should get married and you'll come with me to America." I began to think that my getting sick was God's will, so I agreed.

While we were waiting to leave, we rested, we relaxed, and we began to send letters through the Central Committee to all the DP camps in Austria and Germany asking for lists of survivors. I received a letter from my sister's brother-in-law, the older brother of the man I had seen in the ghetto, which said he was coming to see me. When we saw each other again the crying and the excitement was unbearable, and then he told me that my sisters were not alive,

15 Underground army in Palestine before Israel gained independence in 1948.

that their children were not alive and that no one from his family had survived, which meant my sister's husband was not alive either.

This man naturally assumed that he and I would marry each other, but Reuben told him that he had asked me to marry him, although he had not yet done so, and since he thought Reuben was the finest man he had ever met, he told me I should marry Reuben and that he would pay for the wedding. Then Reuben said we should get engaged and married so we would not be so lonely. I really must have been lucky because quite a few men were interested in me, like my sisters who had married young.

My brother-in-law's brother lived in Gnadenwald, a little town near Innsbruck, where the *Hagana* had a kibbutz training-center on the top of a hill in a hotel with an absolutely splendid view overlooking Switzerland and Italy. I lived in the American zone of Austria and the kibbutz was in the French zone, which meant I needed papers to go there, like crossing from one country to another. After being told by the Central Committee in Salzburg that they could not issue the documents, I got them from the Mayor of Lenzing, where I was then living in abandoned workers' housing.

A jeep driven by a soldier in the American army drove us to the kibbutz where a Jewish man, not a rabbi, married us and an older couple who had found each other after the war gave us away under the *huppah*. Also present was a survivor who was a ritual slaughterer, and they slaughtered a cow and made all the food for the Sabbath. We were married on a Friday and celebrated the wedding throughout the day on Saturday.

I stood under the *huppah* and knew I was not going to be alone anymore, but it broke my heart that I had to look for somebody who I had never seen in my whole life to give me away.

When we went back to Lenzing as a married couple, we learned that a lieutenant had come asking for Reuben and would come back the following week. We were afraid but we could not do anything except wait. When he returned he introduced himself as Lieutenant Joe Auster and said that he was working for General Clark of the Intelligence Service. He told us he was from Brooklyn and knew Reuben's brother; that, in fact, his father worked for Reuben's brother, and that his name is no longer Ivanovich but Irwin. He said that Reuben's brother, now Harry Irwin, who had left Poland to avoid serving in

World War I, had written to see if any of his family had survived. Joe Auster said he would write back, tell him he had found Reuben, and find out what his brother wanted Reuben to do. In the meantime he brought us food and cigarettes, which Reuben smoked. This news was very comforting because we thought we had someone who would help us.

While we were waiting to go to America we received letters from Harry and packages from his daughter Yolanda. One package contained my first lipstick and some Maybeline cream, which I still use to this day. Because I had come of age in Auschwitz I had never seen lipstick before, and Joe Auster showed me how to put it on. One of Harry's letters said it was difficult for him to bring us in and that the process would go more quickly if we were brought in by HIAS (Hebrew Immigrant Aid Society).

While we were waiting we would hitchhike on U.S. Army cars and trucks and look for members of our families who might possibly be in DP camps in Germany. Even though I had heard that they had been killed, I was still hoping to find someone in my family who had been spared. But whoever I talked to told me that everyone from my town had been sent straight to Treblinka and that the only people who survived from Końskie were a small number, like me, who had gone into hiding. Then I knew, finally, that no one had survived.

All of a sudden we saw the name David Ivanovich on a list hanging on the wall and my husband started to scream that David was his nephew. We found him right away at the DP camp office, and when Reuben and David met there was wild hugging and kissing, crying and hysteria. David told Reuben that no one had survived from either his immediate family or from Reuben's.

We had David added to the HIAS list and he waited with us in our one room in Lenzing until we heard from the U.S. Consul that we could leave. Until then we used the small amount of money we made selling cigarettes from the Joint packages to buy food.

Finally, around the festival of Purim, 1947—the best Purim present ever—we were told to go to the American Consul in Munich. We went via Salzburg and the Joint arranged our transportation to Munich, to a place called "the golden doors," even though it was so decrepit that rain came in and we did not even have a real apartment, just a compartment in a big building, and we did not have enough to eat because the German ration cards purchased such a small amount of food. But apparently the name was accurate because it meant that sooner or later we would be getting out of Germany.

In Lenzing Reuben had a friend who had survived with him. He was alone, with no family in America, and when we left he cried hysterically. Without family the wait was very long. I knew that if there was someone in America who promised to give you work so you would not be a burden on the country and said he would find you a place to live, you could get there a lot faster. When I got to America I went to HIAS and told them this friend could live with us and signed my brother-in-law's name, promising to give him a job in his business that manufactured men's clothing. I was afraid that if I asked my brother-in-law about this he would refuse and then we would not be able to keep our promise to help this man to get to the United States.

While we were in Munich we spent our time filling out forms and going for medical examinations. The doctors kept taking X-rays of me, but whatever the problem was it did not clear up. So, after living in those terrible conditions for three or four months, I told my husband and his nephew they should go to America without me. They refused and I went back to the doctor and started crying and telling him that we could not live in those conditions any longer, that we were getting sicker rather than better by being where we were. The doctor then said, "Don't cry. Your X-rays are O.K. now. You'll be able to go. I'm signing the papers." I have forgotten what was wrong with me but it had something to do with a blood count showing that my body was fighting an infection.

But the waiting was not over. While we were waiting we went to Hamburg where a 15-year-old boy from Końskie, who I had helped when we were hiding, was living with his mother. When his mother met me she started crying and thanking me profusely for helping her son to survive. This woman had known my parents, so it felt good to talk with her, and she even told me stories about them that I had not known.

As we were walking around Hamburg with her my husband suddenly became pale and began to cry. He said that he had just seen an SS man who had been very brutal to him in the camp. I asked if he was sure and Reuben said he recognized the man's walk because he had a limp. I do not know where Reuben got the courage but he took the man by the arm, called him by his name and said he knew he had been the SS person in charge at the camp in Poznań. The man tried to deny it, but Reuben would not let him and said, "I'll never forget your face." The man said, "Leave me alone and I'll give you the diamonds I collected." We called the German policeman who was standing right there, and he was taken to jail. We told the Americans about this so that he would not be released from prison, but the Americans said they needed another witness to testify to his identity. We asked them to contact all the other DP camps and issue bulletins that whoever was in Poznań should come forward to identify this particular SS man. About three witnesses came and this SS man was tried and condemned to jail for the rest of his life. I know this because the story was reported in the New York Yiddish daily, *The Forward*, soon after we got to America.

About a week after the doctor gave me a clean bill of health, we were sent to Bremerhaven and embarked on a big transport ship with sleeping bunks filled with Jews. The journey to America took two weeks and we landed in New York on June 7, 1947. I had been seasick for the whole trip and could barely get out of my bunk, but when we arrived Reuben helped me stand on the deck so I could see America. We cried and screamed from happiness. Finally, we thought, we are in what we used to call "di goldene medina" (the land of gold). In Germany, in the broadcasting center in Munich, while we were waiting to leave they used to say that in America you just have to bend down to pick up the money that is lying in the street.

After the first excitement, I looked out at New York and started to cry bitterly. "What kind of country have we come to? How can we raise children here when you can't cross the street?" I was looking at the West Side Highway and it looked like millions of cars going without stopping which seemed terrifying to me because I had seen maybe three cars before the war. But after hearing that all you see in America is factories with no green and no trees, I was relieved to see gorgeous trees and flowers growing alongside the West Side Highway.

Since there was a tugboat strike, we had to stand at anchor without landing for two days. Once we docked they let people come on board to look for members of their families. My husband's brother and his wife came and took us to their home, which was a big private home on 21st Street and Avenue J in

Brooklyn. When I saw the trees on the street and the garden in the backyard, I knew that the people who had said America was a country filled only with factories had been wrong.

We arrived in New York the day before *Shavuot*, and on *Shavuot* we all went to the Young Israel of Flatbush synagogue, where Reuben's brother was a member. The welcome we received there was overwhelming and the rabbi had tears in his eyes as he greeted us. We may have been the first survivors they had seen, because this was not a neighborhood to which survivors were likely to come. A man came over to me, crying, and wished us all the good things in the world and said that if he could help in any way, he wanted to and that when Shabbat was over he would write down his telephone number. The man was Mr. Kestenbaum and I am still friendly with his daughter, Shirley Schulder.

As soon as we moved in with Reuben's brother, who owned one of the country's largest men's clothing factories, located on West 23rd Street, a couple came to us and said they had seen in the papers that someone named Ivanovich had been on our ship and that my husband had helped her sister become reunited with her husband, who was in the Polish army. The sister was now living in New Jersey and her Brooklyn sister had come to us to thank us in her sister's name and to say that because my husband had been so wonderful to her sister, if I ever wanted a job in the nursing home she owned all I would have to do is call her and the job would be mine.

She had made that offer because I told her that while I was in Austria waiting to come to America I had been studying to be a nurse, but I knew I could not be a registered nurse here because I did not have a college education. I felt that the only kind of work I could do would be to help people and that nursing was a way to do it.

After about two months we decided to move out. Housing was very tight because all the returning soldiers wanted someplace to live. After a day of walking all over Brooklyn I found a furnished room on West 6th Street near Kings Highway, but we could not stay there long because our landlady never stopped crying over the son she'd lost in the army. I had lost my whole family and I could not bear listening to her crying.

Luckily, two weeks after we moved there Reuben found us a better place to live. We moved in the next day. I had nothing to bring; I just picked myself up and went to the new place. We really had nothing and my husband's brother was only paying him $20 a week even though he was so educated, intelligent and had begun studying English in college because of his brother in America.

The day after we moved I went to work in the nursing home where I was soon making $50 a week, which was good money. I started studying English at night in an elementary school on Seventh Avenue that the owner told me about, and after a year I began taking evening classes at Erasmus Hall High School and four years later I received my high school diploma.

I wanted to have a baby but I had stopped menstruating when I arrived in Auschwitz and still was not. A doctor whose mother lived in the nursing home helped me, and after a minor operation at Beth Israel Hospital I began to menstruate and became pregnant, which was the biggest miracle of all. On October 15, 1949, I gave birth to a baby boy and named him Moshe in Hebrew after my father, Martin in English.

It was my husband's niece Yolanda who took me to the hospital at two in the morning when my water broke and who found a doctor for me when I became pregnant. She even taught me how to take care of the baby and was always there for me whenever I had a problem, either with Martin or with anything else. In fact, from my first day in this country she was my helper and my interpreter, and I do not know what I would have done without her.

When Martin was born I stopped working but I continued studying. It was hectic. When Reuben would get home the baby was sleeping, his dinner was on the table, I had my coat on and I ran out so I would not be late. An old man who took the same train I did every day said, "You're rushing the life out of you." It was hard but I wanted that diploma, and when I graduated we went out to eat, which was my first meal in a restaurant, and I was very proud.

We had applied to become citizens, and when we took our citizenship test with hundreds of others we answered all the questions correctly. The day we were sworn in at a courthouse in Brooklyn was the holiest day for me, the greatest day of my life, because I had become a citizen of the United States.

When Martin was five he went to Yeshiva (Jewish day school) Kindergarten. I decided to send him to a Yeshiva because I did not want to have to go through what I saw happening with my neighbor and friend, who had to fight with her son every day when he came home from school to get him to go to the afternoon Talmud Torah for Jewish studies. I had been preparing for his education from the day he was born, when I made a vow to put aside five dollars every week for his education. And every Friday when I got Reuben's check, I would put aside five dollars in Martin's name even if I did not have money for things that we needed that week.

When he started school I went back to work for four hours a day at a private hospital run by five surgeons so that we could pay for his education. I did not want Reuben to know that we needed money, so I did not tell him I was working. But when it came time to pay our income taxes I told Reuben I had been keeping something from him. He promised not to be angry so I showed him all the slips for the money I had been earning. I had not slept for nights worrying about how I was going to tell him. I was afraid they would send me back to Poland if I did not pay my income tax.

I also became active in the Yeshiva and served as class mother. I think the energy to do this while I was also working came from my determination to make my mother and father, who I believed were watching me from heaven, proud that I had not forgotten what they taught me.

One day Helen Gould, a United Jewish Appeal (UJA) professional, came to the Yeshiva and said she wanted to arrange a fundraising luncheon for the organization. When she told me that HIAS and Joint were part of UJA, I said, "I owe them a lot, so I'll do whatever you want me to do." I worked with her arranging the luncheon and pledged $18, which I had no idea how I was going to pay, and even lost sleep worrying where the money would come from. But I saved it up quickly and ever since I have been paying back for what was done for me. Those organizations had helped me get out of the most terrible place in the world, Germany, a place in which I could never have borne to stay. And to this day I still work very hard for UJA and am devoted to helping them with their mission of helping any Jew in need anywhere in the world.

I am also involved with Brooklyn College Hillel because Jewish youth is our future. And when the Russian Jews started to arrive in Brooklyn, I told them my story, hoping they would identify with a fellow immigrant, and I encouraged them to become involved with the Jewish community. As a community, I believe we can do everything; as individuals, we are powerless. Jeremiah said, "There is hope for your future." That quote helped me survive in Auschwitz and I think of it often.

ELEVEN YEARS OF SUFFERING

By Lotti Kahana-Aufleger

TABLE OF CONTENTS

INTRODUCTION

These recollections are based on my memories. No one, of course, would have thought of writing a diary while the circumstances that I am about to describe were taking place.[1]

I lived a comfortable middle-class life until September 18, 1939, the day my only daughter, Gitta, turned three. Eighteen days had passed since the Germans invaded Poland, but we were in Czernowitz, Romania, and still considered ourselves relatively safe. That afternoon, as was our custom, we hosted a group of children for the birthday celebration. The children enjoyed themselves at Gitta's party, as did their parents, and it didn't occur to any of us that Poland was on the brink of total collapse, as were our own lives.

That evening, however, when we hosted friends and family in our home, as we did after Gitta's party every year, there was only one topic of conversation—the war. We served wines, liquors, sandwiches and cakes, because such luxuries were still plentiful and available, but everyone was in a downcast mood as we listened to Polish radio broadcasters bellow out "Uwaga! Uwaga!" (Listen! Listen!)—"German planes are bombing us mercilessly, showing no compassion for the flood of refugees filling the roads…" In contrast, the German broadcasts were filled with jubilant exultations and triumphant cries of "Heil Hitler!"

---

1 Translated from the original German transcript by Lotti's daughter, Tova Bar-Touv (Gitta Aufleger); Translated from the Hebrew by Miriam Samsonowitz.

Poland had surrendered on that day,[2] and our hearts trembled, fearing that Romania would be the Nazis' next target.

Our comfortable, sun-drenched, three-room apartment was located on Siebenburger Street, a main traffic artery on the Polish-Romanian border. My parents had lived there with Gitta, my husband and me since antisemitic persecutions had begun in Czernowitz, prompted by the Romanian government's antisemitic policies, which had become extremely oppressive prior to the country's descent into Nazi Germany's orbit. An evening walk through my parents' neighborhood had thus become too dangerous to take unescorted. Jews comprised about four percent of Romania's ethnically diverse population, which also included Germans and Ukrainians in Czernowitz, and Hungarians in Transylvania as well as Romanians. A complicated and volatile political culture dominated prewar Romania and made its Jewish communities particularly vulnerable to history's offenses. Jews who lived in eastern Romania suffered persecution for being the alleged agents of Soviet communism. Jews were also oppressed in Transylvania, where they were associated with the region's pre-World War I Hungarian rule.

Close to one o'clock in the morning, as our guests began to leave, we heard noises in the street that were unusual for that hour. When we went to investigate, we saw that a stream of buses, private cars, motorcycles and Red Cross vehicles had filled the street. Thousands of vehicles blocked the avenue, and traffic was stopped in front of our house.

I approached one of the automobiles and encountered my first Polish refugee: a barefoot woman dressed in a nightgown, who sat there, dazed, with a fur coat thrown over her shoulders. She was the first of many I invited up to our apartment for something to eat.

"Are you a Jew?" she asked in response to my offer. When I answered that yes, I was, she firmly refused to accept anything from me other than a drink of water. I was shocked. From that moment on, I experienced the war as a Jew. I was reminded at every turn that this was not only a war against nations: it was also against all Jews.

My family and I worked tirelessly until morning, distributing tea and bread to

2   Poland surrendered on September 28 [Ed.].

the refugees in the street. When we ran out of bread, my mother cooked a large pot of potato soup. That soup was to become my mother's specialty after we ourselves became refugees.

The Polish refugees gave us a picture of what was happening in Poland, where the war began when German armies invaded from the West and two weeks later, Soviet armies overtook the eastern borders. The geographically vulnerable country—its stretches of plains had for centuries tempted foreign incursions—had been besieged from the east and the west, which had driven thousands of Poles to pack up their lives and flee. Some had managed to take their most important belongings with them and hoped to travel via Romania to England or France. At dawn, we collapsed into bed, dead tired. I felt close to a nervous breakdown and I shook with chills for several hours. All I could think of was what happened to people who were forced to abandon their homes.

Many years have passed since then, but I remember as clearly as if it had happened today how I pulled my sky blue silk blanket over my head and asked myself: How much longer will I be able to sleep in my own bed?

Within days, the front stabilized and became quiet. Hitler's armies changed course, and we watched developments from afar. Unfortunately, we didn't take advantage of that brief cessation in hostilities to escape to Palestine.

Although in many areas life more or less seemed to have returned to normal, we set by a large stock of food just to be on the safe side, thinking that would be enough to guarantee our future security. We also bought many clothes and shoes, worried that perhaps these items would be in short supply later.

My father, my husband, and my brother-in-law, Karl, ran a business paving roads, which continued to flourish. Though we were considered affluent, all of our assets were invested in the business. Our family, which was large and had an unusually close relationship, counted among the most distinguished families in Czerñowitz. Every Saturday afternoon my grandparents had a family get-together with all their children, grandchildren, and great-grandchildren. We were always happy to see one another there.

My mother's oldest sister, Peppi Kibak, was the aunt I most loved, and since she lived in the center of the city, not a day went by when my family didn't drop in for a visit. Because we loved her so much, Peppi had to put up with our frequent calls. I also loved her three daughters, who were very close in age, and were like sisters to me. I, on the other hand, was an only daughter, which I lamented my whole life. Since the war was hanging over our head like a Damocles' sword, plain logic dictated that my parents should not bring more children into the world.

Spring is the season of the year that I love best, and from my window on Siebenburger Street in the spring of 1940 I could see the chestnuts blossoming in a nearby park, the National Gardens. The park was a balm for my eyes and offered tranquility for my taut nerves.

Every evening we heard the triumphant shouts of the Nazis on the radio news, and those voices pierced my dreams. In the morning, when I looked out upon the magic of nature, I could forget my melancholy, but only for a moment. However, a twenty-seven year old doesn't give in to perpetual depression, even when the German army is sweeping through Europe. So to lift my spirits I ordered myself two beautiful summer dresses, one in antique pink with a large pink hat, the second a silk print with a black-rimmed organdy hat.

Once a week my parents and I visited friends, though my husband, Siegfried, preferred to stay at home with Gitta, whom he adored almost to the point of veneration. Gitta was a chubby child with dark hair, a pinkish face and an iron will. One day when she was ill, she refused to take medicine until she got a doll carriage she coveted. My husband rushed to the city to buy it.

Leaving a friend's home one night in early April of 1940, my mother fell and broke her ankle. The doctor came to our home to remove the cast on the day that France surrendered, and I still remember his words: "If France can be vanquished in so short a time, then the end has come for all of Europe."

On June 24, 1940, my mother took her first outing since her accident. As we went down Siebeburger Street toward my aunt Peppi's house, we noticed that the traffic was too brisk for the early afternoon hour. When we reached the police station, we saw a line of open-bedded trucks carrying cartons full of papers and documents. Since the Russians had by then conquered the part of Poland that bordered Romania, they were, in effect, already our neighbors. But for some time, there had been rumors that Russian planes had been passing over our city. Rumors also filtered in from the Russian-occupied section of Poland that were not particularly encouraging. We heard that affluent citizens were persecuted, that people were kidnapped based on unsubstantiated slander, that there was a shortage of food, and that the NKVD (the Soviet secret police force) was terrorizing the population. Nevertheless, to many people the possible occupation of Czernowitz by the Russians appeared to be the least terrible thing that might happen—better, in any case, than a German occupation would be. For several days, all the signs had been indicating that a Russian invasion was imminent.

My mother's ankle became so painful that we returned home in a carriage. For the next three days we listened to the various rumors running through town and determined that no one actually knew what Romania's political situation was.

On June 27, my husband returned from a trip to Bucharest where he had received a large government payment for paving roads. I told him what mother and I had seen, and about the imminent Russian invasion, but he shrugged off the rumors. That evening, the radio news brought us the tear-choked voice of Romania's King Carol II announcing to the nation that he had given up Bukovina and Bessarabia to the Russians.

The residents of Czernowitz still hadn't made peace with being torn away from the Austrian Empire and annexed to Romania in 1918. Now we were to be handed over again— this time to the Russians. The Romanian government had received orders to evacuate Czernowitz without delay, and the Russians were supposed to take over the next day. Many of our acquaintances took only their most essential possessions and boarded a train for the Romanian side of the border. The trains were packed and we heard that sometimes Jews had simply been thrown out of the moving cars.

We, however, decided to remain in the city and accept whatever happened. Because all financial transactions were blocked and no one could collect a debt from either the government or private institutions, we found ourselves with only 20,000 Romanian Lei in cash from our net worth of a quarter of a million Lei. Merchandise for which we had already paid remained in the factory's warehouse and was never shipped. Many factory owners had already crossed into Romania, and those who remained on the Russian side had their entire inventory confiscated.

In this new reality, we had suddenly become penniless. The morning after the regime change, I dismissed the maid who had worked for us for years, explaining that the Russians didn't permit class differences, so she'd be better off returning to her village. She cried bitterly, and said she couldn't imagine how we would manage without her.

The Communist Party, which had been illegal until then, took advantage of the coming transfer of power to grab the reigns and free the Communists who had been jailed by the Romanian government. As an official government authority was not yet in place, the city was in chaos. The streets became dangerous. Ukrainian youths who had previously worn nationalist green ribbons suddenly did an about-face and turned into enthusiastic Communists sporting red ribbons. A joke began to make the rounds: "What's the difference between a watermelon and a Ukrainian Communist from Czernowitz?"—The watermelon is green on the outside and red on the inside.

On June 28, 1940, the Russians officially took control of Czernowitz. Our apartment was near the army camp where the ceremony was scheduled to take place, and we gathered on the porch to watch the historic event. At three o'clock in the afternoon, the first Russian tanks arrived in the streets and several planes appeared in the skies. Ear-splitting noise filled the air. The Russians marched in fully armed, as if a well-equipped enemy were opposing them, when in reality only a handful of frightened Romanian captains were assembled at the army camp. We had never before seen so much war equipment, and this march frightened us and shattered our spirits.

Like many others, my family was divided concerning the Communists. My husband and I were pessimistic about how we would fare under their rule. Still, though I didn't feel much sympathy for the Russians, I believed that they were the lesser of two evils and would protect us from war. My father, a stoic type, viewed everything with composure. My mother was cheerful because she hoped the political situation would improve. Although rumors had filtered in from Poland that the Soviets persecuted businessmen, my mother naively believed that we could hide our status from them.

We found out the next day that the Russians wouldn't exchange Romanian Leis for Russian rubles, though such a procedure was standard in other countries that had changed governments and currency. We couldn't even buy a loaf of bread, though we still had our stored food.

We held a family consultation, and my mother, who always gave excellent advice, presented the following plan: the men would quickly learn the Russian language so they would become eligible for positions, and the women—she and I—would work at any job that presented itself in order to provide for the family.

The men, both of whom had degrees in accounting, studied Russian from morning to evening, while my mother and I turned to cooking. Aunt Peppi owned a successful restaurant, which was always full of Russian soldiers after the invasion. Mother turned our kitchen into a small factory in order to supply her with patties and baked goods, despite the fact that standing on her feet still caused her severe pain.

In addition to helping cook, I also found myself doing the family laundry by myself for the first time in my life. It kept me busy for a full week—of course we had no washing machines in those days. With practice, I became faster.

A few weeks after the Russian takeover, a stream of Russian civilians poured into to our city. They had plenty of money and wanted to spend it, for Russia had a shortage of desirable merchandise. There was virtually nothing they wouldn't buy. Naively, we thought that we would have to live for a long time to come from the proceeds of selling our possessions, so we parted with our belongings sparingly.

After several weeks, Siegfried found work as a substitute for the main accountant in a wood products firm and my father got a job as an accountant in a company that made preserves.

One day my husband returned home pale as a ghost. He had been called before the government authorities and told that they had found out that he had previously been a businessman—a terrible stain. Even worse, he was accused of having tried to hide this fact.

We immediately began destroying "incriminating" documents that Siegfried had refused to sacrifice earlier. We stoked all the ovens in the bedrooms, bath and kitchen in order to finish as soon as possible. When I noticed that the porch floor was covered with soot, I quickly set about getting rid of that evidence too.

The next day Siegfried was called in by the head accountant, who received him amiably and told him that he would do all he could to help him. The days crawled by. Much more than just our income was at stake. The Russians were planning to distribute passports soon, and anyone who wasn't working would be given a 39 passport. In the USSR, nothing could be worse. It marked one as a "bad element" and meant one could expect to be exiled to Siberia.

After several days, Siegfried was notified that he should no longer go to work—since he was a former businessman, he could live off his savings. The head accountant was a congenial man, and he promised Siegfried that he would try to find him work in another company after his class status had been forgotten.

I cannot describe the dread and tension we felt.

Stalin's dictum was quoted everywhere: "Whoever does not work does not have to eat either." I had never before worked to bring in money, but I decided that I had to take part in the struggle for our existence.

I bumped into a German acquaintance who worked in a public restaurant and wanted to obey the Führer's call for the Germans who lived outside Germany's borders to return to their homeland. Hitler needed them. Germans had lived on the outskirts of Czernowitz in a suburb called Rosh for generations, and many of them listened to the German propaganda and abandoned their homes. Later, we heard that they regretted it, but of course they didn't realize that if they hadn't returned to Germany they could have been shipped off to Siberia.

I told my German acquaintance I was willing to take over her position, but wanted to try it out first. In Russia, one didn't leave a bad place of work unless one had another place to go, so if I took the job without trying it first, I wouldn't be able to leave even if I wanted to.

On the first day I worked without respite. My job was to collect the waiters' tips, and I had to watch that none of them slipped the money into his pocket. At ten o'clock that night a man in uniform tottered in and placed his gun on my table. He declared that I had found favor in his eyes and was to accompany him to the courtyard because he needed me urgently. The mass of people around us grew silent—and then the man cocked his gun at me. The crowd expected me to obey him, but I took advantage of the split second when he turned around to vomit and fled. To calm myself down, the next day I went to the park with Gitta, where I encountered several of my acquaintances. At that time, we still allowed ourselves the luxury of spending an hour every day at the park.

Before Czernowitz had changed hands, our conversations centered on the cinema, the theater, clothes, problems with our maids, and so forth. Now we spoke about how to make a living. I told my friends that, after what had happened, I had decided not to integrate into the Soviet work force. In any event, it wasn't possible to live on the wages that they paid. Since I was an accomplished seamstress, my friends now advised me to make a living from sewing.

Thus began the career that supported my family for the next ten years.

After a few weeks, on the recommendation of his former employer, my husband obtained work in a military office, and a stone rolled off of our hearts. But he had found this job only at the last second, after the government had already begun to distribute passports.

After a nerve-wracking wait and several sleepless nights, we received our passports. We were safe, but to our distress, many Czernowitz residents— including some of our family members and friends—had been issued passports stamped with the dangerous 39.

Who could imagine that everything accumulated through the passage of generations would be lost because of the Russian occupation? Even worse, that fine, decent people would suddenly be marked criminals? My mother's younger sister Antonia Klinger and her husband had a textile factory, which the Russians immediately "nationalized" — in other words, claimed for themselves—along with their apartment and its entire contents. They moved the little they had left—only a few clothes—into the apartment of my recently deceased grandparents. Perhaps that old couple had passed away at the right time. They saw all their children living comfortably and happily until the end of their lives.

Things were no better for my relatives who were still in Romanian territory. Perhaps in part looking for a scapegoat to blame for Czernowitz having been torn away from Romania by the Russians, an antisemitic campaign had begun in Romania, under the guise of an anti-Communist campaign. All the Communists the Romanian authorities found proved to be Jewish.

My mother's brother, David Shaiovitz, was a doctor who had a private clinic in Botoșani. A man of great personal integrity, he would treat the poor without asking for payment, and perhaps because of this, he was thought to have a Communist worldview. His sons, my cousins Henri and Jack, were 17 and 18; they were also sympathetic to Communism, and this added to the circumstances that made my uncle suspect of being a communist in the eyes of the fascist

Romanian authorities — circumstances which led to Uncle David's imprisonment.

We had no idea what was happening to our relatives in Romania until Uncle David, after his release from prison, decided to bring his family to Czernowitz. The trip, part of it on foot through a no-man's-land, was especially difficult for my aunt, who had never had to walk more than a hundred meters in her life. They managed to bring only a few belongings along, though they were burdened with illusions, of which they were soon disabused. They had heard that every doctor in the Soviet Union received a villa and had a car put at his disposal. For a family used to luxuries, it was a drastic change suddenly to have to squeeze into one room in our apartment.

After his arrival in Czernowitz, Uncle David was required to report to the police. Everyone warned him not to tell the authorities about his imprisonment in Romania. People who were informed about the Soviet regime claimed that in the Soviet Union, it's better to appear apolitical. But my uncle refused to give up on what he believed was his strong card.

"What, I suffered for nothing?" he protested. Unfortunately, one who doesn't accept advice can't be helped either. My uncle proudly told the police that the Romanians had imprisoned him for being a Communist.

It took only a few minutes after entering the NKVD room before my uncle regretted opening his mouth. An interrogation was conducted, and it wasn't hard for the police to find a reason to imprison Dr. Shaiovitz once again. He was fortunate to have a colleague specializing in hematology who worked in the Party hospital. After one of the investigators spoke with that doctor by phone, my uncle, now disabused of his delusion, was permitted to return to our apartment.

One day in the fall of 1940, panic gripped the public because rumors were circulating that deportations of mainly Jews from Czernowitz would begin that night. At around eleven o'clock, we saw one truck after another heading toward an out-of-the-way train station. Loaded with people, the trucks filed by without interruption until morning.[3]

After sunrise, we gathered in the kitchen and tried to calm our nerves with a

---

3   The Soviets had shut down Jewish national life, and in June 1941 deported 10,000 Jews from Czernowitz and environs to Siberia [Ed.].

cup of coffee. We froze in fear when the doorbell rang. It was a young friend who had been sent to say that the NKVD had appeared the night before at the apartment where the Klingers, my aunt and uncle, used to live. They were now targeted for deportation, and posters everywhere announced that anyone providing refuge would face immediate exile.

For hours I combed the streets, looking for a place for the Klinger family to hide, but no one had the courage to act against orders. Then I remembered a Jewish shoemaker who had a small basement workshop nearby and went to explain our dilemma to him. I suggested that he stop working and rent us the basement for several days. "It's impossible," he said, and I broke into heartrending sobs.

"Madam," he interrupted, "let me speak. You can't put a family in the basement because there are mice. The family can move in with me."

I had no sooner returned home when the doorbell rang again. This time we were informed that my father's brother, sister, and 87-year-old mother had all been taken away in the night. They had been forbidden to dress for the outdoors and weren't allowed to take anything with them.

We organized ourselves quickly. Everyone carried a package containing essentials for survival, and we each spread out to canvass different sections of the train station where the helpless deportees sat waiting in cattle cars. Their departure had been delayed by the search for those who had escaped arrest. We walked back and forth along the tracks all that day looking for my father's family, and it seemed as if all of Czernowitz's Jews had been crammed into that train. Even those who hadn't received deportation orders were there to provide the victims with food and encouragement. This time, it wasn't only the Jews who were affected. The train also contained affluent farmers from the countryside, and even though I never felt empathy with the Romanians — they had always, in general, been virulently antisemitic — it touched my heart to see those people torn from their homes and their land. When evening fell, we stopped our search because a curfew had gone into effect.

When we went back early the next morning, the train station was empty. All traces of the tens of thousands of prisoners had been erased. Later, we discovered that we had been searching at the wrong station all along. The transports from the suburbs where my grandmother lived had left from a station in a different neighborhood.

Life went on. Those who were saved from the catastrophe of deportation continued with their affairs. Those who had managed to hide left their hideouts, but then had to choose between living underground or crossing the border into Romania, which involved placing their lives in danger. The Klingers, who had Austrian citizenship, were able to return to their apartment after leaving the shoemaker's, since at the time the Soviets were still honoring foreign passports.

CHAPTER 1

War Reaches Us

I t was not yet clear, at the end of 1940, whether Germany would dare to invade England or would send its armies eastward. We had already been under the Soviet regime for half a year and were nearing the end of the pact between Germany and the Soviets.

By the end of June 1941, without having heard a declaration of war, we found ourselves in the middle of the fighting. The Germans began to bombard Czernowitz, and we were totally unprepared. Our neighbors sought refuge in the stairwells, as there were no shelters. We remained in our apartment, however, because my father, who had served in World War I, didn't think the stairwells were any safer.

The Soviets spent eight days preparing to evacuate. They drafted all the high school students and pressed them into service. My husband was drafted too, but as he had the good fortune to work in a military office, he was allowed to remain at his job. His heart disease, angina pectoris, would not have earned him an army exemption—the Soviets couldn't have cared less about a draftee's state of health.

Like many of Czernowitz's Jews, we could have retreated to Russia with the Russians, and Siegfried was even offered a place in a car for the journey. But we decided to remain because we didn't trust the Russians.

On the eighth day the retreating Soviets laid waste to much of the city. All the emergency warehouses were set on fire and the army camps and ammunition depots were blown up. Explosions were heard in several of the city's passes, the loudest of which came from the Prut River when the bridge was blown up. We spent an entire night at our windows, watching the burning ammunition depots turn the heavens red. Since we lived near an army camp, we were worried that our apartment building might collapse if the camp and its ammunition stores were blown up, but miraculously, they remained untouched.

The Soviets had entered Czernowitz on June 28, 1940, and on June 28, 1941, the city was empty of them. I concluded that nothing good could ever be expected on that date.

Now we needed Romanian money again. By chance, we had kept a box of Romanian coins for Gitta to play with, and my mother immediately raided it and went to buy milk. She came back quickly, pale as a ghost. She told us that young Ukrainian men and women wearing green ribbons on their arms were downstairs attacking Jews. Suddenly, Romanian soldiers appeared on the scene and shots rang out. We locked the gate to our house and didn't open it for four days, during which we had neither water nor electricity. We could only imagine what terrifying things were happening in the city.

Though they did not coordinate their rampages, the local mobs (which consisted of Romanian and Ukrainian civilians), the Romanian soldiers, and the German Gestapo all ran wild for four days, during which time Jewish homes were ransacked and Jews were murdered and raped. Afterwards, an order was publicized requiring all Jews, including children, to wear yellow stars. Every time a Jew left home, his heart was pounding; each time he came home, his eyes shone with fright. There were many victims, and since they were buried in a joint grave, no one ever knew their exact number. Dr. Abraham Mark, Czernowitz's chief rabbi, was among them. The Gestapo ordered thousands of Jews to assemble in the Cultural Hall and then murdered every tenth person in cold blood.

My friend Ida and her family were forced to stand in a courtyard for an entire day with their faces turned to the wall. They were told that they would die, but in the evening, the women and children were allowed to return to their homes. Ida's husband and father-in-law were taken away, and she had to hand over all her jewelry to free them. There were many more people in prison, and we had to galvanize all possible resources to try to secure their release. We learned to barter for human lives.

The Germans had handed the fate of Czernowitz's Jews over to the Romanians, who were all too willing to follow the Nazis' antisemitic plans. Our tormentors were mollified, and since they wanted to rebuild their businesses, they were willing to employ Jews. One had no choice but to work for the enemy if one wanted to survive. Siegfried was taken to do janitorial work and to help rebuild the bridge over the Prut River. My father was given a position as an accountant, but for a minuscule wage.

And so I became the main provider for the family. My friend Ida and I went into business together. She had a well-developed business sense, and I was a talented knitter. We worked together knitting and marketing suits, woolen dresses and shirts, and we brokered the sale of furniture, carpets, crystal, furs and silver serving pieces. Despite the grave situation, we managed to have a good time, particularly when we sold something we thought worthless to the city's newly-wealthy inhabitants for a good price. Our profits were not bad, and we began to re-stock our inventory of items we hoped would see us through the war.

Ida had been living in Czernowitz for only three years when I met her in the National Gardens park, where our daughters played together. Once we were business partners, we became inseparable.

We sold our own personal effects as well as those of other Jews, and our apartments began to empty out. We did this not because we lacked money but because rumors were flying that the Jews would first be forced into a ghetto and then deported. So, like all the Jews, we were trying to sell our belongings and accumulate money in case further tribulations lay ahead. We invested our profits in dollars, having learned from the experience of three currency changes in the recent past.

Soon, however, an order was issued requiring us to transfer all our gold, silver and foreign currency to the government. We surrendered a few things, just for the record, but the rest we hid—a portion in our mattresses and the rest between two sections of a cupboard in the basement of our building. If we had been caught, the punishment would have been death, but by that point we had become too hardened to let that affect us.

When fall arrived that year, 1941, I couldn't resist sitting in the park for a while every day, surrounded by the brightly colored trees. I always took some knitting along, and one day a young Romanian couple admired my work. Their name was Kazacu and I had the impression that they were lovely people. They commissioned some work, and over time we became friends.

Early one morning — I think it was October 11 — the Kazacus appeared at our door unannounced. They told us that posters had appeared in the street giving all 70,000 of Czernowitz's Jews until six o'clock that evening to relocate to the ghetto, which was comprised of several streets in the Jewish quarter. Anyone caught outside of the ghetto after that hour would be punished by death. The Kazacus said they had come to help us and added in an undertone that implied secrecy that we would probably also be deported to concentration camps beginning that very day. They had heard that during the deportation we would be able to take only our most essential belongings with us.

Despite the danger involved, the Kazacus said they were willing to watch over our belongings. We were stunned by their news, but grateful for their generosity. Without delay, we packed all our remaining valuables and had them transported to the Kuzacus' apartment. Among the items were some embroidered pictures that I had worked on for years. One of them, called "The Secret," was as wide as our bedroom wall and had taken me two years to finish. We also gave them some small Persian carpets that I had woven myself and had refused to sell. That same day we sold several other items for absurdly low prices. Nothing had any value any more.

Then each of us filled our knapsacks and loaded a rented wagon with crates of foodstuffs, linen, furs, coats—everything we thought we couldn't do without. Fortunately, my mother's sister, Mrs. Reiner, lived on one of the streets within the ghetto, and so my parents climbed onto the wagon and set off to join them.

The streets looked like a scene from a movie depicting the migration of an entire nation. The ill, the elderly, the very young—everyone, rich and poor, clutched packages and dragged their other belongings along in laundry vats, baby carriages and every possible contraption. Some were even trying to take their furniture with them. Since Jews were forbidden to use the tram, anyone who owned a means of transportation took advantage of the situation and demanded huge fees for every trip. The wagon we rented didn't even take my parents all the way to their destination but let them and their belongings off midway. My parents had to carry the backbreaking load the rest of the way by themselves, and took turns watching over the dwindling pile and dragging the crates to the ghetto.

My husband and I also carried many loads from our apartment to the Reiners' well-kept apartment, which soon resembled a refugee camp. A total of twenty-four souls—including all of my mother's sisters and their children—gathered with their possessions in one three-room apartment. We could hardly move, but the chaos had a good side—none of us had time to think about our depressing situation. Rumors of many suicides soon circulated throughout the ghetto.

At night, after curfew, the streets outside of the ghetto were empty of all but the armed patrols policing its borders. Inside the ghetto, things bubbled like a boiling pot, as people tried to gather information about what would happen next, and tried to scrape together enough food for a meal.

Our own situation was relatively good, because at least we had a roof over our heads. All the cellars, attics, and corridors had been claimed as living space that first day, and the streets were packed with people who hadn't been able to find shelter.

As we spread our sheets on the floor to sleep, it seemed to me that we had gone back in time hundreds of years and were once again subject to the caprice of sadistic enemies. Keeping our sheets had been against the Kazacus' advice, and it soon occurred to me that they would have been more than happy to leave us naked.

After a sleepless night punctuated by groans coming from various corners of the apartment, we rose at five o'clock. We were not yet used to sleeping on the floor. The ghetto had been buzzing with activity all night, and that morning the streets resembled an agitated ant mound as commerce got underway. Knowing that we were confined inside the ghetto, Romanians showed up to make easy sales, and the farmers among them wanted exorbitant prices for their produce.

It was rumored that the deportation would begin that day because the Romanians feared disease would spread from the ghetto to the rest of the city. A list was posted of the names of streets whose residents were ordered to leave for the train station. And another order demanded, again, that Jews surrender their gold, silver, jewelry and foreign currency.

That first morning, my family gathered together to make a plan, and each member was given an assignment. The older women baked bread with their jewelry inside. My cousin Marta and I sewed knapsacks. The men experimented to see how much they could pack into the knapsacks without them being too heavy to carry.

The first lines of wagons loaded with deportees moved slowly through the streets toward the cattle cars waiting at the station. People stood for hours in the burning sun, waiting to be loaded. Many people tried to escape to streets whose occupants were permitted to remain, but the Romanian soldiers chased them toward the train station at gunpoint.

Soon another announcement was made: one could take nothing but sliced bread along in the trains. I opened the stitches on one of Gitta's dolls, removed some of the stuffing, and hid my jewelry inside.

The Kazacus visited us in the ghetto and gave us updates about all these orders. They were willing to exchange plain watches for our gold watches, and gave their solemn promise that everything would be returned if we came back to Czernowitz. By now we had so many other worries that we couldn't spare much attention for our valuables.

The ghetto was confined to a smaller and smaller area after each deportation, as the streets from which the Jews had been deported were closed off. Soon, we were so tightly confined that we almost couldn't cross the street it was so full of people. Finally, our street was listed and we were scheduled to leave the next day. That night, none of us could sleep.

Early the next morning, soldiers chased us out of our house. We loaded our packages onto wagons as ordered, but then had to stand for hours in front of the house. Every so often one of us would go back in to rest a little. The apartment looked as if it had been sacked. Our treasures were lying about for the taking, things we had managed to salvage from our original homes but now were forced to leave behind.

Our line finally began to move slowly up the street, and the way back was closed off behind us. The sun was scorching, and we felt the heat even more intensely since we had all dressed in heavy clothing. The children were tired and thirsty. We brought them water from the apartments of strangers. We didn't think we would reach the train station, which we had heard was in total chaos, until evening. Organization had never been one of the Romanians' strong suits, and now they were trying to transfer many thousands of people in a single day.

Our group took a chance and guessed that since chaos and disorganization reigned, the soldiers who were watching our wagons might be willing to accept a bribe. We let them know that we did not want to enter the train cars at night, and after some negotiations, they agreed. At the fixed time, we all left the line and entered one of the streets that was still part of the ghetto. For the moment, we were saved, though we no longer had a roof over our heads.

Remembering that my cousin Marta's sister-in-law lived on one of the ghetto's few remaining streets, all twenty-four of us went there to appeal to her. Her apartment was already full of people, but we gladly joined them, happy for a sliver of space on the floor where we could finally rest.

My aunt Antonia Klinger and her ten-year-old son were among the twenty-four members of our extended family who spent the night on that floor. The Klingers possessed Austrian passports, which had been a liability under the Russians: as a citizen of the greater German Reich, Aunt Antonia's husband had been deported to Siberia. But now, since Germany was Romania's ally, Antonia's citizenship brought her certain privileges. Perhaps the greatest of these was that she was allowed to enter and leave the ghetto at will. She had used this freedom in the past to get heart medicine for my husband from the city, and now, after our narrow escape from deportation, she went to reconnoiter. Returning from her trip outside, she told us that the city seemed to have emptied out and everyone felt the Jews' absence. She had also heard that Romanian public opinion had recently shifted somewhat in the Jews' favor. We were so despondent that we found it difficult to believe that our situation could improve, but the next day the Romanian government surprised us by announcing that lists would be compiled of experts who would be allowed to remain in Czernowitz. Thus began a new period of nerve-wracking waiting as the horse-trading for these special permits got underway.

Various members of that group of twenty-four — the Shaiovitzes, the Klingers, and my own immediate family — were soon granted permits to leave the ghetto. We — Siegfried, Gitta, my parents and I — returned to our old apartment, which had been thoroughly sacked. I still remember how Gitta wept as she searched the empty rooms in vain for her baby carriage.

The first days after we returned from the ghetto, we were afraid to go out in the streets, because all along the route from the ghetto to our apartment the Romanians had given us hateful looks. We were also still consumed by concern for the Jews who had remained in the ghetto, particularly our family members.

We had learned on the example of the Kibak family that it was possible to successfully forge an exemption permit. Apparently, some of the permits to remain in Czernowitz had been issued to families that had already been deported to Transnistria.

The Kibaks, who had never in their lives broken even the most minor law, decided, on the advice of an acquaintance, to take one such family's permit and change the names and dates to match their own. I still can't comprehend why the Romanians didn't catch the forgery, or maybe they just shut their eyes to it because others also got away with it.

My husband and I decided to use the Kibaks' technique to get my friend and business partner Ida, her husband, and her daughter out of the ghetto. Her family had been wandering through the ghetto from one street to another for weeks. They had even been sent to the train station, but Aunt Antonia used the power of her Austrian passport to get them away from there. Though neither my husband nor I was the hero type, and there was considerable risk involved, we did manage to forge a permit, thus engineering a successful escape for Ida and her family. But their respite from the threat of deportation did not last long, and Ida was soon to need our help again.

Though our entire family — all those twenty-four who were together in the ghetto—eventually managed to escape the deportation, we remained heavy-hearted, for we knew it was just a temporary respite. Like us, the other family members returned to their apartments, which had also been sacked. Then another order appeared, requiring each stay-permit to be reviewed, and the days of terror returned.

There were two types of permits: official permits of residence, called "Calotescu" after the city commander who had originally given them out, and the "Popovici" permits of residence, which had been issued by the mayor, a decent man who had hoped they would save Jews. People who had managed to hide in the ghetto and later found a way to leave it could get Popovici permits, but to exchange them for official Calotescu permits one had to scrape together a small fortune and then find an official who would be willing to accept it.

We needed to raise 150,000 Lei for the Kibak family and a similar sum for Ida's family, all of whom had only the forged Popovici permits. These were huge sums even before the war, and all the more so now that everyone was impoverished. Each municipality had a committee that was to examine the documents, and we all went into action for the Kibak family, searching until the right contact man was finally found.

Ida's sister in Bucharest had sent her the needed money, but it was slow to arrive. Ida also had an expensive fur coat that had belonged to a relative who had been sent to Siberia, but it wasn't easy to find the right buyer for it. She was growing increasingly distraught.

On the day the Romanians celebrated the occupation of Odessa,[4] Jews were forbidden to go out into the streets, but despite the great distance between us, Ida skirted the victory marches and cheering crowds and came to visit me. She had found out that an Italian professor who had helped many Jews was living in the Palace Hotel, and since Ida was an Italian citizen, she hoped that maybe he would help her.

Ida was blonde, with large grey eyes and long lashes. She was an expert at flirting, and many a man fell for her. She hoped to use her charms to impress the Italian, though in truth she was enamored of her husband.

Ida asked me to accompany her to the hotel, which was tantamount to entering the lion's den. The Palace Hotel contained the German headquarters and was brimming with high-ranking Romanian officers. Gripped by fright and anxiety, we went into the street without wearing the yellow star. While Ida didn't look Jewish, I was more recognizable as a Jew—brown hair and brown eyes— and when we entered the hotel lobby I felt exposed, as if I had been thrown into the lair of wild animals that were waiting to tear me apart.

But Ida remained cool and confidently approached the reception desk to ask for the Italian's room number. We knocked and were admitted to an elegant room by a man dressed in a bathrobe. He and Ida spoke in Italian, and she translated the details for me afterwards. He was prepared, he said, to take Ida

---

4 Odessa was occupied by the Romanians and the Germans on October 16, 1941 [Ed.].

and her daughter to her sister in Bucharest on condition that she agree to travel as his wife. Unwilling to leave her husband behind, Ida refused. Still willing to help, the Italian gave her the name of a Romanian officer who might be able to get her a Calotescu permit in exchange for her fur coat. We immediately set out to find this officer. But the Romanian officer, though he was interested in the coat, had been transferred to a different position that very day and was no longer authorized to "buy" it for his wife.

We hurried home, thinking that our luck had run out, only to discover that by some miracle a messenger had arrived from Bucharest with the money from Ida's sister. Within hours, Ida had her permit in hand. I will never forget her joy at that moment. Even her daughter, Ruthie, understood that now she could remain in Czernowitz with her friend Gitta.

CHAPTER 2

To Transnistria

By now, 50,000 Czernowitz Jews had been deported to Transnistria, a region in the western Ukraine that had been conquered by German and Romanian forces, and none of the news of them that reached us brought anything but anguish. There was nothing we could do to help them, though some of us appealed to the Joint Distribution Committee (American Jewry's overseas relief and rehabilitation agency) and others donated items for relief packages, only a few of which ever reached their destination. Many of the deportees died even before reaching the camps. They were forced to march through the Podolia swamps, while soldiers clubbed them mercilessly to keep them moving. Those who fell were shot, often before the eyes of their surviving family members. The bread they had brought along from Czernowitz quickly ran out, and though winter arrived early that year, people were nonetheless willing to trade their clothes for anything edible the local Ukrainians made available.

By the end of November the deportations from Czernowitz had drawn to a halt, although we heard rumors that they would resume. Siegfried was working in the public library sorting the books of those who had been sent to Transnistria. He did not receive a wage, but at least he was considered "vital" to the economy, and we hoped that would save us from deportation.

We had serious financial problems, and my husband tried to retrieve some of our belongings from the Kazacus, but they slammed the door in his face. Later, when Siegfried met them in the street, they threatened to have us deported if we dared to confront them again.

After that meeting, Siegfried suffered a heart attack from which he barely recovered.

He never complained about his pains, and I hadn't taken his heart problem seriously, but now I was seriously worried, both for him and about how I would provide for us. There were few sewing jobs available. Most of my clients had been deported, and those that remained were preoccupied with other matters and didn't plan to update their wardrobes. To make matters worse, my sewing machine had been stolen from our apartment while we were in the ghetto.

And so Ida and I set up our knitting salon again. Our first clients were the Tomascus, a Romanian officer and his wife. Ida and I also resumed our work as brokers, for the Jews were now selling whatever they still owned dirt cheap to the Romanians. Our business kept us afloat and had the advantage of helping us forget the threat of deportation.

Though nearly all the men had been sent to the border to dig trenches, Siegfried was able to remain at the library after his heart attack, which, considering his fragile health, literally saved his life.

And so, our family of five stayed together and spent the winter of 1941-42 crowded into one room, since that was all we could afford to heat. When spring arrived, I didn't even think of going down to enjoy my beloved park. When we left the house, it was only to make a living. Rumors continued to circulate that the deportations would soon resume, and so, when we saw lights on late one night in all the houses on a street where only Jews lived, we knew that people were baking bread and packing knapsacks again.

Exactly six months after the last deportation, people were again taken from their homes. 1,500 people were loaded into freight cars in a single day, carrying no more than the one knapsack per person they had been allowed. My uncle, Dr. Shaiovitz, went out in this transport. His wife Sally and their two sons hid in the apartment of a Christian friend for three weeks, but finally could no longer bear it and gave themselves up. Aunt Sally could only hope that in Transnistria she and her children might be reunited with her husband.

On June 27, 1942, the day before 2,000 people were scheduled for deportation, Ida's husband Ernst died after undergoing a minor operation. He was buried that same day. After the funeral, Ida tried to make me promise to spend that night with her, but my family decided it would be better to go home. We left her, miserable and broken, alone with her six-year old child. At home, I rolled jewelry and what money we still had into protective plastic packets so that, if necessary, it could be inserted into one our rectums. My father saw what I was doing, and I still remember his comment: "My daughter, why are you bothering? We have Calotescu permits!" He was recovering from a serious gall bladder attack, and I didn't respond because I didn't want to aggravate his condition. We suggested to him that we all go into hiding in Siegfried's library until the deportation was over. Siegfried had a key to the library, and no one would see us enter because it was Sunday and no one was working there. But my father refused to join us, so we all decided to stay home and spend a watchful night.

The next day was June 28, a date we had already come to dread. At six o'clock in the morning I looked out the window and saw a soldier and two citizens approaching. I wasn't surprised when the doorbell rang. My husband, Gitta and I were on their deportation list, but my parents were not. Nevertheless, my mother was the first to pick up a knapsack. My father, who was still weak from his gall bladder attack, tried to make my mother promise to remain, but she refused to listen to him. Prodded by the soldier, we got ready quickly.

Before leaving, each of us went to the bathroom and inserted the rolls as planned. We had even bought Vaseline to make it easier. Each of us tied a cooking pot to his knapsack, but the soldier took a liking to them and declared them the property of Romania. I was the last to leave and managed to pack a regular pot and something called a "wonder pot," which could even be used to bake bread. They proved to be invaluable.

A group of Jews, accompanied by policemen, were waiting for us below. We were marched through side streets toward the Maccabi stadium. My husband's brothers saw us leaving from their windows and could do nothing for us but look worried. Other Jews joined our column, pouring in from all the side streets.

Back when the Russians were conducting deportations, they had put freight trucks at the disposal of the deportees and had allowed them to take along whatever they wanted, even urging them to equip themselves with warm clothing. The Romanians, in contrast, sent us to the trains on foot, carrying knapsacks we wouldn't have been able to lift in ordinary times. Terror had imbued us with super-human powers.

I was very worried for my father and my husband. It was almost July, and we all wore at least two sets of clothes. We were soaked in sweat and Gitta's cheeks were beet-red.

After a few hours' march, we arrived, exhausted and apathetic, at the collection point, which was so densely packed with people wearing dark clothes that the whole place appeared to be black. A committee of officials checked everyone's residence permit, and representatives of the Jewish community were also present. My husband gave one of them our permits; I am still not sure why those permits didn't exempt us from the transport. I wouldn't be surprised if they made their way to other people, who made use of them.

After hours of waiting, which was a torture in its own right, we were sent onto the trains. Romanians lined the sides of the road the entire way from the collection point to the station. One woman, the wife of an officer, ran after me and tried to convince me to leave Gitta with her. I can still hear her saying, "Why are you taking your daughter with you? She is going to die. Isn't it better that you leave her with me and I will be a good mother to her?" I answered that if I was not going to live, my daughter did not have to live either. I saw tears in her eyes, but in those days, I didn't believe that there were still people who could feel another's suffering.

Arriving at the Maccabi sports stadium, I found that various members of my family were also there — Aunt Sally Shaiovitz and her two sons, as well as some other cousins. A huge freight train awaited us at the train station. Forty people were crammed into each car, and representatives of the Jewish community came along to distribute two loaves of bread to each of us. Although the train remained at the station for several hours before leaving, we were locked in. At least there were benches in the cars, and people managed to arrange themselves and their bundles, but it was so crowded we could barely breathe. I had packed a small potty for Gitta, which now served all of us, and a large pail had been provided for solid wastes. It wasn't long before no one was ashamed to use either of them. It seemed strange how quickly a person could cast off all vestiges of civilization.

Finally, the train departed. We went through a torturous night with nothing to drink followed by a day even hotter than the previous one before we finally disembarked near the Dniester River, on the other side of which lay the region of Transnistria. Then we were marched several kilometers to the bank of the Dniester where we spent the night. We were thrilled to be able to refresh ourselves a little in the river and take care of our needs behind the bushes.

My mother, my husband and I still had all of our treasures in our rectums. After forty-eight hours we were relieved to be able to take them out. But since we were afraid there would be another examination, we reinserted them. We had already endured one examination in the Maccabi stadium and the bundles had escaped detection, though our wedding rings had been confiscated.

That night on the banks of the Dniester remains etched in my memory. First, a violent storm broke out. We sat on the ground with only the shelter of a few ineffective umbrellas while thunder and lightning shook the earth and rain flooded down. After each round of thunder, we could hear the children weeping.

The rain stopped as suddenly as it had begun, leaving us drenched to the bone, and then the temperature fell and we began to freeze. Lying down on the saturated ground was unthinkable. Gitta was of the opinion that the train car — where she had undressed completely — had been preferable, and she advised that we should try to return home because she missed her bed. She looked at me and said, "You are laughing and crying at the same time. Why?"

I pressed her little body against mine and wondered what was to come.

In the morning we succeeded in making a fire and prepared our first tea in the wild. The pot I had stolen out of our apartment was the object of everyone's envy, and soon it served the entire group of forty people who had been together in the train car. The morning sun infused us with new strength. Our clothes dried and our frozen limbs warmed up. Then we were ordered to line up and the soldiers inspected us. Anyone who did not stand properly was hit with a rubber club. We heard shots, but they were directed into the air.

Several of the men organized a committee to bribe the soldiers to treat us a bit more humanely. Meanwhile, a lone ferry had arrived which was to transport all 1,800 of us across the Dniester. We stood in line under the scorching sun the entire day, but at least had the protection of our umbrellas.

Once across the Dniester, we were on Romanian-occupied Ukrainian soil and were forced to undergo a body search. Once again, our hiding places remained undiscovered. We had also successfully hid some silver in our knapsacks. Many others returned from this examination completed demoralized, their last items of value gone forever.

Towards evening, we were loaded into train cars again, and our journey to the unknown continued. Thanks to the bribes we had paid to the soldiers, every so often the door of the train car was opened and a whiff of cold air entered, making the night a little more bearable. We were all so exhausted that we slept sitting up. And since it had been only two nights and a day since we'd left our homes, we still had something to eat.

The next morning, we were taken off the train at a place called Volcineţ, where a committee of Jews from the city of Mogilev was waiting for us. The members of this group had already spent eight months in Transnistria and had endured every misery one human being could impose upon another. They had come to see if any of their relatives were on our train. We cried when we saw the state they were in, and they cried because they knew what awaited us. We also received two loaves of bread per person from the Joint. After several hours, we were put on the train again and spent two days and two nights making our way through Podolia to Cariera de Piatrá on the Bug River.

This was the camp where we were to spend the first year of our exile.

Cariera de Piatrá (stone quarry) on the banks of the Bug had been a Soviet penal camp before it was taken over by the German and Romanian forces. There were several barracks, which lacked windows and doors, situated some distance away from a few crumbling farm homes, and nothing else but the sky, the river and the quarry. All 1,800 of us were to live there.

Before we were allowed to enter this paradise, we had to spend a full day next to the Bug. The daytime heat was suffocating and relentless, and we sweated profusely. The night was freezing cold and we had to keep moving the whole time to stay warm. Though it was the height of summer, such extremes were typical of the season in this region.

Against orders, we prepared tea on two bricks, and I don't think we ever enjoyed a hot drink so much, despite the smell of smoke that accompanied it, threatening to give our illicit act away. Early the next morning, camp commander Deputy Vasilescu appeared, accompanied by Sergeant Poinescu. We stood in formation while the commander explained what was forbidden and pointed out the barracks. These, he said, could be used as sleeping quarters — but only for sleeping. For reasons of hygiene, we'd have to spend the days outside, along with our belongings. This man was a pharmacist in private life, and he promised us that he would be inspecting our level of personal hygiene every morning. Anyone who had lice would be beaten twenty-five times with a club, as would the head of his division.

One division head was chosen for every eighty people, and to my great distress, Siegfried was among those chosen. There was no appealing this decision, for the camp commander made the appointments himself.

We stood in formation for hours until all the formalities were finished. Once, my cousin Henri Shaiovitz turned around to give me a few words of encouragement, and he was hit on the head with a rubber club.

Then a disinfecting contraption was brought and we were told to strip naked. Those who put their clothes into the container first got them back as rags, no longer wearable at all. Among those unfortunates were people who had been taken from an old age home and inmates from psychiatric hospitals who had no other clothes to wear. They had to cover themselves with blankets, which only added to our overwhelming despair.

We gathered money to bribe the soldiers not to burn our clothes, and everyone contributed something to clothe those who were in greatest need. At that point, we were still shocked to see humans clothed in rags.

At sunset, we were taken to the barracks we had been eyeing from afar all day. We were so worn out by then that even four walls without windows or doors seemed like a luxury.

The barrack to which my family and I were assigned was number 25, and it excelled in the discipline and cleanliness it maintained. Most of its residents were academics. We slept in the room with twenty other people and when all of us stretched out to sleep, there wasn't a narrow strip of ground between us. Anyone who had to go out during the night had to crawl over the others. Despite this, on our first night there we were satisfied just to be able to stretch out, cover ourselves with the blankets we had brought, and put our knapsacks under our heads. We hadn't slept as well for weeks as we did that first night in the camp, and we naively thought the war of nerves was behind us.

The next day reality assaulted us. Deputy Vasilescu appeared for the daily inspection at six o'clock in the morning, accompanied by his sergeant and several fully-armed soldiers. When he had told us we could not remain in the barracks during the day, it had not been a vain threat. Deputy Vasilescu made clear that his instructions must be followed to the letter.

The camp resembled a disrupted anthill or a gypsy camp without wagons. Opposite our barrack was a structure that had served as a stable in the past. We were able to spend the hottest hours of the day in there. Our greatest concern was keeping clean. Twice a day we went down to the river to wash, and we laundered our clothes in the river as well, all in full view of the German soldiers.

The saddest cases among us were the former inmates of the psychiatric hospital. They had been allocated a separate barrack some distance away, but they wandered around the camp freely, and their hunger brought them to us. We gave them a little of what we had because we couldn't bear it when they came to the open windows at night and begged: "Bread! Give us bread!"

Vasilescu promised that the neighboring farmers would be allowed to come once a week so we could trade our possessions for some food. On the first market day, a Saturday, we were allotted just one hour to sell the belongings we had taken from our knapsacks and buy what we needed. But the day ended in failure. Even though each family sent only one representative, that still meant that 500 people fell upon twenty or thirty farmers.

The farmers wanted to take advantage of the situation, and they demanded shirts in exchange for bread. We hadn't yet reached the point of starvation, so each representative spent some time calculating how many shirts he had in his knapsack. Before we could make up our minds, the militiamen whistled that our hour was up and began to use their clubs. We were chased back into the camp without buying anything and had to make do for another week. We still had some leftovers from home—rice, tea, dry bread and sugar—and we used them extremely sparingly.

We fared far better than those who had been deported before us. They had been forced to contend with the rigors of both winter and typhus. We had arrived in the middle of summer, and the sun and the river compensated us a little. Once we had successfully passed the morning's "cleanliness inspection", the hardest part of our day was behind us. However, if a louse was found on any camp inhabitant, we were all forced to stand for hours for inspection, and we also had to watch the "guilty" man or woman be beaten with the rubber club until blood flowed profusely.

On the second market day, more sellers appeared, and this time we wasted no time. Men's shirts were exchanged for 10-kilogram buckets of potatoes. Every potato was counted, and we calculated how many each of us could eat until the next market day. We did everything we could to guard our health, for our only goal now was to survive the war.

The currency then being used in the Ukraine was the German mark. We had several thousand Leis—the Romanian currency—with us, and one day when fetching water, Siegfried encountered a train worker who was willing to exchange Marks for Leis. This worker returned to the camp several times to change more of our money.

I usually carried the packet that contained all of our treasures on a cord around my neck, but one day I gave it Siegfried before going to wash myself in the Bug. Before undressing to get in the water, I noticed a crowd of people gathering at the camp and hurried back to investigate. To my shock, I saw a soldier dragging Siegfried and two other men away. I soon learned that he had been imprisoned for changing Leis into Marks.

I was still naïve about strategies for using money inside the camp, but the previous day I had chanced to show my diamond engagement ring to a man in our room who had formed ties with Deputy Vasilescu, and now, seeing my despair, he asked if I would be willing to offer it to Vasilescu in exchange for Siegfried's release. I immediately agreed, but realized that the ring was in the packet I had given Siegfried.

Mr. Arjintaru, the broker, told Deputy Vasilescu that I possessed the nicest ring that he, a professional, had ever seen. He received a promise that Siegfried would be returned to camp the next afternoon. Nevertheless, I remained in deep despair, even began to think of suicide. I didn't believe Mr. Arjintaru's assurances and thought he was just trying to calm me down. Listening to the rush of the Bug, I said to my mother, "Do you hear the river calling us? What will we do without Siegfried?" In the morning I found it easier to cope, and searched out the women whose husbands had been taken with Siegfried. To my shock, I found them calm. "Those clever guys have probably already found a way to get out of this mess," they reassured me.

I spent the afternoon waiting on the slope that overlooked the tunnel and eventually saw soldiers followed by three figures, one of whom, to my delight, I recognized as my husband. The entire camp welcomed the men as if they were victors back from the battlefield.

Siegfried hugged Gitta and me as if he had been gone for years instead of only twenty-four hours. After his arrest, he had told the soldier that he suddenly had to attend to his needs, and was able to hide the packet, which he now returned to me intact. That saved our lives—for the next two years, our survival depended completely on that packet.

When I told my husband about the agreement with Deputy Vasilescu, he was angry at first, though later he was moved that I had agreed to give up my ring to secure his safety.

Soon, Vasilescu summoned Siegfried. Returning from the meeting, he told me the commander had been very impressed by the ring, and he generously offered 500 Marks for it. It was worth 3,000 Marks! He also told my husband that the ring would save our lives. We smiled at this and assumed Vasilescu was only trying to comfort us on the loss of the ring. We soon discovered that we had underrated him.

A few days later we heard an alarm summoning us to the clearing where inspections were held. To our shock, we were confronted by a committee of German officers, rather than the usual Romanians.

The highest-ranking officer announced, "This committee has come to examine your situation. We are interested in improving your conditions. Anyone who wants to can earn his livelihood working in his own profession. We will provide you with a place to live that will be suitable for the winter." The officer asked all the professionals to raise their hands and continued to offer incentives. He closed by saying that buses would be available to transfer us on August 18.

Though we still had no idea about the German atrocities, my family was in total agreement that we would not switch to the German side.

On August 17, Deputy Vasilescu asked our representatives to prepare a list of the professionals who would remain in the Romanian camp, and he stressed that all five members of the Aufleger family should be at the top of the list. It cost 100 Marks per person to get on the list. That night I tried to convince several families to stay in the camp and even offered to lend them the 100 Marks, but the general tendency was to go with the Germans.

It was planned that the 200 people on the list would withdraw into one of the barracks after the morning inspection on the 18th and stay there until the Germans had left. But during inspection that morning we suddenly found ourselves surrounded by a ring of soldiers and Ukrainian militiamen waving clubs. I grabbed Gitta with one hand and my mother with the other, and somehow we slipped through the barricade and reached the designated hideout. My father and husband, who had succeeded in grabbing our knapsacks, were already there. 200 people sat crowded into two small rooms on a sweltering day, listening to Germans bellowing orders, shots being fired, and the cries of the victims.

We could see the Ukrainians plundering knapsacks. It took the entire day to transport some 1,600 people across the Bug. I placed my Gitta on the windowsill, and she sat there all day without eating, drinking, or attending to her needs. Her cheeks were flushed with the heat and her eyes were full of fear.

We had been told explicitly to keep silent and not to attract the Germans' attention, and a baby that could not be soothed was now endangering us all. Its mother took it to the stable opposite our barrack, but her husband remained with us. He kept opening the door to check on his wife and baby, and that was how a German soldier discovered us.

"Jews!" he shouted. "What are you doing here?"

We were sure all was lost. Then Dr. Fichman spoke up, saying, "The Romanian authorities left us here because we are professionals." The German replied, "We'll check it out. If it's not true, you'll all face the wall…"

Terror swept over us and a few people fainted before the German returned and announced that the Romanians indeed had permission to hold on to us and we should remain where we were until the last transports left. We waited until evening and then went out. Instead of the unceasing noise, instead of having to fight for ten centimeters of sleeping space, emptiness and a deathly silence surrounded us. Documents the Germans had torn from people's belongings were scattered everywhere. We felt as if we had lived through an earthquake. We would learn later that we were the only group to have escaped being relocated by "concerned" German committees.

After some time, the camp commander appeared and ordered the men to go outside the camp and bury the dead. The Germans had shot the elderly and the sick because it was not "worth their while" to take them along.

All that night we worried that the Ukrainians, having just developed an "appetite" for plundering Jews' knapsacks, would fall upon us in the dark. We stationed a guard for that night, and then stretched out on the floor to try to sleep.

Aunt Sally Shaiovitz bribed a Ukrainian militiaman to find out what had happened to her husband, who, she had learned, had been in a camp three miles away. She was informed that he had gone willingly to the German side after a German officer told him no Jews had remained in our camp and he would be reunited with his family on the other side of the Bug. We still did not know the full dimension of this tragedy, but the news shocked us nonetheless.

Still gripped by fear, some among us began to regret not having joined the others, but we slowly got used to our new situation and began to make plans again. We even considered escaping to places nearby such as Bershad and Oboduvca, where many deported Jews were living under what were rumored to be safer conditions. Then Deputy Vasilescu offered to send 200 of us to the nearby Ladizhin camp, which also had a remnant of "professionals" who hadn't transferred to the German side. He told us Ladizhin was a clean, well-organized camp that even had a kitchen—no more cooking soup on two bricks. Many of its inmates lived in houses with wooden boards to sleep on. We accepted the offer, and all of us sold something of value on market day to come up with the money that this officer who "was concerned for our welfare" had requested. Ladizhin was further away from the Bug, which meant it was further from the German side, and I think we really believed that our situation would improve if we went there.

One bright, hot August morning we were ready to be on our way. The commander from Ladizhin was to lead the journey on his horse, accompanied by soldiers and the Ukrainian militia. We were to follow on foot, carrying our own loads. Knowing that some of us wouldn't be able to walk twenty kilometers in the August heat even if we did not have to carry a thing, our group had rented a few wagons to take the heavy packages and the small children. But chaos broke out when the Ladizhin commander saw that wagons were being used without his permission. He drew his gun and shot into the crowd, and his militiamen wielded their clubs. We were forced to run back to our camp, and the ever-present Ukrainians took advantage of the commotion to steal the knapsacks left behind on the wagons. Though Siegfried, my father and my Aunt Sally Shaiovitz all had their packs on a wagon, by a miracle they were not taken. Others, however, were left with only the clothes on their backs, and the children were left virtually naked, since they had been wearing almost nothing in the heavy heat.

Back at Cariera de Piatrá, we lay on the floor exhausted. Those who had lost all their belongings were overwhelmed with despair. But soon we began to organize ourselves again because we had no choice. I have no way to explain the source of our emotional and physical strength. We were hanging on to life by our fingernails, but no one thought of suicide. With every breath we prayed that we would live to take revenge on our tormentors.

We went back to our old schedule: selling something once a week on market day, so that we could buy a few more items; cooking tea and bean soup or potatoes on bricks. The nights turned colder. We huddled under blankets and asked ourselves what we would do come winter. The commander again offered to arrange for us to spend the winter in Ladizhin. It was out of the question to spend the winter cut off from the world in our present camp, where the snow would pile above our heads, and our barracks were little more than ruins. Once again, each of us collected the necessary sum to permit our transfer to Ladizhin.

This time the journey passed without incident. We marched for hours and every so often were given a break to rest and collect money to give the soldiers so they wouldn't press us so hard. We arrived in Ladizhin in the evening, and were received warmly by the Jews who had remained there after August 18.

The commander had described the Ladizhin camp accurately. On the night that we arrived, after months, we finally ate soup that did not smell of smoke. Our beds were elevated boards in rooms with windows and doors. We drifted to sleep feeling that we had reached a Garden of Eden. The next morning, though disquieting rumors were already circulating, we paid our fee to use the kitchen for the coming week. But at noon, we were told that the Ladizhin camp was going to be closed and all its residents would join us back in Cariera de Piatrá.

The Jewish committee, which we ourselves had chosen, informed us that the order to combine both camps had arrived from above and could not be changed. We were told that our camp's commander had sent us to Ladizhin to "improve our situation," but we conjectured that he knew about the impending closure and had seen an opportunity to squeeze more money from us. Or perhaps seeing us disappointed satisfied some sadistic urge.

Our knapsacks were still packed and we were already used to our camp's terrible conditions, so we had some advantage over the Ladizhin inmates. Their advantage was that they were fresh for the journey, not already having made it just the day before.

No wagons were available to us, and a long night's journey through forests awaited us. I wondered how we—especially my frail parents and my little Gitta—would endure it a second time. We set out at four o'clock in the afternoon. It was a lovely fall day, but we were too bewildered to enjoy it.

Several soldiers and militiamen watched over us, which relieved us somewhat, as one could "speak" with soldiers through bribes, and they occasionally let us take a break. Nonetheless, many of us were hit with clubs, particularly those who did not march in line as demanded. As long as we could see where we were going, the journey was bearable, but when darkness fell, we entered the forest. I held on to Gitta with one hand, carried her knapsack in the other, and my own knapsack on my back. We often bumped into the roots of the trees and fell, but quickly got up and continued. They drove us like a herd of cattle.

We emerged from the forest to find that the Ukrainians had discovered that a procession of Jews was on the way. They hid in the cornfields and ambushed several people, pulling off their knapsacks. Confusion erupted, the soldiers shot in the air, and the Ukrainians dispersed. We continued on our way.

Losing one's knapsack meant simply that one would die of hunger. Bartering one's belongings was the only way to pay for food on market day.

We arrived back at Cariera de Piatrá at noon to find that the Ukrainians had destroyed whatever they could of the barracks. We found our place of residence in a worse state than ever. Completely spent, we collapsed on the floor, our knapsacks safe under our heads, grateful that the ordeal of the journey was behind us.

The nights were already chilly, and a cold wind was blowing in from the river. It was impossible to close the windows. The young daughter of friends who had had their knapsacks stolen was feverish, and I gave her Gitta's winter coat to wrap up in. Totally exhausted, we slept amid the Ladizhin Jews, for whom Cariera de Piatrá was terra incognita.

Our community had grown, though I didn't know how many inmates there were now. We went on as before—people lit fires and prepared tea, and those of us who had food sat down to eat.

September arrived and we had to get serious about preparing for winter. The first priority was to close the windows, and there was no alternative but to use bricks. There were plenty of bricks in some ruins outside of the camp, and for a fee the soldiers let the men fetch them. We bought small panes of glass from the farmers and affixed them between the bricks. One problem was solved.

Rain began to fall, and the days became colder, but at least we were now allowed to spend the day in the barracks. One day I discovered some tufts of soft grass growing between the rocks and organized the entire family to pick it to stuff into the bedcovers, pillows and blankets we had brought from home. The next day, many other inmates emulated us.

Continuing our preparations, we pulled boards from the unused barracks to make wooden sleeping platforms that could double as benches during the day. Of course, we had to bribe the guards first. We even bought a saw from farmers, but used it only under cover of darkness. Now that we had windows and wooden sleeping platforms, we only lacked cooking facilities and heat.

Suffering inspires creativity. A blacksmith who was in the camp constructed a kind of sink in which we could wash ourselves and our clothes, because of course we could no longer use the freezing Bug. He also built an oven, and though it filled with smoke, we cooked on it. It even warmed up the room a little. To operate the oven, we needed real logs, not just the wood chips we had used in the summer. There were telegraph poles outside the camp, and one Sergeant Poynro had a liking for Doxa watches, so we turned over a large collection of timepieces in exchange for permission to bring in that supply of wood for the winter. While we were trying to survive, he was trying to get rich.

New groups kept arriving at Cariera de Piatrá, which was considered a penal camp. Among them were people who had performed terrible "crimes" such as trying to buy food for themselves. Many were penniless and arrived with only the clothes on their backs.

After all these winter preparations were completed, rumors began to spread that Cariera de Piatrá would be closed down and we would be sent to other places. Lists were formed again, and this time, money didn't help. One needed connections to be sent somewhere better, such as Tulchin, the regional city, which had always had a Jewish community. My Aunt Sally Shaiovitz and her sons managed to move to there in exchange for an x-ray machine, which the family had owned in Botoşani. Those who went to Tulchin really did find their conditions improved, though they too were interned in a Romanian concentration camp, but we remained in Cariera de Piatrá, awaiting the worst.

One day the new commander from Ladizhin came to us, and he made a good impression. After making an initial inspection of our barracks, he said that he had now seen Dante's Hell. He had orders to send a group of people across the Bug, and really had no choice, he said, but to follow instructions. He compromised by gathering together the sickest inmates and those dressed in rags to send to the Germans. I remember standing on a bed platform watching out the window as that group left, thinking we might easily be next.

Meanwhile, businessmen who wanted to buy our remaining jewelry and diamonds kept arriving from Romania. Anyone who had something to sell could buy time to live. An exchange network was created: in exchange for a substantial percentage, certain officers would bring us money from family members who had remained in Czernowitz.

We also received money occasionally from Ida's sister in Bucharest, for I had transferred various valuables to her before the deportation. One of the first messengers to reach us from the external world was Sergeant Tomascu, to whom I had sold fur coats, crystals, furniture and knitted goods when we lived in the ghetto. The sergeant drove right into camp in his car to give Siegfried money from our relatives. If the guards had known of this, we would have had to divide the money with them.

The winter arrived and snow piled up as high as a house. The local farmers had lived under the Soviet regime for twenty years, and they were very poor. They were hostile towards us, and enjoyed alarming us—for instance, they had threatened some months ago that they would not bring us any market goods in winter because the snowdrifts would be too high. Despite their threats, however, the farmers continued to come—not because they didn't want us to starve, but because they coveted our belongings, many of which they had never seen in the

Soviet Union. The camp committee organized a kitchen so that those who were penniless would at least receive a bowl of soup to warm them up.

The days passed. When no telegraph poles were left, the authorities let us chop wood in the nearby forest. We had to give nine-tenths of the wood to them, however. Not only was the chopping hard work, the wood was wet and had to be pulled several kilometers to the camp. Siegfried joined in this work, despite my protests, though the effort was far beyond his physical capacity.

When the snows finally melted, a terrible smell spread throughout the camp. The cesspools overflowed, dreadful flies appeared, and typhus and dysentery broke out. Many people died without medicine or treatment, lying on their miserable wooden platforms.

Those who could still stand on their feet were forced to clean up the camp. When even that didn't stop the epidemics, the authorities took new measures. Those who could work were sent to a farm called Trostinets, and all the others were sent across the Bug to meet the same fate as my Uncle Shaiovitz, whatever that might be.

On a pleasant spring day we were lined up and walked towards the Trostinets farm. Thinking of previous experiences, we were suspicious, especially now that several escapees who had joined us over the winter had enlightened us about the atrocities taking place across the Bug.

But after a daylong march, we found ourselves at a place that was harmonious and pleasant compared to the place from which we had just come. Trostinets was a collective farm on the Soviet model that was run under Romanian supervision. The Ukrainians who lived there loved their way of life. We, however, had no idea how to work the soil, and had been sent there to do hard physical labor.

On the first day, at five o'clock in the morning, we walked in the rain to some far-off fields where we dug potatoes and harvested corn, which wasn't particularly hard. Then came the beets, which we had to learn not to damage. A brigadier supervised us, and clubbed anyone whose work was not up to standards. And woe be to anyone not working steadily and advancing in line when the overseer arrived on his horse. In that case, the supervisor was also punished.

The children were permitted to remain in the sleeping quarters with the elderly women, who had to cook the large vat of cereal that was taken to us in the fields, where each worker was allotted a tiny portion.

During the noon break, we collapsed and wondered if we would last until the evening. After a general consultation, we decided to pay the supervisor a weekly "wage" to allow us to take a short break every so often. We worked near a forest, and now we could take rests there, while the supervisor stood on guard. But as soon as his overseer approached, someone would call out "Bel Ami," and we would run to the field and begin working at full speed.

Our sleeping quarters housed fifty people, but since we were from similar backgrounds and we all got along, it was more or less tolerable. Quarrels broke out in other barracks, but in ours people did their utmost to be considerate. This was not a simple thing, for we had already been in the concentration camp for a year, and the colors of civilization had faded. Or perhaps one could say that by then everyone was more or less showing his true colors.

One day I sold a pair of nylon socks to the wife of the collective farm's accountant, a Ukrainian called Mrs. Hora. Many of our maids had been Ukrainian, so she and I were able to communicate easily. She was looking for someone who knew how to sew, and her husband arranged for me to work for her. I worked all day at the Horas' and even ate with them. In the evenings, I received a loaf of bread and a liter of milk for my family. That job was great luck.

Siegfried also obtained easy work. The town council was looking for an accountant, and he got the job. After a time, we moved into a room where "only" twelve people lived, and hoped we would manage to survive under those conditions until the end of the war. I got food from the Horas, and every so often Siegfried received a bottle of oil in exchange for his work—it was dark and sometimes bitter, but we thought it was manna—but we all remained malnourished. Many of us developed sores and poor vision, especially at night. I will never know how my elderly parents were able to survive with such extremely poor nutrition, sleeping on hard boards with nearly empty knapsacks under their heads.

My mother was thrilled when they let her help in the soldiers' kitchen, where she could get a chicken liver for Gitta every so often. But one day she was attacked in the kitchen by a drunken soldier who called her a "niece of Stalin," and we made her promise to stop working there.

Throughout the summer we tried to find out what was happening at the front. When we heard of the Nazi reversals, we were in seventh heaven, and we despaired when we heard of their victories, but we never got exact details.

The Ukrainians, including the Horas, also had their mood swings about the war. They did not want the Germans to win, but were afraid that if Stalin won, he'd take revenge because they had not fled from the Germans. Mrs. Hora told me again and again that they had wanted to flee, but the Germans had barred their way. When I told her about my family's life before the war, they didn't believe one could live so well under a capitalistic regime. One day Siegfried told me he had heard from the council head that all the men would soon be sent to work elsewhere. The head of the council gave Siegfried a key to the farm's sugar factory, which was not then in operation, so he could hide there until the danger of this newest *Aktion* was past.

The Jewish head of our farm camp, Mr. Stier, was a sycophantic man who tried to fulfill the authorities' orders exactly. When he was told that we wouldn't be going out to work the next day, I understood that the *Aktion* was at hand. I knew that Mr. Stier would do nothing to protect my family, because he had it in for me. For several weeks he had tried to a send a young girl who also knew how to knit to work for Mrs. Hora instead of me. She was a lovely girl, and I didn't protest. She deserved a little rest from the work in the fields. But Mrs. Hora had become my friend and thought my work was better, and she didn't agree to the replacement. Mr. Stier had to grit his teeth and let me keep my post.

I decided to hide in the cornfields to watch what went on in the camp. I saw soldiers surround it and then chase the men, including the elderly and the sick, outside. They were forced to line up, their names were called, and Mr. Stier ran about trying to make sure the soldiers' orders were carried out.

When it became clear that three men were missing, among them my husband, Mr. Stier advised the soldiers to take hostages from each of their families. Instead of my husband, my father was taken, and instead of the other two men, their fifteen-year old daughters were taken. As soon as I saw them pull my sick, old father into that line, I came out of hiding and demanded to take his place. Mr. Stier, now satisfied, announced that we could go on our way.

We were taken to the village police and delayed there an entire day while the authorities waited for the missing men to show up. The two girls and I were interrogated every so often, and asked where the men were. We kept silent.

"What are you doing, Mrs. Aufleger?" a woman who had brought her husband a package asked me. "You are causing your daughter to lose not one parent but two."

The next day we walked fifty kilometers to Tulchin, equipped with some food our families had managed to organize. The way was dusty and difficult, made more arduous by our fear of what awaited us. In the evening, we encountered some Jews who were paving a road and convinced the soldiers to let us take a short break. We took advantage of the opportunity to send a note to the director of the Tulchin camp, Dr. Fichtman, who was a friend of my family. In it we asked him to do everything in his power to ensure that we would not be sent across the Bug River.

We reached an assembly point where other people had gathered and found ourselves the only three women among 500 men. We ate our last pieces of bread and lay down on the ground, exhausted from the trip. The next day we marched, or to be more exact dragged ourselves, to our destination, a work camp called Nestervarca. The people there were rough, mean and dirty, and I understood that everything up to that point had been a honeymoon. I didn't realize how much having been able to be with my family and other congenial acquaintances had provided vital support that kept my spirits up.

The first night, we slept on boards in a huge barrack, feeling like we were in the hold of a ship. A single old oil lamp cast a dim light and the place felt haunted. The room reeked, the air was heavy with smoke, and I could hardly breathe.

I don't know what would have happened to us if two chivalrous men in our group had not taken it upon themselves to protect the three lone women. We were not afraid of being raped—the men were too weak for that—but they might have ripped our clothes off our backs, because they themselves wore only sacks. These men were forced to work in the peat mines all day and sometimes into the night.

There was activity in the barrack all night, and each time another group was taken out to work there were shouts and sometimes a clubbing. Early in the morning of our first day, we newcomers held a consultation and tried to figure out how to escape from this hell. We met people from Czernowitz who lived in other barracks, where more humane conditions prevailed, and they told us who to approach to get our own living quarters.

I was also able to contact Aunt Sally Shaiovitz in Tulchin and explain our situation. She immediately contacted the Tulchin committee, and they arranged a decent barrack for us. A few days later, the whole group from Trostinets was ordered to begin work building bunkers for planes.

We walked almost three kilometers to a meadow that apparently surrounded an airport. It was still August and the days were very hot, while the nights were cold and humid. Our work was to dig "bricks" from the grass-covered earth and use them to erect walls to protect parked airplanes. I don't know who came up with the idea, because even while we were building them, we were sure they would collapse like a house of cards.

Our "wages" were a bowl of soup in which swam something indeterminable. The work was backbreaking, but to our good fortune there were a number of farmers' houses nearby where anyone who had something to sell could buy bread and apples. With this supplement, we managed to hold out. There was also a lake nearby in which we could wash ourselves and launder our clothes.

One day we learned that several people who had crossed the Bug a year before were now working not far from us, and I was allowed to go there during one of the breaks. During this meeting I learned that my uncle, Dr. Shaiovitz, had died—though I did not yet know any details. I also heard the tragic story of our fellow deportees who had crossed the Bug. Of this particular camp across the Bug River, all deportees were exterminated with the exception of a single family, the Schorrs. When I returned, heavy-hearted, I told only a few people what I had heard, for there was no point in demoralizing them further.

Everything was tolerable as long as the weather was decent, but soon the rains arrived. We had a doctor among us, Dr. Pistiner, and he found us shelter for the night in a farmers' granary. Everyone else had to sleep in the pounding rain with only the trees for protection. I still cannot understand why we did not catch pneumonia, though many of us did suffer from sores and diarrhea.

A month passed, an entire month separated from my family and with no news of what might have happened to them or whether they had heard something about me. One day a delegation arrived that included the commander of Tulchin. He tried to be polite and asked us if we wanted anything. We asked for permission to visit our friends in Tulchin the next Sunday and he promised us that. He also told us that when the project we were working on was finished, we might be allowed to return to Trostinets.

As soon as the high-ranking visitors left, we discussed why we were being offered these concessions and decided it was probably tied to the bad situation at the front. The Romanians, worried for their future, might want to turn a new leaf in their relations with the Jews.

I was longing for my family and especially for my child. The others also suffered from the separation, and we doubled our efforts to finish the job so we could go "home." Also hanging over us was our fear that the autumn rains would destroy everything we had built.

One morning when the ground was a swamp and it was impossible to work, our overseer chose a group to go to Tulchin and I was among them. In Tulchin, we were permitted to visit our friends for a few hours and I was able to see Aunt Sally and her sons. They lived in a decent room, and because they were able to give a certain sum from time to time, they were not bothered. But they were terribly worried for my uncle, from whom they hadn't heard in a long time. I already knew the bitter news and could hardly hide my sorrow from them. But they did not seem to sense a thing, since everyone in the camps exuded a certain melancholy.

After the war, I managed to learn the full story of Uncle Shaiovitz's death. Some time before my visit to Aunt Sally in Tulchin, we had received a letter from her saying she had met an SS officer who had known my uncle and greatly admired him. This officer, whose name was Schweitzer, said that he would bring Uncle Shaiovitz to Aunt Sally. Elated and full of hope, she offered the Tulchin commander her jewelry in exchange for permitting her husband to join her.

Schweitzer also wanted to save another family, the Schorrs, who were with my uncle on the other side of the Bug, and Uncle Shaiovitz insisted that he help them first. Schweitzer was able to successfully smuggle the Schorrs to Czernowitz, where relatives hid them, at great risk, until the end of the war.

But before Uncle Shaiovitz could be rescued, this humanitarian deed became known to the SS, and Schweitzer was investigated and imprisoned. In prison, he caught typhus, and my uncle Shaiovitz treated him in the camp. Though the German recovered, my uncle caught typhus and died.

After the war had ended, Mr. Schweitzer took Aunt Sally a photo of the tombstone that had been erected on her husband's grave. Dr. Shaiovitz was the only Jew who had been sent across the Bug to be buried in a single grave with a tombstone over it. It was a small comfort.

The monument, I assume, was a testament to my uncle's great altruism. Mrs. Schorr has told me stories from those times across the Bug. She said my uncle freely distributed the medications his sister sent him from Czernowitz and never thought to sell them, despite their great value. One day Mrs. Schorr saw him tearing his towel into small strips because, he said, "Soon the people working to shatter stones in these low temperatures will develop sores, and these strips of material will protect them for a little while. I can use a handkerchief instead of a towel."

After the war, Aunt Sally and Mrs. Schorr testified on Schweitzer's behalf when he was tried in Germany, and Mrs. Schorr invited him to Israel to plant a tree at Yad Vashem where he was honored as one of the Righteous Among the Nations.

My relatives knew more about the political situation than I did, and their motto was "Hang on, it can't go on much longer." I returned to work slightly more composed and continued to dig sod bricks with full energy, though many others had grown so weak that they could only lie under the trees and be tortured by stinging flies. Finally, the day came when we were told that we only had to plaster the walls of the building and we could go.

I will never forget the last day! We didn't have paintbrushes, which apparently wouldn't have helped anyway. Several men dragged lime from a lime pit for workers who stood on a scaffold to pour along the length of the walls. Of course, there were mishaps when the lime splattered in people's eyes. We women tried to keep the soldiers distracted from the imperfect work that resulted by telling them we would never forget their humane treatment of us. We even invited them to visit us in Trostinets.

The next day we left our creation and prayed it would last through the rains. This time a few wagons were provided for those who were incapable of walking and the fifty-kilometer march ahead no longer frightened us. We were anticipating our reunion with our families, for Trostinets was now "home."

Towards evening of the next day, we were greeted with great emotion by all of Trostinets's residents. I found my family in even worse condition than I was, for the fear that I might never return completely dispirited them. I hugged my daughter tightly and I thanked God I was with my family again. My mother told me that Siegfried had returned the following day and had collapsed when he heard I had been taken. He had run to the police to ask that he be exchanged for me and was promised that this would be done, but he was needed in the office, so there he stayed.

Typhus had broken out while I was gone, and it was impossible to set up quarantine quarters, so the sick remained where they had always slept. People grew weaker. My father suffered from a fearful pain in his eyes, and in the end became blind in one of them. We got permission for him to travel to see a doctor in Tulchin, but he needed an operation, which she could not do, and he returned even sicker. On the way home, he was beaten viciously by soldiers looking for someone on whom to vent their frustration, because there had been bad news from the front.

Siegfried had also lost weight. He was only forty-two years old but looked much older. The only one who didn't seem to have been affected by life in the camp was Gitta. She remained sweet and was our only joy. I remember watching her organize our knapsacks on the wooden benches and covering them with a blanket so they looked like a couch. She placed a suitcase covered with a towel in the middle, and on it put a can containing wildflowers. Then both of us sat on that couch and talked as if we were still in our apartment in Czernowitz. It was a game of which she never tired.

One day, a twelve-person room was vacated and Mr. Stier organized a new group to live there, including himself, which he invited us to join. Apparently, he wanted to correct his past mistreatment of me. Though we were not happy at the prospect of living with him, the other people were pleasant and the room offered many advantages, including electricity and a small vestibule where one could cook. Of course, it was also more comfortable there than living with fifty people. Mr. Stier had a daughter, Anita, who was slightly older than Gitta. They became good friends.

CHAPTER 3

The End in Sight

Winter of 1943 was approaching, and though we were physically very weak, our situation was much improved compared with that of the previous winter. We received newspapers and were able to deduce from them that our enemies were doing badly. Days passed in mounting anticipation. There was an accordion player in the camp who was occasionally invited to the village to play for the German officers. Returning from such an assignment one day, he reported that the officer at whose party he had been playing had been called to the phone. When he came back, he was pale and had changed into his uniform. The party was called to an end, and the accordion-player was led to believe that the German situation at the front had become much worse.

While we were analyzing that news, the farm commander appeared in our room, and told Mr. Stier to accompany him. After some time, Mr. Stier returned carrying a horse's bridle that the commander had asked him to guard so it wouldn't fall into the hands of the partisans. The Romanians were preparing to flee, but they had been notified that if they did, they would have to take the barracks' inmates with them.

At first, we agreed that we should not join in the retreat, but the next morning, we saw things in a different light. Siegfried had gone to the village, as he was authorized to do, and he returned to relate that both the head of the council and the German commander had advised him that the Jews "should disappear" because Nazi SS officers might arrive and carry out a purge. They promised Siegfried that they would not pay any attention if small groups of Jews were seen making their way to a hideout.

Outside the snow piled higher and higher, and wind whirled the snowflakes into a churning sea. In this weather we were supposed to leave under cover of darkness, in our inappropriate clothing, and take our elderly and feeble compatriots with us.

The entire camp waited to see what our group of twelve would decide, since they had opted to follow our lead. That whole morning, the committee debated where to go.

I lay down for a few moments to gather strength for the journey ahead, and when I woke up, the room was full of German soldiers! Paralyzed with fear, I remained in my place. My initial reaction was that at least we wouldn't have to go out into the snowstorm. The decision of whether or not to leave was now out of our hands.

But these were German soldiers on their way to the front, not the SS, and so there was no purge. The train in which they were traveling had been stopped by the piled-up snow. These soldiers, though German, were sympathetic to the plight of the Jews: when they learned who we were, some of them hurried back to the train and returned with cans of preserves, coffee, and containers of gasoline to light the Primus burners. They stayed with us until late that night, and asked us to tell them about everything we had experienced in the concentration camp. Then they told us what was happening in Germany, where they had just been—whether on leave or receiving treatment in a hospital. The soldiers hinted that the war would not last much longer.

The train was stuck for a few days, and every time the soldiers visited, they brought us something. Once they gave Siegfried a shirt and material for a hat. Sometimes they confiscated eggs from the farmers, claiming that we needed them more. One day they caught a rabbit and my mother cooked it for them in wine. The result was outstanding, even though she had never prepared rabbit before, and they invited us to join them. Though we were starving, we found that in their presence we just could not get the food down.

The soldiers warned us about the SS troops, whom they called "the black demons." They sang popular German songs such as *Lili Marlene*, and once one of them said, while looking at one of the young girls among us, "What a shame if they had killed such a beautiful girl." Then the rail lines opened up, and the soldiers departed. Who knows which of them survived the war?

One day a German officer was looking for a seamstress to sew for his Ukrainian mistress, and Mrs. Hora recommended me. I took an acquaintance with me from the camp, a Mrs. Sass, and a German soldier marched us along to the woman's house as if he had arrested us. The "lady" needed suitable clothing in which to accompany the officer to Germany. The officer had brought her the material from France, but we were more impressed by the breakfast they offered us. I still salivate when I think of the meal—fried sausage, fresh eggs, homemade bread, and pickled tomatoes.

When we sat down to work, Mrs. Sass and I decided not to hurry so we could remain in this wonderful convalescent home as long as possible. However, when the bottle-blonde Ukrainian woman appeared, she told us that everything had to be finished in two days. If we finished in time, she would pay us, otherwise, she would take the unfinished clothes with her to Germany and we wouldn't be paid at all.

We began to work with alacrity. I remember the lunch we ate there, too— nothing I'd eaten for years came close—Tshorba soup, roast meat, and dumplings. By afternoon, we had four dresses ready to be tried on. At four o'clock, we were served tea and pastries that melted in our mouths. Unfortunately, each of us received only two pastries. Yet by lavishing praise on the Ukrainian lady, I managed to secure several pastries for Gitta when I left, which filled me with joy.

Only a person who has lived on the verge of starvation for a long time can understand my preoccupation with food. For finishing the four dresses in two days, Mrs. Sass and I each received eight Marks and a loaf of bread. This wage kept us going for a few more days, but shortly thereafter the farmers started refusing to accept money, and were willing only to barter items for food. They, too, had heard what was happening at the front and understood that the mark would have value only as long as the Germans controlled the Ukraine. Our knapsacks shrank, and we received no more money from our relatives.

One day, a messenger arrived from Tulchin with instructions from the Jewish Agency for Palestine to draw up a list of the orphans in the camp. The Romanian government was permitting orphans to return to Romania. Mr. Stier and Siegfried spoke with this messenger at length, and in the evening, Siegfried called me aside, as he always did when he wanted to speak privately.

He and Mr. Stier had come to an agreement with the messenger, he said, and Gitta and Mr. Stier's daughter Anita would appear on the list of orphans. In exchange, we would give up a gold bracelet. I did not want to hear anything about such a plan, but Siegfried told me that the moment the retreat began, our situation would not be any different than it had been the previous January. It only made sense, he said, to take this opportunity to save our child. Weeping, I came up with every reason I could think of against the plan. When I returned to the main room, however, I saw that Mrs. Stier was already making a list of all the things with which to equip the girls.

Many people came to me and congratulated me for having a chance to save my daughter. No one thought such an opportunity should be thrown away.

It is in the nature of children to see the rosy side, and for the girls, leaving the camp was a new adventure. I can still hear Gitta saying, "Mutti,"—mother in German—"I'll go home and fix up the apartment, and I'll make you a long robe." She had never been able to make peace with the fact that I had not brought my warm robe from home.

The day finally arrived when a Jewish Agency messenger took the children to the train station. The moment Gitta left, I collapsed and cried and cried. I remember looking at the lamp light that night and seeing it surrounded by the colors of a rainbow. That was the beginning of my glaucoma, from which I have suffered ever since.

After Gitta left, I became completely apathetic and thought only of my daughter, and how she would have to depend on the kindness of strangers, an orphan whose parents were still alive.

My family was very worried about me. I had always been the one who pushed the others, but now I had no interest in anything. My husband and my parents were also suffering from the child's absence, but they hid their anguish and tried to act as if she had been sent to summer camp.

After two or three weeks, we received a letter from Mrs. Stier's cousin and two pictures of Gitta and Anita. Our joy knew no bounds. All was well with the children, the letter said, and we should hold on because the separation would not be for long now. All the camp inmates shared in our joy, and I could find some meaning in life again. "Hang on" became my motto.

Winter of 1943-44 was almost over and wild rumors spread about what was happening at the front. We even heard that the Russians were just three kilometers from us, and would reach us within a few days. We were told that the Russian commander had called the barber in Trostinetz to make an appointment for nine o'clock the next morning. We thought that was a joke, but we saw more and more wagons outside that were preparing to leave, signaling that indeed the Russians might soon arrive. Mr. Stier, in his capacity as the camp director, went outside to investigate and was told that whoever wanted to join the evacuation could do so. No one accepted the invitation.

Throughout the night we could hear the thunder of cannons. Planes flew over us, and the village was bombed. Military men—officers, the wounded, the Ukrainian collaborators—all were on the move. We still did not dare to show our joy, however, because we feared that the SS would notice us. No one dared to go outside. We could not rely on the Ukrainian farmers not to attack us, so the only thing left to do was to sit and wait.

A day passed, and the night arrived. Our enemies had evacuated, but we still did not see our liberators. Luckily for us, the Ukrainians were as afraid as we were, and they did not leave their houses either.

Suddenly we saw a line of marching soldiers coming towards us in the dark. They were bent over with their rifles poised in front of them, but they did not have to shoot a single bullet. The enemy had already fled.

Once we were sure that these were indeed Soviet soldiers, we went outside and welcomed them enthusiastically. Some of them came into our room and took stock of the only things we still possessed—bread, butter and cheese. My mother wanted to prepare sandwiches for them, but they refused. They sat in a circle, took out their own bread, and dipped it in the soft cheese.

Finally, we left the farm in order to watch the arrival of the Red Army. For the first time in almost two years, we stood as free people among the locals. Freedom was an idea that took some getting used to, but we had no trouble rejoicing, and we clapped our hands until they hurt.

After some time, five Soviet officers on horseback rode by. They looked at us as if we were a curiosity, and one of them drew near and asked us in Yiddish if we were Jews. "Yes," we answered.

The officer said that he would return shortly with several friends. When they arrived at the farm later that day, one of the officers told us that he was going to write to his father that after covering 5,000 kilometers he had finally met live Jews. The officers told us about the Holocaust: that the Nazis had imprisoned Jews in extermination camps, and had succeeded in murdering most of European Jewry. Until then, we had had no idea of the dimensions of the tragedy that had befallen our people. Before leaving, these officers opened the farm warehouses and gave us potatoes, beans and wheat.

Later, some soldiers caught an SS man who had been hiding in a bathroom, and they said they wanted to shoot him in front of us. We heard him wail, "Let me live, I'm only twenty years old," and beg them just to take him away. We did not want to see what they would do, but we left the decision in the soldiers' hands.

Two things helped us to manage between the time we were liberated and when we arrived home. One, we had rubles, which I had bought while still in Cariera de Piatrá on the advice of a cousin. He told me then that if we were lucky enough to have the Russians free us, we would need rubles, and if not, it would make no difference what we did with our valuables. He was right. We needed rubles from the first day, and they saved us from hunger.

The second thing that helped us was a reparations "down payment" of sorts that we received from the Germans. A short time before the Germans' downfall, a train carrying foodstuffs to the front stopped a short distance from our farm. The Romanian authorities' preoccupation with their preparations to escape provided an opportunity for everyone from the camp, including the Ukrainians, to go to the train and fill their knapsacks with wonderful things such as coffee, meat and fruit preserves. Even my father joined in, despite the fact that at that time it still was not clear what awaited us, and despite our dread of the SS.

On the morning after the Russians arrived, I ran straight to the Hora family to hear what they thought about what had taken place. I found their kitchen full of soldiers who were drinking vodka despite the early hour. The Hora family was heartsick. Our roles had reversed: we camp inmates were now far more tranquil than the Ukrainians, who in the eyes of the Soviets were now traitors. I felt sorry for the Horas, since they were basically decent people who were only trying to survive.

The Russian soldiers planned to continue their journey westward, and asked us how many days it would take to reach Berlin. They taught us an old Russian saying, "The main thing is, we managed to save the bones. The meat will come later." Shortly thereafter, they issued an order that all men aged sixteen to sixty had to enlist in their army. We did not know if that also included our men, but it was decided that if they did not enlist, our liberators would view it as a lack of loyalty.

Miraculously, Siegfried was saved from the draft, perhaps because of his medical condition. Certainly, even weaker men than he were drafted; most of them fell in combat, particularly during the battle for Jassy. For the former prisoners who entered the war arena, it became the last station on a long journey of tribulations, or so we heard from the very few who survived.

It was April of 1944. Outside it rained and occasionally snowed. Siegfried and my father were both very weak, but I had recovered from the nervous breakdown caused by my daughter's departure. My longing for her now energized me—if it had been my choice, I would have made my way home on foot in the hopes of hastening our reunion.

Our last thing of value was a gold coin, a Napoleon, but we were afraid we'd get caught selling it, and the death penalty awaited anyone who did such a thing in the Soviet Union. At this stage, we certainly did not want to jeopardize our lives. We still had a few sheets, which had turned black from continual use. My mother laundered and hung them out to be bleached by the sun, and we sold them to some Ukrainians. With the proceeds, we bought vodka, honey, butter, coffee and other foodstuffs.

Finally the day arrived when we and another group hired a truck to take us to the train station. Rain laced with hail began to fall, weather typical for April, but nothing could dampen our joy. Finally, we could go wherever we wanted. After a long wait, a freight train with open-sided cars arrived, and we climbed on and rode for hours, completely exposed to the rain and wind. At a junction called Shmerlinka, we encountered other Jews who had assembled there from all kinds of camps, all of whom were eager to continue on their way.

At Shmerlinka, the NKVD allowed us to board a freight train that was supposed to be traveling west, but after a while we were taken off the train and sent to a Russian secret police commander for punishment, for what crime we did not know.. We were each ordered to pay a 100-ruble fine, and when we said that we did not have 400 rubles, they threatened to search our bodies. We still had the gold Napoleon and were afraid that if they found it on us, the consequences would be terrible. After much begging on our parts, the commander agreed to compromise on a fine of 200 rubles.

We sat in the station, still 300 kilometers from Mogilev, with no idea of what to do next. We found some free space in a corner at a neglected checkpoint, cleaned it out, and asked permission to stay there for the night. At least it provided some refuge from the cold and damp. My mother went to the market to buy potatoes so that she could cook her famous soup on two bricks.

Siegfried and I hurried back to the train station to ask for information about how to continue our journey, and someone explained what we had to do. As soon as a train appeared, we should approach the station director with a bottle of vodka. In exchange, we would receive a permit to travel on the train with the soldiers.

The next day when the train arrived, we made our deal with the director and called for my parents to hurry, only to find that my mother was at the market. The train left at the very minute she reappeared. I exploded with anger and told my mother that because of her potato soup, I would never get to see my daughter. But when the soup was ready, we were all happy to eat something hot.

Several days passed. We stayed in the little corner we'd found, but the conditions were frightful. We were exposed to the rain and cold, there was no place to wash ourselves, and we ate only dry food because my mother no longer dared to leave the area. We were on the verge of despair when a train finally appeared and we clambered on.

All the cars were unbearably crowded. Every so often the train would stop, and we worried that there would be an inspection and we might be thrown off in the middle of nowhere in the middle of the night. The Russian soldiers on board treated us properly, however, and whenever we noticed that one of them was weary, one of us would stand so he would have a place to lie down and rest. We knew there were difficult times ahead for them: they were being sent to the front.

We had thought that when we got to Mogilev, the worst would be behind us. But when the train pulled in to the city, we found out that a draft was going on from which even a mouse couldn't escape. In addition, there was a severe lack of places to live because so many returning deportees were using Mogilev as a base while they looked for a way to cross the Dniester, which was the border between the Soviet Union and Romania. After hours of wandering, we finally found a place to stay in exchange for some of the coffee we had taken from the train back in camp.

We stayed in Mogilev for eight days. Siegfried's beard grew whiter and whiter. He was only forty-four years old, but he looked seventy. I went to the bridge several times, trying to learn what one had to do to be able to cross it. At five o'clock one morning I watched two young men give the guards bottles of vodka and cigarettes, and then they crossed without a problem. After waiting a while, I approached the guards and asked them if they would be at their posts the next day as well. "Yes, you can come too," they answered.

The next day, after surmounting the obstacle of the bridge, my mother slipped on a rain-slick path and sprained her ankle, which swelled badly. But she plodded on with us for some twenty kilometers until we reached the first village. We were in Bessarabia, and I viewed every farmer as an enemy, since so many had collaborated with the Germans against the Jews. But by that point, they left us alone—perhaps afraid that those of us who had survived might take revenge.

We dragged on for another kilometer or so, always keeping to the edge of the forest, which we were afraid to enter. We passed a few bands of young people who had been drafted and were on their way to a training camp. Finally, when we were ready to collapse from exhaustion, we plucked up the courage to approach a farmhouse. The farmer felt compassion for us and let us take shelter in his granary. There, I put wet compresses on my mother's foot, then we ate what little we had left with us and fell asleep.

The next day the farmer told us that he had a neighbor who drove to the next village every day, and after lengthy persuasion, the man agreed to take my mother and father with him. I was thrilled because I worried that my mother's sprain would delay us.

Only now, when I am not in the best of health myself, can I truly gauge the extent of my parents' self-sacrifice. They had joined us of their own free will and endured every tribulation with us.

Siegfried and I walked the twenty-five kilometers to the next village. We were both frail, and Siegfried was forced to stop and rest every so often. But I was so anxious to get home that it felt as if the ground was burning under my feet.

We arrived in the next town, Edineți, totally exhausted. As in Mogilev, there were crowds everywhere—apparently, the Russians were not allowing anyone to cross the Prut River. It was not easy to find my parents in that anthill. We wandered around for hours, until I finally saw my mother looking out a shop window. We went into the shop, where my father had fallen asleep from exhaustion, and I insisted that my mother also rest. She lay down on the floor— the store had no furniture—and I put a wet compress on her foot. Each of us ate a thin slice of stale bread with a little butter. We were dead tired, but it was too noisy to fall asleep: the whole city was as frenetic as a train station. Nonetheless, we decided to remain in Edineți for at least two days until my mother's foot recuperated.

That afternoon, however, we met people who had come from Czernowitz to look for their relatives, and they told us that the only way one could still enter that city was through the suburb of Horecu. From there one could cross the Prut by boat. We immediately rented a wagon with the last of our money, and set out on the final stage of our journey.

When we finally neared the Prut, it began to rain, which made it easier for us to reach the riverbank without arousing attention. We crossed the river and barely had enough strength left to climb the last hill and finally look down on Czernowitz.

The sun had come out and the city's roofs and gardens sparkled in its rays. Overwhelmed by joy, tears sprang to our eyes. We had survived! We had returned! At that moment it was totally unimportant that we were beggars, that we were physically and emotionally broken. The main thing was that we were all still alive, and that seemed like a miracle. An entire family had survived. We were truly an unusual case. We started down the hill to the city, but when we reached the wall of the Horecu cemetery, my father was overcome by exhaustion, and we had to rest.

CHAPTER 4

Reunited

A s soon as we reached my aunt Peppi Kibak's house on Russian Street, Gitta rushed out to greet me. When she threw her arms around my neck, I felt as if I were in a beautiful dream.

My brother-in-law Karl, with whom we had been in the paving business before the war, had gone to fetch Gitta from the orphanage as soon as the borders with Botoşani had opened. It was great good fortune that he did so, because right after we arrived in Czernowitz, the Iron Curtain descended, and it would have been impossible to reunite the family.

The Kibaks immediately made a room available to us, and we were now twelve people in a four-room apartment. After we had rested somewhat and our strength returned, we had to deal with the problem of finding jobs. Siegfried was able to return to the place he had worked in 1940, this time as a technical manager, but his monthly wage bought us only two weeks' worth of food.

One day, when dining at my brother-in-law Karl's, his wife, who specialized in making handicrafts, showed me how to make cord sandals. I had only a single pair of worn-out shoes, so the next day I immediately began to make myself a pair of sandals. The first time I wore them on the street, a Russian asked me where I had bought them. Full of pride, I told her I had made them myself, and she immediately commissioned a pair. Thus began my new career as a sandal-maker. This was not my only source of income, but it was the main one.

The entire family took part in my work. I prepared the soles and my father sewed the cords to them. Then I added the uppers, which I made from old felt hats or from wide bands that I had knit. Later I learned to make real leather sandals on a mold. My husband bought old rubber tires to cut up, and we pasted rubber on the bottom of the cord to make the sandals stronger.

In addition, we traded whatever we could get our hands on. My brother-in-law sent us slaughtered calves, which I butchered and sold from home until I heard that someone had been sentenced to eight years in prison for a similar enterprise. When I told my brother-in-law that I was not willing to take the risk any more, he said, "In Russia, one must give up sleeping soundly if one wants to eat." I replied that I did not survive Transnistria only to end my life in a Soviet prison.

Our alcohol trading ended on a similar note. On the designated days when one could buy vodka in the supermarket, the entire family would visit the store twice, purchase the alcohol, and head for a nearby tavern where we sold it for a slight profit. This was "capitalism" and was absolutely illegal under the Soviets. We continued doing it, however, until the day my mother slipped on the sidewalk right across the street from the NKVD offices. It was a miracle that none of the four bottles of vodka in her shopping bag broke. I saw that as a sign from Above, and we stopped the activity.

Gradually, our situation improved somewhat. Since he was a civilian employed by the army, my husband had the right to rent an apartment, and we found a two-room place in the same building as the Kibaks. We bought two suits for my husband and father from Russian soldiers who had gotten them in Germany. We also bought linen embroidered with someone else's initials. Through Siegfried's office, we acquired a few pieces of furniture, and finally we bought a sewing machine—a very serious purchase.

Then the Russians began to send women to work in the Dombas mines. We were told that anyone who already had a job would not be sent away, so Siegfried arranged work for me through his office. My job was to guard the furniture warehouses. I sat in the garden in front of the closed warehouses and watched to make sure no one broke the locks and took furniture without permission. Even high-ranking officers were not allowed to help themselves. I did not think I would be able to face down an officer and hoped it would never come to that.

A short time afterwards, I found out that a work card was not always protection against being sent to Dombas. So when the authorities began to conduct raids, looking for women under the age of forty, I hid my hair under a kerchief and dressed like an old lady. I stole my way to work, walking stooped over and using only side streets.

One day I was sitting in the gatekeeper's room at my place of work when a militiaman knocked and entered. He demanded my papers, and my heart pounded while he looked at them. I immediately put a bottle of vodka on the table. He took a drink and we began to talk. When I lamented about my economic situation, the militiaman said, "What are you complaining about? You have a bed, closet and even a night table. In the Soviet Union, a person is considered poor only if he sleeps on a pile of straw in a corner and has to share an apartment with several families."

After the man had taken several more drinks, he advised me not to show myself for a few days until the transport to Dombas had left. I ran a zigzag route home to warn everyone at the Kibaks'.

My young female relatives and I were all in danger, and we decided to hide out between the attic and the roof, where there was a tiny room. We climbed up using a ladder, which was removed afterwards by the family members who had remained below. It was very unpleasant there and cold at night. After the transport left for Dombas some days later, we deserted our hiding place in the attic.

Winter arrived, and our apartment was very cold. The house was old, the sewer frequently froze, and we could not use all the heating stoves. We kept a metal stove going in the kitchen, and the men, who were still frail, slept there. Siegfried suffered terribly from his angina, and the cold made it even worse. He also suffered considerable frustration at work. His manager was not particularly honest, and he demanded that Siegfried adjust the account books to cover for him.

Suddenly we got news that anyone who had lived in southern Bukovina before the war would be allowed to leave Russia. My husband wanted to register us as having come from southern Bukovina. I was reluctant to do this, since all our documents stated that we were from Czernowitz. When I went on a scouting mission to the NKVD building, I noticed many Czernowitz natives who were now claiming to have been residents of southern Bukovina.

I told Siegfried what I had seen, and said I thought it argued against our trying to get away with such a deception. I had never before seen him so angry. An opportunity to leave the Soviet Union was so rare, he said, that it should be taken advantage of immediately. The crack could close at any time and we would remain prisoners of the Soviets for the rest of our lives.

The next day I mustered my courage and made sure I was among the first in line at the NKVD building. We were registered without difficulty. After some time, it was announced that those who had registered to emigrate should assemble on the other side of the city, where the names of those for whom passports had been approved would be read out. We left our jobs and stood there for hours, but our names were not called. Some people whose names had been called had been afraid to appear because of the rumor that this was all just a ruse to ferret out the dangerous subversives who did not want to live in the Soviet Union.

My brother-in-law Karl loved to take risks, and he claimed the passport of a man whose name had been called for several days without a taker. While the lucky group of émigrés was preparing to leave, I was deluged with orders for my special warm slippers. Though they were very nervous when they reached the border, Karl and his wife did manage to leave Czernowitz. Then, suddenly, the border was closed, and run-of-the-mill life returned.

Meanwhile, our small "industry" continued to develop. My work was illegal and involved some risk, but we had no choice. There was no way we could manage on Siegfried's wage alone.

My cousins and sister-in law worked outside their home. Their mother remained alone in the house with the door locked, since the authorities often tried to confiscate their rooms. They were a family of eight living in three rooms, and the Soviets considered that too luxurious.

One day as I looked out the window, I saw a Russian officer approach our building. Soon, I heard him ring their doorbell. My aunt would not open the door, and I stayed in my apartment down the hall—in the Soviet Union, even where relatives were concerned, it was best to appear deaf and dumb. After a while, my cousin Trude came home and let the man in. An animated discussion ensued, and, not able to hold myself back anymore, I joined them.

This was the problem: It was some kind of holiday, and everyone had been ordered to display the flag. My cousins had removed the Swastika from a flag they had left from the Nazi period and painted it red. But the painting was not uniform, and anyone looking at the building from afar could make out a light stain in the shape of a swastika. The NKVD officer was not willing to believe our claims that we were Jews, that the Russians had freed us, that we hated the Nazis and their symbols. They imprisoned my cousin Trude who claimed that she had hung the flag, though her elderly mother had actually done it.

They also imprisoned my cousin Marta, and searched all the other relatives, including us. We tried to find a contact who could help us, but as soon as people learned of the NKVD's involvement, they did not want to hear more.

The next morning Marta was freed. She had been arrested because the NKVD discovered she worked in the Party hospital. She had been arrested as a prelude to extortion. The commander asked her to procure a certain medication for syphilis. When she said that she would try, she was released.

Marta told us that Trude had been interrogated in a cellar the entire night. They had found a prewar photo in her wallet that showed her standing next to a radio receiver. One must remember that listening to the radio was forbidden in the Soviet Union. Later that day, Marta told the hospital director—a Jewish doctor from Czernowitz—the whole story, stressing that they were trying to frame her sister for spying. The doctor immediately gave Marta the medication, and that afternoon Trude was released.

A short time later the authorities phoned Jenny, the third of my aunt's daughters, who was a department supervisor at the Party hospital. They demanded that she report to the NKVD on the Party members who worked there—in other words, that she serve as the NKVD's spy. When the poor girl tried to beg off, they threatened her personally. She sought advice from the hospital director, and he told her that they had demanded the same from him. He advised her to give them petty information and to classify everything she reported as secret and important. In time, he said, they would leave her alone, and in fact, they did.

All of us were happy that at least the winter was coming to a close. By that time, I was sewing every day from six o'clock in the morning until midnight. I unraveled old knitted clothes, including a green woolen dress that had served us for two years in the concentration camps, and knit them up anew. From this period, I mainly remember only the most dramatic events that transpired, one of which was Aunt Antonia's deportation. When the Russians had been forced to swiftly evacuate Czernowitz in June 1941, they took only male prisoners with them. Now, after returning as victors, they suddenly remembered the women and children they'd left behind.

One day they arrested these women and children and put them in freight cars for transport to Siberia. My aunt Antonia (she of the Austrian passport) and her son were among them, as they were still considered suspect due to their foreign citizenship. We managed to buy a sack of food and took it to the train station to equip them for the trip, and we were allowed to stay with them until they left. My aunt's son, Albert, was then twelve years old, and we suggested perhaps trying to have him taken off the train. But Albert said he would stay with his mother to help her. I can still see that scene: my petite aunt, her eyes red from crying, and the courageous little boy standing next to her.

They were sent to the same camp in Siberia where my uncle was imprisoned. All three of them managed to survive, and in 1949 they left for Vienna and then emigrated to Canada.

In January of 1946, the registration to emigrate to Romania was reopened. The iron curtain borders reached up to the Berlin wall. Leaving Romania for the West was totally forbidden, except for people like the Klingers, who had Austrian citizenship. Of course, we registered again. One Friday afternoon I was in the middle of an urgent job preparing slippers for someone who had to leave Czernowitz on Sunday morning. My aunt Kibak called for me loudly from the stairwell and when I went down I saw my Siegfried lying on the floor. He had suffered a heart attack, and had died instantly.

I lack the words to describe my anguish and pain. Never before had I felt so overwhelmed with despair. I had lost my life partner at such a young age and I was gripped by fear of the future. The burden of caring for my elderly parents and my nine-year-old daughter was now entirely on my shoulders. I had to make all the decisions and could not break down because I had to be the strong one. Gitta, sick with the measles, had witnessed her father's death from her bed. For a long time she did not speak about what had happened.

Soon, most of my clients emigrated, and I prepared slippers without having prior orders. I tried to sell them to women in hairdressers' shops.

After a short while, however, we received our passports, including one for Siegfried. Various men offered me substantial sums of money to take them out on Siegfried's passport, but I refused to hear of it. The ground was still frozen, and I wanted to wait to leave until it had thawed so I could put up a tombstone on my beloved husband's grave. I continued to provide for us by preparing slippers.

When the Kibaks received their passports in April, we decided we would all emigrate together. They, too, were women living alone with their elderly parents and a little girl, and we clung together.

That year the winter never seemed to want to end, and it was still impossible to set up a tombstone on Siegfried's grave. But rumors began to circulate that the border would soon be shut, and we decided that we could not wait any longer.

Through Siegfried's workplace, I managed to engage a freight truck that would take us to the border. We were soon on our way. We had changed everything we could into dollars, and my father hid our valuables in a false bottom he made for the wooden crate we used as a suitcase. This helped ease the tension we felt when we arrived at the border and the soldiers searched our bodies, but then they began checking the crate. My father just stood beside it looking disinterested, and busied himself playing with a knot. Apparently, our belongings were so skimpy that the Russian soldiers did not bother doing a more thorough search.

Shortly after we crossed the border into Romania, the Iron Curtain fell again for many long years.

CHAPTER 5

New Home

Despite having left the place where we were born, the place where our families had lived for generations, we felt immense relief. We reached a village called Sered where the Joint Distribution Committee had prepared a transit camp for Jews from Czernowitz. Though so many had not survived the war, there were a lot of us there. Recognizing that I had common destiny with these people somehow relieved some of my anguish. How could I complain when everyone here had suffered similarly? In any event, I had no time for sorrowful thoughts—though sometimes I let them steal their way in at night.

We had to leave the transit camp in Sered as soon as possible: there was a danger that an epidemic would break out because of the terrible crowding. In addition, there was no way to make a living. Before we could leave the transit camp, we had to procure authorization from the Romanian government, which the Jewish Agency and the Joint took care of.

After a week in the camp, we received authorization to move to Mediaş in Transylvania, where we went with the Kibaks and other friends from Czernowitz. Mediaş was a small town, and the options for making a living were limited, but we had no choice but to go there. In any case, from the beginning of our travels, we viewed Romania only as a temporary stop: we hoped to reach the Land of Israel as quickly as possible. We hated Romania, for we had seen the violence and disregard of human dignity of which the Romanians had been capable.

The trip to Mediaş took a week, since the train made many long stops on the way. Transylvania was beautiful, but who could enjoy the view when the future was so unclear? We were still penniless and malnourished, and now we were in a strange land. We reached Mediaş close to Passover, and settled into the community together with the Kibaks. We were given a room that had served as the vestibule and dressing room for the community's *mikveh*, the Jewish ritual bathhouse. An adjoining room had a spring—the old *mikveh*—and mice. The walls seeped with damp and I soon developed arthritis. We spent four years in that room before we immigrated to Israel.

The local Jews had survived the war in better circumstances than we had. They hadn't been sent to camps, they hadn't lost their possessions, and their economic situation was generally good. For festival meals, each of us was invited to join another family. Their intentions were proper, but we felt humiliated. We didn't spend the holiday together as a family, and for the first time in our lives we ate the bread of charity.

But in the end, we benefited from the invitations and met people who helped my cousins and me find work as seamstresses. It is unimaginable how much one can curtail one's needs. We had two sewing machines, which we placed on wooden boards. During the day we moved the boards aside as we had in Transnistria. Here we worked and received clients. In a corner was a gas burner, where my mother and her sister Peppi cooked the meals. My father prepared cord soles, and my uncle did the shopping. Gerda and Gitta went to school.

My parents, both of them ill, did whatever they could to help. My father, now sixty-six years of age, suffered from glaucoma and terrible attacks from gallstones. He was a talented accountant, however, and was able to get a job in a glass factory. This made things much easier for us, because the income from my work alone could not keep up with inflation. Meanwhile, my mother ran the home.

After some time, the Kibak family was able to rent a room with a kitchen, while we continued to live in the community building. I found a job selling tickets that were redeemable for slaughtered chickens, which provided a cover for my illegal sewing and sandal making. It also made me eligible for bread rations. The Romanians had forbidden any business ventures, and anyone who was caught was severely punished. Nevertheless, businessmen from Mediaş and the surrounding areas put their merchandise up for sale in the *mikveh* room that adjoined our residence.

One businessman left behind a suitcase with leather soles in it when he was caught for some crime and thrown into prison. (His punishment was to walk around the city with a sign around his neck proclaiming that he was an "exploiter of the people." The Romanians were looking for a scapegoat for their financial failures, and the Russians were expert advisors.) I was very concerned that the man would reveal to the authorities where he had left his merchandise, and that might get me into trouble. I hid the suitcase in a shed and called the man's brother-in-law, demanding that he free me from responsibility for it. After escaping from this episode intact, I swore to stop my business ventures.

Still hoping that we might regain our lost treasures, which would help to ease our daily struggle for existence, I tried to find out what had happened to the Kazacus. However, they had completely disappeared. In the end, not having the means and time to carry it on, I gave up my search.

After I stopped my business, the threat of finding no work hung over my head. Then someone sent the Russian wife of the director of the town's silk factory to me to do alterations on a dress. At first, I was suspicious of her, but I quickly discovered that she was a lovely, intelligent person. Her name was Mrs. Zanigna and she became not only my client, but also a friend. In addition to the altering that I did for her, she consulted with me on various matters and showed her appreciation by giving me foods that could not be bought, since they were considered luxuries.

I sewed for her and her daughter, who lived in Leningrad and was married to a Jewish engineer. Even though I could not do fittings for her daughter, the clothes I made for her fit her exactly, and she asked her mother to thank the seamstress with the "golden hands." When Mrs. Zanigna moved to another city in Transylvania, she would send her driver for me. Thanks to her, I was able to save a little towards our Aliya, our immigration to Israel.

When Israel's Independence Day was declared on May 14, 1948, our whole community cried and laughed together. When the War of Independence began, all of our thoughts were focused upon our homeland.

Emissaries reached us from Israel, and Gitta studied Hebrew with them. She was diligent, and was not satisfied with learning Hebrew simply as a second language in the Jewish school.

Shortly after we had reached Mediaş, a Jewish organization was founded to represent the interests of the refugees. The Romanian government wanted to (slightly) redress the injustices done to us, and they authorized a pension for several war widows. The pension was small, but I received back payments, and this money, too, helped to pay for our trip to Israel.

My cousins in the meantime had procured jobs. They worked in a textile factory, and with that income were barely able to keep themselves alive. We were women in our thirties, and the years were just passing. There was no possibility to marry in Mediaş.

Jenny, my middle cousin, left Mediaş for a city called Timişoara. She found a job there, and after a while met a man who had lost his wife in Auschwitz. They married, illegally left Romania and arrived in Austria. From there they immigrated to the U.S., which greatly helped the Kibaks. Jenny regularly sent them packages, and in 1962, she paid $6,000 to the Romanian government to bring the family to the U.S. They are living there in a good financial state. The reader will perhaps ask himself why I have been writing so much about this family. The simple answer is that not only were they my relatives, but my best friends, in both suffering and our common destiny.

Three and a half difficult years passed and all that time my thoughts were on Aliya. Now and then we heard it mentioned that in a village called Sighişoara, about an hour away by train, emigration forms were being given out. One day I gathered my courage and traveled there together with a small group from Mediaş. We went straight into the lion's den—the Ministry of Security. We were received by one of the clerks, while an officer sat opposite him. He confirmed that the forms in question did, indeed, have to be filled out in order to emigrate. When he gave me the forms, I shook his hand, and left 500 Leis behind in his palm.

A short time later, my parents received their exit permits, which were valid for one month only. I didn't know what to do. How could I send two elderly people by themselves? But everyone advised me not to let this opportunity slip away. Not wanting my parents to arrive in Israel penniless, I deposited a sum of money with friends in Bucharest to transfer to Israel for them.

My mother was in relatively good health, but my father was very frail. I accompanied them to Bucharest to help them with the many arrangements, including visiting the Israeli consulate. Jewish Agency officials at the consulate made it clear that they preferred young immigrants, and it took a great deal of effort on my part to secure entry visas to Israel for my parents. Finally, my parents and I traveled together to the port of Constanţa, where we said good-bye. I returned to Mediaş alone, holding back my tears.

My neighbors claimed that the separation had already aged me many years. A few days later, a friend from Sighişoara brought the news that Gitta and I had also been issued exit visas. The news spread through Mediaş like fire, and everyone streamed into the community courtyard to congratulate me. It was one of the few moments of happiness I had experienced in recent years, a moment that will remain engraved in my memory forever.

Everyone was permitted to take one suitcase weighing forty-five kilograms. My parents had taken part of our meager belongings, and it was clear to me that Gitta and I together had less than ninety kilograms, so I also took a crate of linen and crystal for my friend Ida, who was then living in Bucharest.

At that time, you could still sell the most insignificant things, and Gitta, who was then fourteen, stood in the market and sold everything we didn't want to take with us, even my father's worn-out razors.

My parents wrote from Israel saying, "Here it is just wasteland, wasteland, wasteland," and I got the impression that the State was nothing but one vast desert.

Despite my mixed feelings, I energetically set about arranging our Aliya and tried to interest the Kibaks in getting exit permits. "Why are you exerting yourself so much?" one of my Kibak cousins responded. "The day is not far off when the Romanians will want to get rid of us all. They will provide us with trains and trucks. Everyone's turn will come."

Another ten years passed before that cousin could make Aliya.

All of our friends and acquaintances accompanied us to the train. That was the custom. When someone left, almost the entire Jewish community came along to say farewell. I was thrilled to be leaving Romania, where I had spent such a difficult period of my life. We left Bucharest on Yom Kippur eve, September 18, 1950 and in Constanţa boarded the ship "Transylvania," which held 1,800 immigrants. Rain began to fall. We received four blankets, and I managed to trade two of them for a mattress. Making ourselves comfortable on the deck, we began our three-day journey.

We reached Haifa at night. We stood on the deck and Gitta suddenly felt sick, either because of the excitement or the food she had been served. Since I had to take care of her, I missed the first reunions of families who had come to greet their relatives. The formalities took a long time, then, with pounding hearts, we stepped onto the shore. I expressed my desire that that step should bring us good luck.

My prayers were answered.

These memories begin on a September the 18th, and they conclude on the same date eleven years to the day later—eleven years of suffering, fear and humiliation.

I hope I will be permitted to describe the good years that followed.

POSTSCRIPT

My mother, Lotti Kahana-Aufleger, wrote this memoir in her native German about twenty-five years after the events she describes had taken place.[5] The purpose of her putting these words down was twofold: To tell future generations what had truly happened; and to serve as a kind of therapy— to release the deep layers of distress that still remained.

The first goal was achieved to some degree. In addition to this account, she gave her testimony to Yad Vashem, and her story is filed in its archives. She wanted to ensure that a detailed record would be left by a person who had experienced that fearful period.

The second goal—the catharsis—was, to my mind, not achieved. Until her last day, my mother had nightmares of those years. In contrast with other people—those who decided to keep silent because they could not speak about the "other planet," as K. Zetnik called it—not a day went by when my mother did not speak about the Holocaust to every ear willing to listen. My grandmother, Adela Gottesman, of blessed memory, who is mentioned often in my mother's memoirs, was the same. My husband, Yaakov, has become an "expert" on Czernowitz, the ghetto, and Transnistria, despite never having been there.

I, Tova—or as I appear in the memoirs, Gitta—could not bear to hear anything about that period. The experience had the opposite effect on me—I

---

5   Tova Bar-Touv translated her mother's memoir from German to Hebrew.

was revolted by it. This is also the reason why, for a long time, I could not translate the memoirs from German, despite having promised my children Yair and Chedva, and my mother, to do so one day.

As soon as the *shiva* mourning period for my mother ended, I began to translate her memoirs. I felt that it was my duty towards her, and towards the individuals whose names her writings recorded for posterity.

Tova (Gitta) Bar-Touv (Aufleger)

SURVIVING A THOUSAND DEATHS
MEMOIR: 1939-1945

by *Margit Raab Kalina*

TABLE OF CONTENTS

INTRODUCTION

August 31, 1939.

Yesterday we finished packing our personal things—dresses, coats, linens, shoes, my wedding outfit, pictures, silver, most of our movable possessions. Today we are leaving via Kraków to Rzeszów, to my father's sister Ethel. It is mobilization, the third since last year. We are on the train, my mother, my brother Poldi, and I. My father stays behind; he will join us later. The train is moving. For a fleeting moment I have a feeling that I will never return to Karvina, in Czech Silesia.

I am excited, what an adventure! I am sixteen years old. On the train, there are students from Belgrade, whom I met during vacation at the swimming pool. The train is packed. Around my neck I wear a string on which I carry a bundle filled with money—50,000 zlotys. I have a smart little suitcase with the most necessary clothes, and, following the government command, I also carry a gas mask. All the other luggage was sent ahead yesterday.

In Kraków we wait for a long time. A woman cries that all her money was stolen. In Rzeszów, in front of the railroad station, there are coaches with horses waiting instead of taxicabs. In Czechoslovakia this kind of transportation did not exist anymore. We hire a coach and drive through the city to its rural outskirts, to a small village with farmhouses and wide fields. Our relatives live here. They own a farm and also have a grocery store. Their comfortable apartment is just next to their store. I meet them for the first time.

There are five children—four beautiful girls and a son, Ignatz. My aunt is a good-looking, large, energetic woman. My uncle has a short beard. The youngest daughter, Rozia, is the same age as I. I like all of them.

Next day, September 1, the war started. I cannot believe it—people are going to kill each other, in the twentieth century! Squadrons of German airplanes are flying over Rzeszów and bombing the city. Rozia and I are in the store. My aunt gets hysterical. She cries: "Twenty, forty, eighty airplanes are bombing." She looks so funny. Rozia and I start to laugh. She gives each of us a slap on the face.

Mother and I go to the train station to pick up our luggage, but it never arrived. The train was bombed, and all our belongings were lost. In the city there is again an alarm. Soon the Germans will drop bombs. People with their valuables are rushing to their bunkers; chaos, shouting, crying. The German army is advancing fast to the East. Young Jewish men are in danger. They have to leave. Father has not arrived yet. We have to wait for him. Poldi and Ignatz have to leave right away, maybe to Lwów.

Next day Father arrives. In Karvina he loaded part of our business stock on three trucks and drove in the direction of Rzeszów. The roads were already full with refugees and were being bombed and shelled. In order not to fall into the hands of the fast-advancing German army, Father had to abandon the trucks near Katowice. He continued his trip to Rzeszów by whatever means he could, hitchhiking or by foot.

Too bad that Poldi has already left, just yesterday. My parents buy a cart, a horse, and hire a coachman. Our journey to the East begins. The Germans are moving fast behind us. The roads are jammed with carts, people on foot, cattle. We cannot move fast enough. Bombs are falling, behind us the Germans are shooting with machine guns. Dead people and dead horses line the roads. We are tired. The driver and the horse need to rest. We stop at a small farm where we rent a barn for the night. We sleep on straw. At last I can sleep and forget about everything. At 3 o'clock in the morning, Father wakes us: "Up, up, fast, the Germans are close!" My face and body are covered with black spots from the straw. We rush to the cart, all panicky. The horse is scared and runs as fast as he can.

We pass Galician cities—all look alike to me: a square market place with stores, the city hall, and a church. Between the cities are bad roads, now jammed. Bombs are falling. We have to leave the cart and lie down in a ditch. The airplanes fly low and shoot at us. At one point we hide under a roof of a farm house. A plane is after us. I can see a German with a gun aiming at us. We run around the house. He has fun shooting at us, but he misses.

Again we are on the road and again hiding in a ditch. We hold each other, our heads bent, waiting for the bomb to explode. Father gets up, looks around. Papa, please, please, come back; if we should die, then let us all die together. During the nights the shooting continues with machine guns and flame throwers. People are hysterical—they shout, cry, panic. The human caravan moves slowly. We pass Stryj, Borysław, Drohobycz. Drohobycz is rich in oil. There are large oil reservoirs here. We are clogged together on a bridge. The oil tanks are burning. Right and left there is fire. Some tanks are not yet burning. Soon they will explode. We are stranded—we cannot move to the front, and behind us carts block the way. We feel the heat from the fire. My mother stands up in the cart, raises her hands, and shouts: "Grosser Gott, wir brennen!" ("God Almighty, we are burning!")

Around September 17, the bombing and shooting stop. Poland is defeated and divided between Germany and the Soviet Union. The dividing line in the south of Poland is the River San, near Przemyśl. Luckily we are on the Russian side of the river. Now we drive at a leisurely pace and stop in a town in eastern Poland, Kałusz. I take out a mirror and look at myself. I am surprised: how come my hair hasn't turned gray? I still have blond hair. Mother has a weak heart; she suffers from angina pectoris. Before the war she sometimes had dizzy spells, yet she has not had one spell during our journey. She says that people are stronger than iron, they can take the unbearable.

CHAPTER 1

Living with the Soviets

W e stay with a professor's family for a few days; they help us to find a room across from their house. Kałusz is a typical Polish-Ukrainian-Jewish town, with a square market place and one main street. I enroll in the local high school, but I don't like it there. I am restless, sad, have nothing to wear. The room we live in belongs to a woman with a small child. We heat the room with an iron stove, where Mother also cooks. Father buys a cartload of wood, and I help to unload it. Father chops the wood. It is getting very cold, and all our pipes freeze. Father has to cut the ice out of the toilet drain. We have difficulties making a fire in the stove: We take turns blowing into the stove, and the room gets full of smoke. At night we dress in stockings, socks, and sweaters. In the morning the milk is frozen.

The train starts rolling again. Mother and I go to Lwów to look for Poldi. We stay with friends whom we met last summer in Krynica, a resort in the Tatra Mountains. Our friends have a textile business, as we had in Karvina. Mother buys clothing for all of us, mainly for me; a girl needs pretty dresses. We walk on the street, and there, on the opposite side, I discover my brother. Poldi has lost weight but he is still handsome. He wears the same trenchcoat in which he left. The coat has a hole in its side—from a bullet. Only the coat got it. Thank you, dear God! Poldi is eighteen years old, energetic and smart, and knows what he wants. He wants to be a doctor. Yet it is difficult to get into medical school. He stands in line a whole day and night to enroll for the entrance examination. He is accepted with a scholarship and pays for his room and board. He sleeps in a student's dormitory.

We all move to Lwów—a beautiful, lively city with many parks and gardens. I attend a Yiddish high school and learn to speak Yiddish. I like the school, but since I have lost one year, I am in a lower class than I should be. That doesn't suit me, so I change to another school, this time a Ukrainian high school. I am accepted into the last class for a trial period of three months. I pass the trial easily. In my class there are only boys. It is a strange feeling to be the only girl, but I will get used to it.

We live on Zielona Street, a nice quiet street, and share our apartment with a family from Bielsko. One day we have visitors. My mother's brother Zisiu, from Ostrava, and my eighteen-year-old cousin, Poldi Weitzner (the son of my mother's sister) from Bohumin arrive. My father's brother Max and his son Heinrich from Karvina also have come to Lwów. The Germans sent them to the Polish-Russian border near Nisko. They had to cross the border under gunfire. On the other side, Russian soldiers shot at them, barring them from entering Soviet territory.

Poldi Weitzner has started to study at a *Polytechnikum*. He is a good piano player and plays evenings in restaurants or bars to earn some money. Father has arranged himself a position as an accountant. The Polish złoty is devalued, and we lose the rest of our money. Mother has had to sell some of her jewels. She is sad, complains about the loss of everything we possessed—our home, livelihood, business, our whole way of life. We assure her that it doesn't matter, that material things are not important, that the main thing is that we are all together.

Poldi has a girlfriend, who is also a medical student. His studies are going very well. He is now a member of Komsomol, a Communist youth organization. I go to school, have friends, see movies, go to the theater and opera. I also date. Every Sunday there are concerts in the lovely Stryjsky Park.

In the autumn of 1940, a public announcement is made: all refugees from German-occupied Poland who wish to join their families left behind should register, and they will be allowed to return home. Zisiu and Max register, for Zisiu's wife and daughter Lily stayed in Ostrava, and Max's wife and two of his children, Marta and Herta, remained in Karvina. Yet they never do reach their families. Instead, they are sent to Siberia. (Zisiu and Max died somewhere in the USSR.) Since the prescribed quota of people destined for Siberia has not yet been filled, the Soviets also start to take refugees from the street and, later, from their homes. Thus, we don't dare go out.

Mostly during the night, NKVD men in white uniforms, looking like ghosts, search the houses for refugees. It is night, we are all dressed, waiting. Poldi is with us. Two NKVD ghosts enter and want to take us. Poldi shows them his Komsomol identification card. They start to talk. It turns out that both men are Jewish. They give us a *Bumazhka*, a permit to remain in Lwów.

Father has lost his job as an accountant and now works in a restaurant. Sometimes he brings home salami from the restaurant. It has a sweetish taste. Isn't it from horsemeat? Never mind, it tastes good anyway. Poldi becomes a convinced Communist. He argues with Father—nothing the Russians do can be wrong, he has answers and excuses for everything. Father asks why then, as a good Communist, doesn't he work as a laborer and dig ditches instead of studying medicine?

There are new regulations. All refugees, being "unreliable elements," have to leave Lwów. We are reluctant to leave. Mother and I go to the NKVD headquarters to talk with the commandant of the NKVD. We wait in line for hours and hours. At last it is our turn. Mother pleads with the commandant to let us stay in Lwów. She shows him the *Bumazhka*. "Nichevo, grazhdianka," you all have to leave; "davai," next.

We move to Zimna Woda, a suburb of Lwów, some forty minutes by train. Poldi comes with us. My parents buy a kiosk in Lwów where they sell ice cream. The business is going very well. What they don't sell they bring home. We eat a lot of ice cream.

We receive letters from Siberia, from Zisiu and Max. They are hungry most of the time and cold. They work in a forest cutting trees. Many of the refugees are sick and suffer from *skorbut* (scurvy). Mother sends them warm clothes and food packages.

Life appears to be quite normal again. All of us travel to Lwów every day. From time to time Poldi and I quarrel, sometimes even fight. For example, I am playing the guitar. He is preparing for a difficult exam. He wants me to stop playing, and I refuse. So we fight. Saturday evening I have a date in Lwów.

Mother doesn't want me to travel at night alone. Poldi accompanies me to Lwów, where we part. He is going out with his girlfriend. We meet again at the station and take the late train home. Father is still up, expecting us. I like candies. One night I am half asleep when my parents return from work. Father comes to my bed and puts a wonderful-tasting chocolate candy into my mouth.

In May 1941, Poldi and I finish our final exams. It was my last year in high school; Poldi finished the fourth semester of medical school. He is an honor student. The political situation is worsening. Will Germany attack the Soviet Union? Father is restless. Father: "Besser eine Kugel im Kopf als unter die Deutsche zu fallen" ("Better to get a bullet in the head than to fall into German hands"). Mother: "Sprich doch keinen Unsinn, zum Sterben hat man immer noch Zeit genug" ("Don't say such nonsense, there is plenty of time to die"). Poldi assures us that we don't have to worry. Voroshilov said that the Soviet army is going to defeat Germany on the enemy's territory. My parents maintain that the Red Army is a giant on wooden legs.

Sunday, June 22, 1941. It is 4 o'clock in the morning. Father has to go to work at the kiosk. Mother is tired and has not been feeling well lately. She is still in bed. I get up to prepare breakfast for Father—scrambled eggs. I am sleepy and grouchy. I don't like to get up so early. Father leaves, and I go back to sleep. It was the last time I saw my father.

We hear airplanes. It is probably a training exercise. We listen to the radio. Germany has attacked the Soviet Union. War again. I help Mother prepare lunch. I am draining noodles when we hear bombs exploding in Lwów. I am afraid for Father. I have a terrible feeling that I will never see him again. In the evening Father does not come home. Poldi catches a train to look for him and for Poldi Weitzner, our cousin.

Monday morning somebody calls my name. I look from the window and see Poldi and Poldi W., but Father is not with them. "Where is Father? Poldi doesn't know. The kiosk was bombed. He is afraid to tell Mother. But she has to know. Next day Mother and I will go to Lwów. The trains are not running anymore. The railroads are destroyed. We walk. In Lwów we go from hospital to hospital, from cemetery to cemetery, looking over lists of people who died or were killed during the last couple of days, looking for his name, hoping not to find it. We are devastated.

For me it seems the end of the world. Even if Germany is defeated, to return home to Karvina without Father? I wish the whole world would collapse. How did he die? Did he suffer? I imagine him sitting in the kiosk, his head bent, waiting for the bomb to explode. I remember the terrible feelings I had Sunday at one o'clock that afternoon, the feeling I will never see him again. His last thoughts must surely have been with me. Was it telepathy? I don't dare cry in front of my mother. Poldi and I try to console her: Maybe the Russians took him with them—after all we never found his body. I look at Father's photographs and cry. Poldi takes the pictures from my hands. Why do you torture yourself? Are you a masochist? Father was forty-eight years old.

The Germans are advancing fast. We can already hear the machine guns. Poldi wants to leave for Kiev. Mother doesn't want him to go, she is afraid something could happen to him, the Russians might send him to Siberia. I don't want him to go. You cannot leave Mother now that Father is gone. He stays.

The Germans are already here. We cannot stay in our apartment, so we move to a small farmhouse. Poldi W. is staying with us. Food is scarce. Poldi W. and I go to the fields and steal corn. Many people from Lwów came to Zimna Woda. We have new friends. Mother is depressed and worried. I didn't want that kind of life for you, children.

The young men are called to the *Arbeitskommando* to work on the roads. Girls are supposed to clean military barracks from time to time. Winter is nearing; it is bitter cold. The boys dig ditches in the frozen ground. Poldi W. gets frostbite, and the skin on his face opens; he returns home soaked and covered with blood. It is difficult to procure food, as the food stores are almost empty. Mother and I venture deep into the country to exchange our valuables with the peasants for potatoes and flour. We carry the heavy sacks home. The boys have good appetites.

In Lwów it is much worse than in Zimna Woda. The Ukrainians have a field day with the Jewish population. They are free to rob, beat, or kill them as they please, without punishment. Many Jews are being arrested and put into prison. The biggest prison in Lwów is set on fire by the Russians before their retreat and burned to the ground with all the inmates inside.

CHAPTER 2

Return to Poland

M other is scared. She doesn't want to remain in Zimna Woda. Poldi W. is worried about his parents. The whole Jewish population from Lower Silesia is being relocated. After World War I, Lower Silesia, also called Zaolzie (a Polish word meaning "behind the River Olza") belonged to Czechoslovakia and, in 1938, was occupied by Poland. Now the Germans annexed it to the *Deutsches Reich*, and the Jews were deported to the General Government of Poland (the districts of Warsaw, Kraków, Radom, and Lublin). Lower Silesia has to become *Judenrein*.

Poldi Weitzner's parents, Pepi and Joseph Weitzner, who owned a big textile business in Bohumin, were transported to Będzin, a city situated between Katowice and Kraków. Not far from Będzin is another small Polish town, Oświęcim, later to be known as Auschwitz. My mother's and Pepi's youngest brother, Iziu, the manager of the Weitzners' business, is arrested and imprisoned in Kraków. After being badly beaten, he is let free and deported to Tarnów. Poldi W. wants to join his parents in Będzin. My mother intends to move to Tarnów where her brother Iziu now lives with his fiancée, Nelly, and her mother, also from Bohumin.

On August 1, 1941, eastern Galicia is incorporated into the General Government of Poland. Mother arranges our transportation to western Galicia—to Tarnów for us, and to Będzin for Poldi W. It is illegal for Jews to move from one city to another, but it can be done with large sums of money as bribes.

One night in January 1942, we leave our apartment. We take with us only the most necessary things; all the rest of our belongings remain with our friends. The country is covered with snow. We travel by a horse-sledge through back roads and forests, like thieves. The roads are bumpy, and the horse falls down. The sledge turns upside down, and we find ourselves buried in deep snow. Luckily, nobody is hurt; only our clothes are wet. On the main road, we wait for an army truck, which will take us to Tarnów. The truck arrives packed with people like us, who are also looking to flee the Ukrainians. During our journey we stand at the open end of the truck. The top of the truck is covered, so nobody can see us. We have to hold on tight to some handles in order not to fall out. It is freezing, and I start to lose all feeling in my hands. In the morning, when we arrive in Tarnów, our clothes are frozen to ice.

Uncle Iziu lives, like the majority of the relocated Jews, in a restricted area at the outskirts of Tarnów. They dwell in little shacks, scattered between peasant houses with their small farms. He shares his hut with Nelly and her mother.

Our new home is located close by. In the meantime, Poldi W. joins his parents in Będzin, but his stay with his family does not last long. He is promptly taken from his home and sent to an *Arbeitslager*—Gross Rosen. There he later died of malnutrition.

Iziu is forty-one years old, four years younger than my mother. He has a slight limp, supposedly from a childhood illness. He is very smart, like all members of the Hornik family. People visit him often and ask for advice. My brother starts to work as a saddler and later works for a building firm, Montana, as a laborer. Mother provides food, cooks, cleans, scrubs the rough wooden floor, washes our laundry by hand. I help her with the chores and also earn some money by knitting sweaters. We have to wear white armbands with a blue Star of David. The armbands have to be snow white, starched and neat. After 7 o'clock is curfew—no Jew must be seen outside. We have new friends, some from Bohumin, some from Katowice, others from Bielsko; there is also a family here from Karvina, a young couple with a small redheaded boy.

New SS-men have arrived in Tarnów. The most dreaded is SS *Obersturmbahnnführer* Grunow. He strolls the streets, stops Jewish boys, beats them up, or kills them. He walks into Jewish homes and shoots everybody present. He shot to death our friends from Karvina, the young couple with the red-headed boy.

May 20, early at night. I am in bed and have a terrible feeling that something bad is going to happen. "Mutti, ich hab so eine Angst, kann ich zu Dir ins Bet kommen?" ("Mommy, I am scared, can I come to your bed?") I hold my mother tight the whole night.

May 21, 1942. Mother leaves in the morning to buy some food. Poldi goes to his job. I sit at home near the window and darn socks. I see two SS-men getting out of a car, approaching our house. They enter. One of them is Grunow. He is looking for my mother. He pulls out a letter and orders me to read it. It is a letter my mother wrote from Zimna Woda to her Czech friends in Moravia. She tells them about the death of her husband, about not having any means to live, about her worries about what will happen to her children. After I finish reading the letter, Grunow hits me in the face. Both men start to search our room. They take out from the closet flour, sugar, leather for shoes, and a diamond ring. Grunow turns to me, points to the items, and starts to hit me in the face again. He slaps my right cheek, my left cheek, again and again. The other man tells him: "Aber lass doch." They start to pack our things into two big suitcases which Iziu has given us. They order me to carry the suitcases to their car. They are too heavy for me. The other man helps to carry them. Before they enter the car, they tell me that my mother has to report to the Gestapo. I plead with them not to harm my mother. The other SS-man assures me that nothing bad will happen to her. Two *Ordnungsdienst* (Jewish policemen) enter and wait for Mother. When Mother learns what has happened, she exclaims: "Was wird mit Margit passieren?!" ("What will happen to Margit?") Then she faints.

We take a bus to the Gestapo; the two policemen accompany us. Mother unbuttons her sweater and wants to leave it with me. Are you out of your mind, Mother? She enters the building, but I am not allowed to go in with her. I wait outside. I wait and wait. It is getting dark. In the corner of the street is a little stand with snacks. I go there and buy some candy. I return to the Gestapo building and wait. A Polish policeman approaches and tells me to go home; it is prohibited for Jews to be out so late in the evening. Mother doesn't return home.

The next day at the Jewish police headquarters we are told that Mother has been shot to death.

How did she die? Did she see the gun pointing at her, or was she told to run and then was shot in the back? Why did I have to go buy candy? Maybe just then my mother was led out somewhere and looked for me. These thoughts torment me for a long time to come. We never find out where she was buried. Mother was forty-six years old.

Before Grunow and his companion came to our home, they stopped at Iziu's. Nelly's mother was home alone. Grunow killed her on the spot.

Poldi and I move in with Uncle Iziu and Nelly. A small textile plant has been established in Tarnów. The owner of the plant was Julius Madritsch, an Austrian from Vienna. He was wounded on the front, leaving him with a limp. I start to work there. In the beginning we knit gloves and socks for the German army; later we sew shirts. We get no pay but receive bread and margarine. We were also provided with an *Arbeitsausweis* (working certificate), which later proves to be important enough to save one's life.

CHAPTER 3

The Madritsch Factory

On my way home I see Polish children playing on the street. I always try to avoid them, for they insult Jews or throw stones at them. Once, when returning home, a big dog comes running after me and bites me on the leg. Did a peasant let out the dog and send it after me? I wonder. I need medical attention. A young doctor from the neighborhood takes care of the wound. His name is Carlo Silbermann, and he has come to Tarnów with his parents. In Bohumin they owned a textile business, and my parents and the Weitzners knew them well. Carlo is twenty-eight years old and very handsome. He became my good friend. Poldi says that he is too old for me. I was then nineteen.

Outside Tarnów is a small forest [Zbilatowska Góra]. The Germans load Jews, mostly old and sick, on a truck, drive them to the forest, where they shoot and kill them.

On Sunday I am walking on a street. Two trucks packed with Polish students drive in the direction of the forest. A Polish woman stops us and says that because of the Jews Poles are being killed.

It is difficult to secure food. We eat mostly potatoes or food made from flour and *Mamalyga* (cornmeal). Meat is impossible to get. People sometimes eat pigeons, despite the fact that killing pigeons is strictly prohibited.

I "organize" two pigeons. Tomorrow we will have a good meal, roasted pigeons.

On the evening of June 10, 1942, we are notified that the next morning there will be a transport. People will be sent to Germany to work. Everybody can take one suitcase. We have to be ready by 6 A.M. The next day, the first to arrive are the *Ordnungsdienst*, who send us to wait outside. Soon the SS-men come with dogs, whips, and shouting insults. "Antreten, los, schnell, schneller, ihr verfluchten Saujuden!" ("Come on, let's go, fast, faster, you damn Jews!"). We fall into line by fives. They check our *Kennkarte* and *Arbeitsausweise* (identification cards and working certificates). Boys who work with the Montana firm can step out. Poldi doesn't have to go on the transport. We see two trucks coming. They load the trucks with old and sick people, pregnant women, and children whom they throw in like sacks of potatoes. Uncle Iziu has also been shoved in. He looks at me from the truck, moves his head as if to say: This is the end. All passengers are taken to the forest and killed.

We march to a marketplace in the Jewish quarter of Tarnów. The marketplace will become the *Appellplatz* (roll call place) for all transports. During our march I remember the two pigeons I had prepared for cooking. I am worried the SS-men will find them and punish my brother.

At the *Appellplatz* there are two tables, behind each of which sits a SS-man. After checking the identification cards, they send the people to an empty place where they are ordered to get down on their knees. A few, mostly young people, are sent home. Nelly is sent to the kneeling group. When my turn comes, I manage to go to the SS-man who seems somewhat friendlier. I show him my *Arbeitsausweis*, he asks me a few questions, puts a stamp on my ID card, and sends me home. In leaving the *Appellplatz* there are still two more checkpoints. I get by them and at last am on the street. I cross a corner, and suddenly a German Youth is standing there with an iron stick. He hits me on the head with it with all his strength. He does the same to everybody who leaves the *Appellplatz*.

Carlo also returns from the transport, but his parents do not. For a long time no one knows the destination of the transport. Eventually we learn that it went to Bełżec, in eastern Poland. There, upon their arrival, people were packed into sealed gas chambers and poisoned with gas issuing from diesel engines.

About 12,000 Jews from Tarnów are deported to Bełżec and exterminated there.

Just a handful of people from our area are left. Carlo moves in with us. He and Poldi occupy one room, and I sleep in a small kitchen. Somebody brings me a letter from Aunt Pepi from Będzin, who has learned what has happened in Tarnów. She writes that from now on she will take care of me just as my own mother did. She also suggests that I should not sleep in the same room as Carlo. A few months later, Pepi and Joseph Weitzner, together with all our friends from Bohumin and Karvina living in Będzin, are sent to the Auschwitz gas chambers.

On June 19, 1942 a decree proclaiming the establishment of a ghetto is issued. Jews from the surrounding smaller places are gradually concentrated there. We also have to move to the newly created ghetto in the near future. We decide to escape from Tarnów and live with Aryan papers in Lwów. We acquire Aryan passports. My name on the new passport is Maria Raczyńska. Three weeks after the transport, we are ordered to move into the ghetto in Tarnów. Carlo leaves with his false papers for Lwów. We are to follow later. The son of a neighboring farmer tells me that I should stay with him, that he will hide me. I refuse.

Poldi and I prepare for our escape to Lwów. I will go first, then Poldi will join me in a few days. I learn the basic "facts" of my new life and memorize a couple of Polish prayers. At last the day of my departure arrives. I take with me some of my mother's jewelry. A friend of mine, Bronia, comes along. We smuggle ourselves out of the ghetto, remove our armbands, and go to the train station. In Lwów we go to the address where Carlo is supposed to lodge. A woman opens the door, and when we tell her that we are looking for Genek (that was his new name), she gets very agitated. She tells us that Genek was caught on the street and shot. She doesn't want us to stay, but she gives us an address where we can spend the night.

We walk to the bus station and take the bus to the given address. All the time, in the street and in the bus, it seems that people are looking at us with suspicion. I am afraid that somebody will recognize us as Jews. Mostly we fear the Ukrainian militiamen, whose business it is to catch Jews hidden under false names. We arrive at the address we have been given and rent a room in an apartment belonging to an older woman. Around 11 o'clock we are already in bed, the woman knocks at the door and tells us we have to dress because a Ukrainian militiaman wants to talk to us. He comes in and wants to see our passports. After we show them to him, he asks me whether I know the Polish prayer "Father in Heaven." I recite it to him. Then he asks Bronia, but she has forgotten it. Then he accuses us of being Jewish. We deny it. He orders us to come with him—he will take us to the Gestapo, and they will decide whether we are Jewish. We leave the house. On the street we start to plead with him to let us go. I give him a heavy gold bracelet that belonged to my mother. Finally, he lets us go free.

We don't know where to go, where to hide. We make up our minds to return to Tarnów. We go to the station and learn the next train is due only in the morning. We go to the ladies' room. The washroom attendant watches us with suspicion. We move on, go to the platform, and notice some Ukrainian boys apparently in a good mood, joking and laughing. We join them, tell them that we were at a party and had a wonderful time. We giggle and entertain them. They are pleased to have company while waiting for the train. In the morning we board the train and find it packed with German soldiers.

And so we repeat the comedy we played the night before. When we return to the ghetto, I actually feel relieved: I cannot live as a hunted animal. In light of my last experience, it is out of the question for Poldi to try to live on Aryan papers: if he is caught, they will be able to prove right away that he is a Jew.

The apartment we stay in is crowded, with all kinds of people thrown together. There is a couple from Polish Cieszyn with their ten-year-old son Otto. The husband was a confectioner (pastry maker) in Cieszyn, and even here he bakes pastries and makes candies to sell in the ghetto. Their marriage is very strange. His wife assists him when he bakes, they share the same bed, but they never talk to each other. He often shouts at his son, and his wife claims that she hates her husband. Still, during the next transport, when the Germans took Otto to be shot, husband and wife join Otto of their own free will—to be killed together.

There is also another young couple, with a five-year-old son Shlomek. Shlomek is an amazing little boy. He is surprisingly clever, talks like a grown-up, and understands everything that is going on. Everybody likes him, and his parents adore him. Yet when the transport comes and Shlomek is taken from his parents, his parents do not have the courage to go with him. Little Shlomek goes to his death alone.

In the same house there is a beautiful four-year-old girl with dark brown curly hair. One day the Germans pick her up on the street and take her with them. They are very friendly to her, and for a while she becomes their pet. They feed her, dress her in beautiful clothes, take her for rides in their open car through the ghetto. This lasts for two weeks. Then they kill her.

In the evenings young people gather in one room or another, where we entertain ourselves. Somebody plays the guitar or accordion, and we sing Polish, Yiddish, and Russian songs, or we dance. We also smoke. Sometimes we make our own cigarettes by filling paper hulls with tobacco. Poldi usually spends the evenings with his girlfriend, Sarah Vielfreund. Sarah, twenty-one-years-old, has come to Tarnów with her parents and her year-younger brother and sister, Olek and Rozia, who are twins. Sarah is very pretty, practical, and has a sense for business. She is quite efficient in selling and buying—in short, in "organizing" necessary items for her whole family. She also works at the Madritsch plant.

The inhabitants of the ghetto are apprehensive, for they expect a new transport. "Transport" is an awesome word. To go or not to go with a transport can often mean the difference between life and death. Poldi states that he will never let himself be taken on a transport and that neither should we. Some people build hiding places in their apartments or in cellars, where they dig tunnels in which to hide in case of a transport.

A second transport is announced early in the morning of September 10, 1942, with shouts of "Raus, raus, alles heraus, ihr dreckigen Schweinehunde!" ("Out, out, everyone get out, you shitty swinedogs!") The horrors of the previous transport are repeated—the brutality, the dogs, the insults. The difference is that by now everybody knows that the transport is not being sent to work but to certain death. From the window I see a family escape through a chimney, only to be apprehended and shot as they descend from the chimney one by one.

We march to the *Appellplatz*, where we stand under the hot burning sun until the evening. We are thirsty and have nothing to drink. Many faint from thirst. I start to eat the toothpaste that I brought with me. The selection is in a full swing. SS-men stand on a podium in their high shiny boots, point with a stick at people whom they choose for the transport. First they select children and the old. A young mother with a baby in her arms steps forward. A SS-man wants to take the baby but she will not let him. He tears the baby from her, yet she still does not let go. Finally, he takes out a gun and shoots the baby first, then the mother.

In front of me a family of five is standing—mother, father, two daughters (one eighteen years old, the other nine), and their grandmother. First the grandmother is selected, then the little girl. The mother, father, and older girl join them of their own free will. The family of an *Ordnungsdienst* is taken to the transport. In order to save them and get them released, the *Ordnungsdienst* discloses to the Germans the hiding place of his friend's family; subsequently, the whole family—grandparents, parents, and children—are deported.

During the nights after the transport, the whole ghetto echoes with crying, prayer, the calling of names of loved ones who have been taken away.

During the deportation another 8,000 Jews lose their lives in Bełżec. Sarah lost her mother and sister Rozia. Her father and brother Olek have remained with her. The population of the ghetto diminishes substantially, and the size of the ghetto is being reduced. We have to move to barracks that are in a desolated state. People sleep in rooms without doors and in corridors on bunks placed one over the other. The majority of the inhabitants of that part of the ghetto are working.

The third deportation takes place in November 1942. About 3,000 Jews die.

The last deportation is on September 2, 1943. Poldi, Sarah, and I are sitting in a room contemplating the transport, which will be tomorrow. What are we going to do? Shall we hide? Where? All at once Poldi goes to his bunk, lies down, closes his eyes and says: "I don't want to hear anything, just leave me alone."

Next day on the *Appellplatz*, after the usual selection, an announcement is issued: everybody who works should join their firm. That seems to us a good sign. Maybe after all we will be sent to forced labor and not to death. The supervisors of each firm call out the name of that firm: Montana here, Madritsch here, etc. Poldi takes leave of Sarah and me. Before going, he says to Sarah: "Sarah, please take care of my sister!"

The first transport leaves. Poldi's firm Montana goes with it. When I hear that, again I have a premonition that I will never see my brother again. But then I pause and think it through. Montana has been the safest place to work. The elite of the ghetto, only healthy and strong young men have worked here. Surely the Germans will make use of them. The same day we learn that the train has gone west—that means not to Bełżec. Thank God.

Thank God, it is better to be sent anywhere than to the east, to Bełżec.

Probably they will be shipped to forced labor. I hope Poldi will be safe. He is strong, healthy, he will survive. But it does not turn out that way. The train went to Auschwitz. Upon arrival, all were sent straight, without selection, to the gas chambers. Poldi was twenty-two years old.

CHAPTER 4

Nineteen Months in Camps

I go with the last transport that leaves on the evening of the same day. We are loaded onto cattle cars. Children are not permitted to board the train. Instead, they will be taken on trucks to the forest and shot. In front of the train are groups of children. Mothers who choose to join them are free to do so. They line the platform, standing with their children, looking with desperation at the "fortunate ones" allowed to be deported.

A father succeeds in smuggling his small child onto the train. He hides him there. Soon SS-men with dogs enter the boxcar and order everybody out. They find the child, seize him, and throw him into the group of children. His father joins the little boy.

A ten-year-old boy is taken from his mother. The mother stays. The boy turns to her, stretches out his hands, and cries: "Mamusiu! Mamusiu!" The mother does not move. Weeping, she says: "Nie mogę, nie mogę, oj Boże przepacz" (I can't, I can't, oh, God forgive me). She repeats this sentence throughout the whole journey.

Sarah, her brother Olek, and her father are also on this transport. The train starts to move. We look through the cracks to see in which direction we are going. To the west! To the west! Everybody is relieved. We arrive in a strange place I have never heard of before—Płaszów. Płaszów was a Nazi forced-labor camp on the outskirts of Kraków. In September 1943, I am one of 3,000 Jews from the Tarnów ghetto brought here.

The night is pitch black. We are driven on foot through a forest, where every few meters Germans in uniform, men and women, stand with flashlights and guns in their hands, pointing at us. It all looks eerie, not real. Are we in hell?

At last we come to the camp. Sarah and I are placed in a barrack located on a hillock somewhat apart from the other barracks. It is built on top of a cemetery, which was destroyed before the camp was built. There are rows of bunks, three tiers, each over the other. Sarah and I occupy the highest tier, which is considered the safest and cleanest. There are no mattresses or blankets. In order not to lie on the hard board, we take out all our clothes and try to sleep on them. But we cannot sleep. The barrack is infested with bed bugs. Our bunks swarm with them. Secretly we go outside to sleep on the grass. We manage to do that for three days. Then the block *Kapo* notices us and we have to return to our bunks.

Later Olek organizes blankets for us. The men occupy another part of the camp; sometimes they manage to come for a visit. That way we can support each other with food or whatever is needed.

At the Madritsch plant we work in shifts—one week during the day, the other during the night. Sarah and I take opposite shifts, so that nobody else can sleep on our bunk or steal our blanket. We march to work in formations, in columns of five girls in a line. It takes us about an hour to get there. First we cross a check point, where we are counted, usually by an *Ordungsdienst*. One of the policemen is extremely nasty. He holds a whip and likes to hit people with it. He aims mainly for the eyes. (After the war he is sentenced by the Polish tribunal to death by hanging.) After the checkpoint, we climb a hill and pass a pit with a smoldering fire and strange smell. Prisoners are forced to undress and stand at the edge of the pit. They are shot and their bodies fall into the ditch. Later, when the ditch is full, the bodies are incinerated.

The Madritsch plant is one of the best places in Płaszów in which to work. We sew men's overalls for the army. We work in groups of five and create our own assembly line. Each girl works on different parts, and then we assemble them. Sometimes we put together the wrong parts and they don't fit. So we stretch and pull them until they fit. Once, the overseer checks our product, pulls slightly at the overalls, and they fall apart. He is also a prisoner and is sympathetic. We get away with it. The more we produce, the more bread we receive. We take the bread back to the barracks and exchange it for soap or other necessary items. Sometimes Julius Madritsch visits our plant. He is always kind and polite, and protects us from deportations. When a transport is in progress in the camp proper, he keeps us at the plant day and night.[1]

The night shifts are harder for us. We are sleepy, and all the time somebody in our group ends up falling asleep. This is strictly forbidden. When we see the *Kapo* checking on the prisoners, we wake each other: "Judith, don't sleep, Hela, Edith, Malka…" This goes on every day. To keep awake, we sing. Some nights, to our great enjoyment, the sirens start to howl and we know that soon we will have air raids. The lights are turned off, we sit and wait, hoping and wishing for the bombs to explode here.

On our way from work, we go to the kitchen to get our ration of soup. We are hungry, cold, and tired. In front of the kitchen an *Ordungsdienst* is posted. He is also a sadist. Sometimes he lets us wait in front of the kitchen for a long time, or he orders us to walk around the kitchen barrack three times before we get our soup.

In the mornings and evenings there are roll calls, usually in front of our barracks. We are counted and recounted. One day in November we are standing in the roll call. It is raining and very cold. We have to stand at attention in exact and straight rows. The SS-man walks around and checks the evenness of the rows. If somebody is slightly out of line, he gets whipped. The ground is soaked from the rain and covered with mud. Suddenly, he commands us to lie down. We lie down in the mud. Then he shouts: "Everybody crawl!" I watch ourselves crawl. This is absurd, macabre, like in a black comedy. I start to laugh, loud, I can't help it, I am not able to stop. It is a hysterical laugh. I see the SS-man approaching. He wears high boots and a raincoat. In his hand he holds a whip. He walks smartly, swinging his whip playfully. I force myself with all my might to stop laughing. He stops behind me for a second, then moves on. Fortunately, he does not notice me.

Płaszów also has an important *Appellplatz*, used on deportation days for selections and other purposes. For example, if a prisoner tries to escape, all inmates have to remain standing for hours, often through the night or for as

1   Julius Madritsch has been honored by Yad Vashem as a "Rigtheous Among The Nations".

long as the fugitive is not caught. He usually is apprehended and brought back to the camp. Then he is driven to the *Appellplatz*, with a board fastened on his body on which his crime is spelled out in large letters. He has to pass along each row of prisoners so we can read it. At the end of the *Appellplatz* there is a podium on which the gallows is placed. Here the fugitive's journey ends. He is hanged while everybody has to watch the whole procedure. That way attempts to escape are discouraged. Also each escape is followed by long hours of standing in roll call and by additional beatings or killings. These should also serve to discourage us from flight.

Near the *Appellplatz* are barracks for children. Some children sleep there; others are brought here by their mothers while the mothers go to work. One day we are standing in roll call. A record player with a loudspeaker plays music, sentimental German songs about a mother's love for her child, the Italian song *Mama*, and a Yiddish song *A yiddishe mame*. In front of the children's barracks there are trucks. Children are dragged out of the barracks and tossed onto the trucks, one on top of the other. Hell breaks loose at the *Appellplatz*. Children are crying, mothers screaming, Germans shouting, shooting, and all the time the music is playing.

The newest invention is the selection of women. The whole staff of SS-men stand in a row. The women have to undress and file naked in front of the Germans. They amuse themselves, laugh, make comments, and, at the same time, select those to be put aside. Then the women are loaded onto the trucks, taken to the pit, and shot.

Another day we have visitors at the plant. SS-men from Płaszów are showing their menagerie to their colleagues from other places. They are accompanied by their dogs. They shout: "Everybody out, fast!" Outside it is bitterly cold. The ground is covered with frozen snow. Everybody has to grab a rock and run with it up the hill, down the hill. If somebody takes a smaller rock he is called back and punished. The Germans hurry us on: "Schnell, schneller, dalej, dalej!"

The dogs chase us. It is slippery, we run for our lives. If somebody falls down, he is doomed. The dogs tear into him.

The Madritsch plant is dissolved. We are transferred to a different job: *Barackenbau* (construction of barracks). But we don't build anything. We carry stones from one place to another. We have to jump over ditches with the stones.

We are cold, our shoes are torn, socks and clothes are wet. We wrap our feet in rags that we fasten with strings. We are constantly hungry. In the morning we receive a small piece of dry bread for the whole day. Sometimes we eat the daily ration at once. Then, at least for a while, we are not hungry. And later? Who cares.

In the spring we are again deported, supposedly to another labor camp. At the station we have to hand over our belongings, which we are to get back at our destination. I have in my hand a pocketbook with photographs of my parents and of my brother. I don't want to give it up. I plead with a German to let me keep it. Instead he gives me a slap on my face. We are forced into a box car where we are packed in like sardines. We stand, hardly able to move. The car is shut hermetically, and the train starts to roll.

Soon it gets so stuffy that we have difficulty breathing. We take turns to get near the cracks of the car to get a little air. At the final station, when the boxcars are opened, prisoners in striped uniforms enter. They direct us out and tell us that we are in Auschwitz. The name doesn't mean much to us. We ask them what it is like here. Not too bad, they say. On the platform SS-men are posted. As we pass them one points with his finger to the direction in which we should go: older people to the left, younger to the right. In front of the railroad is a puddle with rainwater. Some people drink it. We are led to a wooded area to an open barrack, where we are left alone. We can go into the barrack or we can stay outside. The ground outside is strewn with clothes, jewelry, and money. Money lies everywhere. There must have been another transport shortly before us.

We wait there through the night. There is a foul smell all around, the same as in Płaszów when the bodies were burned. There must be a similar pit close by. Behind a fence is another building where people are led in groups. It is the *Sauna*[2] with showers. Soon our turn will come. We have to undress and remain waiting, naked. Then we are led to the *Sauna*. We go to a basement with a long corridor. Prisoners in striped uniforms sit on a chair and shave the newcomers. It goes fast. Each prisoner shaves a different part of the body. At the end of the

2   In this building, which went into use in late 1943, newly arrived prisoners were registered and subjected to disinfection before being exploited as slave laborers. This is where they were assigned the numbers that were tattooed on their forearms, received their striped camp clothing, and had the hair removed from all over their bodies. The periodic delousing of prisoners and their clothing was also carried out in the *Sauna*.

corridor a SS-man is standing and directs people once more either to the left or to the right side. We go to a waiting room where there are benches and hooks for clothes. But we don't have any clothes anyway. At last we go to the adjoining room where there are rows of showers. After we shower with cold water, we are given some clothes and told to wait outside. I look for my friends. We hardly recognize each other—we look funny with our shaved heads. Here is Sarah, Judith, Hela, Ruth. Malka is missing. She was the smallest and weakest of us.

Sarah tells me that now I look like Poldi. Sarah's father and brother were sent to Mauthausen. Both perished there. We see four chimneys with high flames and dark smoke coming out of them. We are told the smoke and flames are crematoria in which people are first gassed and then burned in ovens. Some of the newcomers don't believe it. "They just want to scare us," they maintain.

We are next led to a women's camp in Birkenau B2B. This camp was, until recently, occupied by whole families deported from Theresienstadt. It was called *Familienlager* (family camp). My mother's younger sister, Mania Taubeler, with her husband, Erich, and two children, Turi (Arthur), nineteen years old, and Gerti (Gertrud), seventeen, were here. Both children had red hair. Gerti was a beautiful quiet girl, quite the opposite of Turi. He was very talkative and had a tremendous imagination. He wanted to become a journalist. Before the war they lived in Slovakia, in Turciansky Svaty Martin. Erich was an accountant, Mania a teacher of French literature in high school. They were brought to Auschwitz via Theresienstadt. One day all the inmates of the *Familienlager* were taken to the crematorium, they, too.

The wooden barracks in the camp look the same as in Płaszów: rows of bunks with three tiers each. Sarah and I again take the highest tier. One half of the barracks is occupied by girls from Płaszów, the other half by girls from Hungary. It is still dark outside when the Hungarian girls wake us up: "Felkelni, felkelni" ("get up, get up"). The roll calls start very early here. At one end of the barrack is a small room belonging to the *Blockälteste* (the boss or head supervisor of the barrack). Her cubicle is arranged rather cozily. In it she receives male visitors from the men's camp. The *Blockälteste* and *Kapos* enjoy the highest status among the prisoners. They have all the privileges the camp can offer: better food, clothes, and amusement. They also have limitless power over the other inmates. They can beat, torture, or kill them as they wish. For the most part they are German or Polish prisoners chosen from the ranks of criminals and prostitutes arrested for crimes they have committed. The most powerful of the camp inmates is the *Lagerälteste* (the head of the camp). The *Lagerälteste* of the B2B camp happens to be a Jewish woman, Zuzi Gross, who before the war lived in Prešov, Slovakia. She wears riding breeches, high boots, and an omnipresent horsewhip. She walks around the camp like a queen. Usually during roll call she comes for inspection and, if the rows in the formation are not straight enough, she uses her whip.

After roll call we have breakfast—dark water (supposedly coffee) and a slice of stale bread. For the main meals we have soup, usually made of turnips. The food is brought to the barracks from the kitchen in cauldrons. The inmates are hungry, starving. They fight over pieces of bread or steal from each other. In front of the kitchen I see women fighting to get hold of the garbage cans and eat the garbage. Like animals, I think, and at that moment I make a pledge never to let myself lose my human dignity, no matter how much I might suffer.

Then there are the *Muselmänner*. They are living skeletons, just skin and bones, with no flesh left on their bodies. They walk like shadows, dragging their legs behind them. They are beyond any help, in the last stage of starvation before death. We can actually see perfectly healthy prisoners slowly change into *Muselmänner*. First they become slightly disoriented. Then, gradually, they lose all energy and the will to live. They stop talking and eating altogether. The healthy prisoners avoid them like lepers, and they become the outcasts of the camp.

We are tattooed on our left arms. From now on during a selection, done periodically by Josef Mengele and others, the tattooed numbers of the selected women are written on a list. Later their numbers are called, and they are moved to a so-called "death barracks." They are shut in here and eventually taken to the crematorium.

Those marked for death during selection are the *Muselmänner*, the sick-looking, and women with wounds, or even just an infected pimple on their bodies. Sanitation in the camp is completely inadequate. There is no water with which to clean ourselves or wash our clothes. Only occasionally are we allowed to use the *Sauna* where, under slowly dripping water, we can take showers. The barracks are infested with lice. Evenings we sit on our bunks and try to remove them from our clothes. From time to time we are taken for *Entlausung* (disinfection of our clothes).

I am so hungry that during the day I doze off now and again, just for a split second. Immediately I dream about food.

To clean myself I sometimes use coffee. It gets so I can't stand it anymore, can't go on like this. How can I remain a human being without water, without food? I have to do something to help myself.

I remember that when we first arrived at Birkenau I visited a barrack where women from Slovakia where housed. I wanted to get some information about my uncle, my mother's older brother, Salo Hornik, his wife, Greta, and his son, Kurt. They lived before the war in Žilina, Slovakia. It so happened that one woman in the Slovak barracks also lived in Žilina. She knew my uncle but couldn't tell me where they were. Deported to Auschwitz already in 1942, she works now in the *Revier* (the hospital barracks).

I decide to ask her to let me work in the *Revier*. And indeed she takes me in. From now on, every day after the morning roll call, I leave for work. The *Revier* looks like the other barracks, the only difference being that the sick are lying all the time on their bunks, too weak to move or attend roll call. They suffer mostly from diarrhea. They come for the most part from Italy and Greece. They are unable to eat anything, yet for some reason they long to eat raisins. There is no medicine whatsoever. One Italian girl who spoke a little German asks all the time for water: "Marguerit, Wasser, bitte Wasser!" She is so grateful when I attend to her, but she does not last long. Every now and then the sick are sent to the gas chambers and burned in the crematorium.

My job consists of cleaning the barracks and taking out the buckets with waste. In the beginning it was sickening, but later I get used to it. In the *Revier* there is plenty of water and soup. I can even take soup for my friends.

One morning in the late summer of 1944, when I am at work, an order is issued stating that all inmates belonging to the Płaszów transport should line up in formation. *Kapos* go from barrack to barrack shouting: "Płaszów antreten!" (Płaszów line up!) I hurry to our barrack, where people are already standing in rows of five. My four friends, Sarah, Judith, Hela, and Ruth, are waiting for me. They don't want anybody else in their row. They tell me quite happily that we are going to be sent to another camp. After being counted, our formation starts to move. I look at the smoke rising from the chimneys. The ovens are apparently in full operation, and suddenly I feel a terrible disgust from the realization that soon I might turn into smoke. I do not feel fear, just disgust. I tell my friends that we should not go, that we should hide somewhere. They don't want to hear about staying in this horrible place, for anywhere will be better than Auschwitz. But I refuse to go. I stay behind, very slowly move backwards, and, when I reach the rear of the formation, I run to the *Revier.* Here I hide on a bunk on the upper tier, lying down and covering myself with a rag. One tall Hungarian girl who also works in the *Revier* sees me. She approaches and advises me to report to the transport lest I be shot. I tell her to shut up and go away. The *Kapos* are still shouting: "Płaszów antreten! Płaszów antreten!" In the evening the shouting stops, the transport is gone. The roll call starts, so I return to my barrack. The *Blockälteste* counts us, but the count doesn't match. There is one person more than there should be.

I step forward and explain to the *Blockälteste* that I have not gone with the Płaszów transport because I was scared. She looks at me for a while with astonishment and tells me to line up with the Hungarian girls. After roll call I go to my bunk. The whole half of the barracks formerly occupied by the inmates from Płaszów is now empty. I am there alone. I feel miserable, remembering how my friends waited for me and how glad they were to see me just a few hours before. I didn't go with them, I let them down. I start to cry. Some of the Hungarians come over to cheer me up. They make room on their bunks and invite me to join them. I move over, and from now on I remain with some of them to the end of the war. (After the war I learn that the whole Płaszów transport was shipped to Riga. There they were loaded on an old ship and drowned in the Baltic Sea. Nobody from the transport survived.)

The *Revier* is disbanded, and I work for a while in the *Sauna.* Later I am assigned to work as part of an *Aussenkommando* (a group for outside work). Our commando works in a forest cutting wood. Every day we pass the gate occupied by SS-men. We have to march in a brisk step like soldiers while the *Kapo* shouts: "Links, rechts, links—und links, links—und links!" On our way to the forest we have to sing. Winter comes, and it grows very cold. One day my hands are freezing. I start to rub them. The *Kapo* sees me do it, approaches, and orders me to keep working. I tell her to mind her own business. She takes a branch, hits me across the face with it, and threatens to report me to the SS. I don't care. Some girls start to plead with her not to report me. When we arrive at the gate on our way back she doesn't report me.

The end of December 1944. We work at dismantling the gas chambers. Prisoners from the men's camp also work here. One man from Prague brings me shoes. Up until now I have been wearing wooden clogs.

January 1945. We are deported to Bergen-Belsen, in northern Germany, not far from Hannover. We are put in barracks already occupied by prisoners from different parts of Europe, some of them Russian. The first thing I do in Belsen is look for some kind of work. By now I know that the only possible way to survive is to work. For those who work the nourishment and hygienic possibilities are somewhat better. I also realize that to stay in the barracks and wait for the end of the war is dangerous. Too much hope is almost as dangerous as losing hope completely. Waiting for the end to come is itself endless and frustrating. My camp philosophy is to arrange my life as if the present situation will last for a long time, while still hoping that some day it will all end. In short, I try to make the best of things under the given conditions. I hear that in the *Schälküche* (the potato kitchen) they need a few girls. I go there and wait in the anteroom with many other girls. As soon as the kitchen door opens a fight breaks out. Everybody wanted to get in first. I fight my way in. I and a few others who get in first are accepted.

The work in the *Schälküche* is very unpleasant. We sit in a cold barracks and all the time peel turnips and potatoes. I have the advantage of eating the raw turnips or potatoes. I can even steal some potatoes and exchange them for warm clothes and soap. We put the peeled vegetables in buckets and, when they are full, one of the girls delivers them to the real kitchen, which is across from the *Schälküche*. We take turns for that trip. The kitchen is warm, and the girls who work here can eat warm soup and cooked potatoes. I make up my mind to try to get work in the kitchen. A SS-man who does not look too menacing sits there all the time. He is well nourished and has a ruddy complexion. Before the war he was a butcher. I notice that he likes to look at girls. I will have to find a way to make him notice me. The day when it is my turn to deliver the bucket, I make myself presentable. I put on a tight pullover, and carefully comb my hair, which has grown back. When I come to the kitchen, I do indeed manage to attract his attention. He calls me over and says that from tomorrow on I shall work in the kitchen. My chief task is to take care of the kitchen stove, to heat it and keep the fire burning.

Daily I bring bread and potatoes to my Hungarian friends. I carry them in a small bag made of cloth. One evening on my way from the kitchen, a Russian girl snatches the bag from my hand and runs away. I start to run after her, catch her, and, after a fight, I get my bag back. The Russian girl is hungry, too, but I think only of my starving friends.

One day a woman is pushed into the kitchen by a German. He saw her steal a bucket of turnips. After beating her, he puts the full bucket of turnips in front of her and orders her to eat it all. The woman eats until she collapses.

The conditions at the barracks are horrendous. Sanitation facilities are nonexistent. People die from starvation and disease. The dead are put outside the barracks, and every day the grounds of the camp are covered with heaps of dead bodies. In Belsen there are no gas chambers—they are not needed.

An epidemic of typhoid breaks out. The disease is spread by lice. Everybody around me gets sick. One day I feel sick and dizzy. I know I am getting ill, but I hope I can carry on and tough it out. But one morning I get up and faint. The next thing I remember I am lying in an overcrowded *Revier* with high fever and diarrhea. I get up and stumble over bodies to reach the waste bucket. There is no medicine and no doctors or nurses to help at all. On the bunks the dead and sick lie all about, all mixed together.

CHAPTER 5

Liberation and Recovery

On April 15, 1945, one week or so after I get ill, the British army liberates Bergen-Belsen. I see in front before my eyes the horror-stricken faces of the British soldiers as they open the door of the barracks. They promptly get to work, take off our rags, wrap us in clean blankets, and put us gently on stretchers. They then carry us into ambulances. It is unbelievable! There are people who do not want to harm us, who actually take care of us. It feels good, and at last I can let go, give in to my illness and sleep.

The cars drive off to a military hospital in Bergen. They make a short stop at a disinfection station, where DDT powder is thrown on our hair. But all of that I learn later. At the time I do not know what is going on.

I remember waking up and hearing German-speaking voices. I open my eyes and see German nurses in their uniforms fussing over me. I don't want them to touch me. They calm me down and tell me that I don't have to be afraid. They put some powder into my hair, and I am carried back into the ambulance. Again I fall asleep.

I remain unconscious for three weeks and dream that I am traveling all over England.

Then I wake up, look out of the window, and see that, far from traveling, I am still in the same place. I ask where I am and am told that I am in Bergen. I can't believe it! Still in Bergen?

Boils filled with fluid break out all over my body. Each morning I find myself sticking to the bed sheet. It is very painful. I dream again that somebody takes out my eyes and puts burning coals into my eye-sockets. My whole body burns with pain. I get an infection in my right arm. I keep begging the nurses to cut off my arm because the arm is too heavy and I simply cannot carry it.

As the nurses are preparing me for surgery, the wound opens by itself. They put a basin under the arm, and gallons of pus seem to come out. A Russian girl, Nina, feeds me, for I am too weak to hold a spoon. On the table I see a vase with flowers filled with water. I manage to drag myself over to the table in order to drink the water. Luckily, I do not have the strength to lift the vase. An English woman in an army uniform comes to our room to take down the names of the patients. I have difficulty remembering my surname. Finally it comes to me. Slowly I say, Margit Raab. She also asks me whether I have any relatives. I mention my uncle in Palestine, but I cannot remember his name.

Slowly I recover. I want to eat sugar and cherries and to drink milk. The nurses, who are of every kind of nationality, bring me everything I ask for. My friends, already recovered, visit me and give me sardines. I eat a whole tin of sardines at once. For a short time I get sick again. When I am able to walk, we make trips to the woods to pick blueberries. We spread them on bread—it tastes like blueberry cake.

During the first days of the liberation of Bergen-Belsen, the British give the former inmates a free hand to deal with the SS. The angry crowd throws stones at the Germans and kills some of them. When I am told what has happened, I am sorry that I wasn't there, for I would have thrown stones at them myself.

In July 1945, all recovered patients are sent to Sweden. I am already prepared for departure when a Czech official comes to the hospital to gather Czech citizens who wish to return to Czechoslovakia. I decide not to go to Sweden but to Czechoslovakia. We take a bus to Hannover, and from there we travel by train. On the way we see German cities in ruins, completely destroyed. The train is full of Czech repatriates. It stops often, and we leave the train to look around. Sometimes we pick fruit from the trees. Once a German farmer tries to chase us away. We shout at him, and he gets scared and leaves us alone.

When we reach the Czech border, I become very sad. Why am I returning? Nobody is left from my family anyway.

In Prague we are given addresses of places where we might stay. On my way there I go to the washroom to refresh myself. The washroom attendant wants me to pay, but I don't have any money. Outside I start to cry. I feel so alone and lost. A Czech soldier approaches me and starts to console me, telling me that I should be happy that I survived and that I have returned to my fatherland.

In a tramcar I meet a man from Žilina. He tells me that my uncle, Salo Hornik, and his family are alive and living in Bratislava. The next day I take the train to Bratislava to join my relatives. Uncle Salo, his wife, his son Kurt, and my mother's oldest brother, Oskar Hornik (who, in 1938, emigrated with his wife Ethel from Vienna to Tel Aviv), and I are the only survivors of a once large family.

POSTSCRIPT:

Margit Raab Kalina was born on September 23, 1922, in Karvina, Czechoslovakia, and died on February 25, 1998, in New York City. She completed this memoir in January 1991.

MY ESCAPE INTO PRISON AND OTHER MEMORIES OF A STOLEN YOUTH, 1939-1948

by *Jane Lipski*
(Jadzia Szpigelman)

DEDICATION

For my children, grandchildren, nieces and nephews.

ACKNOWLEDGEMENTS

Many thanks and appreciation to: Judy, Zoltan, Miriam and Chris

TABLE OF CONTENTS

CHAPTER 1

Our Life Before the War

I was born in 1924 on Yom Kippur, the Day of Atonement, the holiest and most solemn day of the Jewish calendar. Like most of the Jewish population in Będzin, a city in southwest Poland, my parents Hadassa and Meyer Joseph Szpigelman fasted and prayed all day long in the synagogue. They sat apart from one another, because according to orthodox Jewish tradition, women did not pray near the Ark and the Torah or sit with the men in the main sanctuary. Rather, my mother and the other women prayed from the floor above, where they could clearly hear the men chanting and observe the Torah being lifted out from the Ark.

In the late afternoon Hadassa felt her first contractions. Not wishing to disturb her husband, she stepped quietly down the stairs and slipped unnoticed out of the prayer house. She headed home with the knowledge that she could call upon the local midwife, who lived in our building and who came to her at once.

Meyer Joseph prayed through *Ne'ilah*, the day's closing service, as the early October sun dipped below the horizon. It was only afterward that he found out, while waiting for his wife by the stairwell, that she had left hours earlier. By the time he arrived home and heard my cry from the bedroom, I had already been cleaned up and a red ribbon tied in my wispy blond hair to protect me from the evil eye.

I came into my parents' lives rather late. My mother had delivered five children before me, of whom three were alive at the time of my birth. My brother Poldek was 15 years old, my sister Helen was 13 and Hania was 6. Even though my parents were probably hoping for another son, having lost two, they were happy with the healthy newborn daughter that God had given them.

They named me Jadzia, after an aunt, Jachet, who had died when she was over 100 and supposedly had been very clever as well as hardy. For the rest of their lives, my parents' called me their Yom Kippur girl, although I could never celebrate my birthday with a party, because everyone would be fasting, meditating and asking forgiveness of God on that holy day. Come to think of it, my family never had birthday parties, and I don't remember going to any, so maybe it simply wasn't the custom.

We lived in an enormous, five-story, double-courtyard building on Kołątaja Street, one of three main boulevards that ran through the city. More than a hundred families resided in the building's one- to four-room apartments. Even the basements and attics were occupied by tenants, except on the side of the attic where everyone hung their laundry to dry. Professional people, such as doctors, lawyers, professors, and schoolteachers, lived in the front apartments where the windows faced the street. The rear apartments were mostly occupied by trades people, including tailors, seamstresses, shoemakers, brassiere and underwear makers, and milliners, all of whom worked at home. The building also housed a bakery, a hair mattress factory, a chicken wire fence factory, and a blacksmith, as well as a school for ballroom dancing, a trumpet school, a merchant's organization, a private school for girls that my oldest sister Helen attended, a sports club called *Hakoach*, where I exercised when I was grammar school age, and a *cheder* (a small religious school), where a rabbi taught young boys to read the Torah. There seemed to be a whole city within the confines of this one urban dwelling, a city densely populated with vivid sounds, smells and characters that I have never forgotten.

Almost all of the tenants were Jewish and everyone knew everyone else. After school, the children played ball, hide-and-seek, hopscotch, and other games in the courtyards. A group of Gypsy men and women often came to perform their folk music; on other occasions, a blind man and his son sang and played the accordion. We children would circle 'round to watch a performance, scramble to pick up the coins that women tossed from their apartment windows, and drop them into the musicians' hats. Something was always going on in my neighborhood. But whereas I felt exuberance for the local happenings, my big brother Poldek adamantly kept his distance and tried to restrain my friendships in the apartment building.

Poldek stood out in our family as the disciplinarian, more rigid and exacting than either of our parents. He used to monitor my actions at home and in the courtyard; for instance, he forbade me to play with children from a poor family that lived in a one-room basement apartment. They were uncared-for and unsanitary, Poldek insisted. A medical student and later a surgeon, he worried that I would learn unwholesome habits and foul language or catch diseases from them. He punished me many times for playing in the courtyard and other such transgressions, and I grew up resenting his iron grip. Along with trying to control my playtime, he pressured me to study assiduously and even had me memorize poems and recite them in front of his friends. While other children played, I was obliged to read books that were appropriate for higher grade levels than mine, books that I didn't understand or care about. Then my brother would test me to make sure I had read them. If I didn't understand a book, he'd punish me. My parents and sisters couldn't protect me because Poldek bossed them around too, and not even my parents could stand up to him. One reason my family treated him with kid gloves is because he was the prized only son, born between the two sons who had died. I recall being able to breathe freely only when he left Poland to study medicine abroad in Prague, Czechoslovakia.

That was in the early 1930s, before the start of the Nazi war, when Polish Jews faced new occurrences of persecution as a result of government policies and popular flare-ups against Jews. Polish universities, for instance, enforced an admissions quota to restrict the number of university placements reserved for Jewish students. Poldek was one of the unlucky ones whose medical school application was rejected in Poland. Nonetheless, in Prague, he rose to the top of his medical class, graduated *magna cum laude* and grew into a skilled surgeon. He returned to Poland filled with hopes and aspirations to practice medicine in Będzin, but because he was Jewish and had studied abroad, he would neither be given a license to practice nor be appointed to a hospital staff anywhere in Poland. His hopes sank. He eventually found a meagerly paid job, working unofficially as a first assistant surgeon in a large hospital in a nearby city called

Sosnowiec. Although he performed effectively at the hospital, he continued to torment our family at home. I looked forward to summer vacations when I could escape his control.

During the summer months, my mother would rent a cottage in the Beskid Mountains in southern Poland. We'd bathe under waterfalls, climb mountains, pick berries and mushrooms in the forests, and visit friends and family. Father, who worked as a brewery sales representative, joined us on the weekends. By no means were we a well-to-do family. Father's income barely covered our living expenses, which included the costs of a Jewish private school education for four children. We had no choice but to attend private schools, because admission quotas restricted the number of Jewish students who could attend the public high schools.

But discrimination didn't dispirit the youth of Jewish Będzin. We were energetic and earnest, ready to help others and solve the glaring problem of hatred against Jews. Most young people belonged to Zionist youth movements or sport clubs. When I was eleven years old, I joined a Zionist group called *Ha-Noar ha-Tsioni* ("Zionist Youth," in Hebrew). My friends and I would meet, learn Hebrew songs, and dance the *hora* and other group dances. Our young instructors—including Israel Diamond, Karola Bojm, Alex Statler, Sheva Ingster, and Sally Gutman—took us camping and introduced us to Jewish history, literature and Zionism. From them, we leaned that the Jewish people must have our own country, that we must return to Palestine, our Biblical homeland, because it was no longer possible to live peacefully and securely in the Diaspora. Jews were not wanted in Europe.

In the summer of 1939, when I was fourteen, I begged my parents to allow me to spend one month with my friends at the Zionist Youth camp in the Beskid Mountains. Though my brother tried to prevent me from going, I cried and pleaded with my parents—I even refused to eat for two days—until they gave me permission. The Zionist camp experience remains one of the fondest memories of my youth. I befriended young people who shared a common goal and desire to build our own state. I made up my mind that summer to immigrate to Palestine as soon as I finished high school in four years. Several of my older friends had already emigrated. Others were preparing to go before the end of 1939, but the war erupted and crushed their plans.

More than forty of my family members lived in Będzin and about 150 more resided in neighboring towns and cities such as Sosnowiec, Katowice, Dąbrowa, and Strzemieszyce. Most of the family, especially the older generation, was religious and observed the Jewish holidays and the Sabbath, during which they did not work, carry money, or ride vehicles. (Very few families had cars, but trams were available.)

Będzin is located in an industrial region of southwest Poland called Upper Silesia, which borders Germany and used to be famous for its coal mines. Jews had lived in Będzin for generations, reaching back to the eleventh century, when the town first began to grow into a center of Jewish life for the entire province of Upper Silesia. By the start of World War II, approximately 27,000 Jews resided in Będzin, more than 50 percent of the total population.

Poldek warned our family that war was imminent. It was near the end of August, he was working in a medical unit that was preparing to head eastward, and he came to see us. I remember he was dressed in uniform and carrying a gas mask. He insisted that we all leave the area and get far away from the German border. Most people did not believe that Hitler would dare to attack Poland. Nevertheless, a few days later, my parents, my two married sisters, Helen and Hania, their families and I fled Będzin. We were a mere handful among thousands of Jewish and non-Jewish Poles, who were making a mass exodus away from the battlefield in the event of an invasion. My family traveled by horse and cart and later on foot to the home of my mother's older sister Gusta, who lived with her family in Jędrzejów, a town sixty miles east of Będzin. In the chaos of travel, my mother and I were separated from my father and two sisters. We kept trudging toward my aunt's town, occasionally getting a short ride on a truck or car. Hearing that the German troops were very close, my mother, some friends and I fled further on foot, travelling day and night through forests and on roads, until we saw a red sky in the distance and heard gunfire and bombing. The Germans were in front of us! Shocked and terrified, we immediately turned around and headed back to Będzin, where we were reunited with my father and sisters.

Germany attacked Poland on the first of September. Two days later, Britain and France declared war on the Third Reich. The two European Allies had promised to defend Poland in the event of a German invasion. But no matter—within weeks, the Polish army was defeated. From Silesia in the south, where we lived, and from Germany and East Prussia in the north, Nazi military units broke through Polish border defenses and marched toward Warsaw, the nation's capital. After suffering a massive encirclement assault, Warsaw surrendered to the Germans on September 28.

In the short time that we were gone from Będzin, the Germans had occupied Będzin and burned down the synagogue and the surrounding old community of Jewish homes. Fortunately for us, our apartment building, which stood outside the Jewish quarter, had not been damaged. The rest of "gentile" Będzin also survived intact.

Hitler immediately annexed most of western Poland in October. That's how Upper Silesia, which encompassed Będzin, Sosnowiec, Katowice, Oświęcim (Auschwitz) and other towns, became incorporated into the German province of Silesia. The northern stretches of Poland, including the Free City of Danzig (Gdańsk, in Polish) along the Baltic coast, became part of the new German province of Danzig-West Prussia. Poznań and part of Łódź, two major industrial cities, were combined into a new province called the Warthegau. By October's end, the remainder of Nazi-occupied Poland was organized into the "Generalgouvernement" of Poland. As if the German invasion was not traumatic enough, the Soviet Union stormed the borders of eastern Poland on September 17 and overtook those communities in accordance with a secret pact between Hitler and Stalin, which had been forged in August. With eastern Poland dominated by the Soviet Red Army and the rest of the country swept under Nazi control, Poland was virtually erased from the map of Europe. Thousands of people including Poldek who had fled to the east found themselves now under Soviet occupation.

CHAPTER 2

Poland Under Nazi Occupation

I n the weeks that followed, the German conquerors imposed a series of restrictions on the entire Jewish population under their authority. They appointed Jewish Councils, called *Judenrat*, in every Jewish community to administer the prohibitive regulations and maintain order. In Będzin we watched as the *Judenrat* shut down Jewish sport clubs, cinemas, theaters, newspapers, libraries, and so forth. Our Jewish youth movements were banned; gatherings of more than six people in public or private settings were prohibited; and Jews everywhere were forced to wear a white armband with a blue Star of David (later replaced by a yellow star).

Jews were forbidden to enter city parks or walk on the main streets. We were no longer allowed to ride the trains or trams. At first we were permitted to stand on the streetcar platform, but soon enough we were robbed of that "privilege" as well. Cars were confiscated from the few families that owned them. Jewish-owned factories and stores were taken over by German commissioners, who forced the former owners to teach them how to operate their businesses.

Będzin's Jewish schools—including three grammar schools, various trade schools, religious schools, and our private co-ed high school—did not open in September of 1939, or ever again. After six years of grammar school and two years of high school, my formal education ended when the war began. I would not be free to complete the remaining four years of my studies. Instead, at 14 years old, I was forced to join the thousands of Jewish children and youth who were left, day in and day out, with nothing to do.

While Jewish boys and girls were being pulled out of the classroom, their parents were being pushed out of the work force. That same autumn, my father lost his job in the brewery. Because our family desperately needed money and food, he got involved in illegal trading, which took him traveling by bus or train to nearby cities. My mother and I stayed at home, cooking, hand-washing laundry and knitting gloves and socks, which we'd sell to relatives and friends for about fifty groszy per pair. Eventually, my father allowed me to join him in his illegal endeavors, because, although the work was terribly dangerous, a father and daughter traveling together would appear less suspect than a man journeying alone.

We would remove our armbands, conceal the smuggled goods beneath our garments, and travel by train or bus to neighboring towns. Before the war began, merchants had stashed away goods such as yarn, linen, socks, and underwear, and now they wanted them delivered and sold in cities and towns outside Będzin. I smuggled linens by wrapping them around my waist under a loose fur coat that belonged to my cousin. Other times, I helped my aunt by delivering meat that she obtained on the black market. One time, my sister Hania and I took a train, unaccompanied by our father, to trade some goods between Będzin and Jędrzejów. We were young and willing to take such risks, because we did not realize the extent to which we were gambling with our lives. Only later did we find out that many young people who smuggled goods had lost their lives. Luckily, my family members and I were never stopped by the authorities, which I attribute to our Aryan looks. I had blond straight hair, blue-green eyes, and a straight nose. I also spoke a beautiful Polish, which set me apart from most of my Jewish friends, who had grown up in families where only Yiddish was spoken at home. Polish was their second language and that detectable difference in the spoken word could expose a Jew who was pretending to be a gentile. I have to admit that I owed my flawless command of Polish to my brother Poldek's demanding language drills.

Despite the new prohibitions, the Zionist Youth group continued to meet in small groups in private apartments with the aim of engaging boys and girls in meaningful social activities. Once a week, a group of half a dozen nine and ten-year-old girls would gather in my parents' apartment, where I'd read to them and teach them songs for an hour or two. We sang softly so as not to draw attention to our gathering. Sometimes we'd shut the lights and sit on the floor around a "campfire" made of twigs and an electric bulb covered with red crepe paper, while I told them stories about the heroic first Jewish settlers in Palestine, known in Hebrew as the *Halutzim*.

After a year or so these meetings came to an abrupt close, because we were forced to share our home with other families, and there was no longer any space for social gatherings. The Nazis had expelled hundreds of Jewish families from Germany and Czechoslovakia, as well as from other cities in Poland, and relocated them to Będzin, where they were forced to live with families like mine. Our two-bedroom apartment became home to a mother and daughter from Czechoslovakia whose husbands had been sent to labor camps in Germany. After they left us, we were ordered to take in a woman with two daughters, also from Germany. And so it went, one broken family after another moved into our home and soon enough moved on. Where did these families go when they left us? We wondered but only learned later that they were sent to slave labor or concentration camps. The largest and closest camp to Będzin was the dreaded Auschwitz-Birkenau, the ultimate symbol of Nazi evil.

The Gestapo regularly ordered Jews to hand over their gold and money, using brutal means of coercion. They beat people up in the streets, cut off men's beards (or the side locks of the religious men), and hung men from trees in public view for everyone to witness until the correct amount of cash was delivered. It was on Zawale Street, where an ancient Jewish cemetery stood, that I first saw men hanging from trees.

To cope with these horrific events, my friends and I sought comfort and strength by banding together and pursuing our favorite cultural activities. For instance, a group that played musical instruments got permission from the Judenrat to give a concert in the Jewish orphanage. I sat in on most of the rehearsals, mainly to listen, but wasn't able to attend the concert because, at the entrance door, I accidentally cut off the tip of my middle finger. It bled profusely and I ran through a main street, on which Jews were prohibited, to the city hospital, which also was off-limits to Jews. Indeed, I was turned away by the nuns, who said they did not treat Jews. Finally I found a Jewish physician, Dr.

Pearl who, though like all Jewish doctors was no longer allowed to practice medicine, kindly treated the wound and dressed my finger in his one-room attic apartment.

That same evening, my father and I took off our armbands and boarded a streetcar to Sosnowiec to visit the surgeon for whom my brother Poldek worked. Dr. Travinski undid the dressing and replaced it with a fresh one. When I asked if the fingertip would grow back, he said, "A lizard's tail grows back, but not a finger." I was sad. My mother sobbed when we returned home that night, because she had worried that we had been caught.

Not long after my accident, the *Judenrat* banned all concerts and some of the young musicians were deported to labor camps—or so we were told. Every so often, young people were arrested in the middle of the night and sent away to unknown destinations, never to be heard from again. The rest of us held fast to one another, seeking comfort in our friendships, trying hard to believe that the world was not caving in on us. Once the Nazis forced us into ghettos, however, there was no escaping the overwhelming isolation and doom.

CHAPTER 3

The Będzin Ghetto

I n the spring of 1941, the building in which we lived on Kołątaja Street was to be converted into an army uniform factory called the Rosner Shop. All tenants were ordered to leave our apartments and move to the outskirts of Będzin, where a Jewish ghetto called Kamionka (and later called Środula Dolna) was later established. My family was given a small house with one main room, a tiny kitchen and an outhouse. My parents and I slept in the room. A young couple that we did not know was to sleep in the kitchen.

The Będzin ghetto lasted a little more than two years. The ghetto was liquidated in August 1943 and its inhabitants were transported to Auschwitz. A group of 150 Jewish men, guarded by the SS, were assigned to gather and ship our possessions—silver, furniture, sewing machines, clothing—to Germany. They burned our books, documents, photographs, and all else that remained. Later on, this group was sent to Auschwitz as well.

As early as mid-August of 1942, about one year after we had been forced into the ghetto, the first mass deportations of our community began. The entire ghetto population, including the young, the elderly, and the bedridden, as well as families who still lived on designated streets of the city, were ordered to assemble at the sports stadium on Kościuszko Street at six o'clock in the morning. Those who could not make it on their own were dragged to the stadium by the militia and the police. Every house, apartment, basement and attic was thoroughly searched. Around 30,000 people gathered in the stadium and waited for what was to come next.

At the time, my brother Poldek, was somewhere in Russia or Asia. Later he was fighting with a heroic Polish army under British command, called Anders Army. My oldest sister, Helen, was terribly ill from typhoid fever. She lay half-conscious and delirious with lockjaw and twelve large boils on her back. Nothing could be done for her. There were no medications. On the day of the selection, her husband left her lying unconscious in bed, because he couldn't carry her to the stadium. A heavy curtain concealed the door to her room, and miraculously, she remained untouched and alive when he returned.

At the stadium, we stood in a long line that moved towards a German officer cracking a leather whip and ordering people to assemble in different areas. One section of the stadium filled with children and older people, another with young, healthy-looking men and women, and a third with people of all ages. The first group was to be sent for extermination. The second group was assigned to work in labor camps, and the last group was supposed to remain in the ghetto. When my parents and I approached the selection officer, he motioned, "Old ones to the right, girl to the left." As I took a few steps to the left I heard my mother crying and I turned around to go toward my parents. I never reached them. I was beaten and dragged back to the left side. The man with the whip had decided our destiny.

The traumatic scene was ruled over by police bearing whips and guns. In the late afternoon, they allowed the people in my line to return to our homes. At midnight, with the streetlights on, we watched the loved ones being herded like cattle towards the orphanage, where another selection process was to take place and transports prepared for Auschwitz. We knew people were being sent to their deaths, because we had already heard horrifying reports about the extermination camps at Auschwitz-Birkenau, approximately forty-five miles from Będzin.

My parents were trapped in the selection process. I stood paralyzed, separated from them and surrounded by cries of grief. I spotted my mother. That day was the worst experience of my life, the first really deep wound I ever suffered. In time, more ghastly things would happen to me, but I hardened with experience and built a shield around my heart.

I was spared prolonged suffering. Probably because the Germans were not yet prepared to send so many thousands of people to be mass murdered in such a short amount of time, some people were released the next day and sent home. Among them were my mother and father. I don't know how many thousands were sent to Auschwitz that week, but very few of the elderly or the mothers with small children came back.

Soon after this round of deportations, my Aunt Regina, my mother's younger sister, arrived at our place with five of her six children (four boys, ages four to ten, and a two-year-old girl). Her husband and oldest son, age 15, had been sent to German labor camps, along with other able-bodied men. Regina and the other children were quickly driven out of their little town of Jaworzno. Given no time to pack, they arrived at our doorstep empty-handed, with not one suitcase. Jaworzno was being "cleansed" of Jews, and the survivors like my Aunt and her children were "relocated" to Będzin. Because of its close location to Auschwitz, our region was used as a way station.

Not long after her arrival, Aunt Regina was deported to Auschwitz along with hundreds of others. Her four young sons (Majloch, Zelik, Izek, and Jakob) managed to run away and come back to us. Two-year-old Pauline stayed with us too; she slept with me on the sofa or in my parents' bed. The boys slept on rugs on the cement floor in the entryway. We lived together in our cramped quarters with hardly any food, satisfied to eat a little watery soup that my mother would make.

The Będzin ghetto consisted of long rows of small houses, with one or two rooms each, without any bathroom facilities. Though the ghetto wasn't fenced in with barbed wire, as many others were, armed police and guard dogs patrolled the space day and night. Their vigilance ensured that Gentiles did not enter or send supplies into the ghetto and prevented Jews from leaving unless one was part of a convoy of laborers walking to and from work. Any other activity that took a Jew out of the ghetto was forbidden under penalty of death.

Most of the previous owners of the houses that made up the ghetto were relocated to furnished apartments in Będzin that had been vacated by Jewish families. At the army uniform factory, in our former apartment building, thousands of Jews were put to work. Labor prolonged one's survival, if only for a short time, because laborers were given food rations as well as identification papers, which stated that they were still needed in the service of the Third Reich.

The Polish owners of the house we now lived in had been given an apartment on Środula Street, which divided the ghetto from the rest of the city. Lotti, who had worked as a live-in maid for my parents before the war, moved into this same building on Środula Street. One day I left the ghetto illegally and went to plead with both Lotti and the former owners of the home we now occupied to take in my two-year-old cousin Pauline, an innocent and beautiful toddler. With her blue eyes and blond hair, she looked like a typical Aryan child. I begged them to help her. Instead, I was ordered to get out of their homes and never come back.

Life went on. Most of us were forced to work in factories set up by the Germans, making shoes and sewing uniforms, shirts and other clothing for the German army. We were marched under guard to work in the mornings and marched back at night. But we never knew if we'd live through the night because that's when the Germans would barge into homes to make random arrests and send people away to unknown destinations. No reasons for the arrests were ever given. No charges were made. These veritable kidnappings were part of the Nazi terror campaign. Nobody knew when his or her turn would come. After a while, many of us thought about bunkers where we could hide and postpone the "end."

Broken families, broken hearts, hunger and sickness. I came down with paratyphoid fever, an even worse case than my sister Helen had survived. I was 17 years old and felt that surely I was going to die. "At least I'll die in my own bed," I remember thinking at the time. I also recall that although I was semiconscious, I recited poems from Greek mythology that I had learned in school. Fortunately, a makeshift hospital had been established in the ghetto, and the staff was able to take care of me. Because I was bleeding internally, I needed a transfusion, but there were no blood banks, of course, or equipment or intravenous solutions. My friends from the youth movement offered to donate blood for me, but in the end my sister Helen became the donor. They put her arm next to mine and did a direct transfusion, cutting into us to find the veins. This saved my life, though I had lost 30 pounds and was too weak to walk. Friends and family brought me whatever food they could find to build up my strength. Gradually, I recovered and my parents rejoiced to have their "little girl" back again.

A few months before I fell sick, the *Judenrat* had gotten permission from the German authorities to cultivate several acres of fields that had not been used for many years. The idea was to plant vegetable plots with potatoes, beans, groats, and so forth and use the harvest in a soup kitchen, where we'd feed people and allay the starvation.

My friends from the Zionist youth group volunteered to help, although we knew absolutely nothing about farming. Under the supervision of one Mr. Strochlic, a graduate of an agriculture school, we tilled the soil with spades, rakes and our bare hands. We awoke before sunrise to plant and water seedlings. Our garden grew plentiful with carrots, parsley roots, radishes, cucumbers and tomatoes. Watching the plants grow and harvesting them filled our hearts with hope. We used natural fertilizer like horse and cow manure and also excrement from the outhouses and the ghetto. We "golden youth"—former high school students and graduates—mixed soil and fertilizer by hand (we had no gloves). The wind blew it all over our legs and the smell was putrid, but the garden kept growing. At the time, nothing seemed too difficult or impossible for us. We were young, still together, and still singing and joking in spite of everything. We slept in separate barracks for girls and boys.

One sunny morning we were tending to the potato plants, when I heard someone whistling beautiful clear notes from a field on the other side of the road. Recognizing several familiar melodies, mainly classical music, I joined in. Now there were two strong and clear whistles, mine and, as I soon found out, Janek's. He was a youth group instructor, about four years my senior, and all the older girls had a crush on him. It felt like our whistling was drawing us together. I suddenly felt so alive and happy to be working in the green fields on a glorious summer day that I could almost forget reality. It was like a breath of freedom. Janek and I went on and on, whistling one melody and then another, until a clanging bell signaled the time to leave the fields. Still whistling, Janek came from his field and I from mine, and together we walked slowly towards our barracks. Janek jumped into a little creek on the side of the road and picked a handful of forget-me-nots for me. We talked and held hands. We were falling in love. Four years older than me, Janek had graduated from high school in 1939 and had been preparing to immigrate to Palestine, where his older brother lived on a kibbutz, but the war put an abrupt stop to his plans. Now, two summers later, against a backdrop of terror, we spent long evenings together, sharing our love, worries and frustrations. But we were unable to plan for the future because we knew there would be no future for us.

The recognition of the depth and breadth of our hopeless situation marked a turning point, not only for me, Janek and our other friends in the Będzin ghetto, but apparently, in many ghettos. It became the pivotal moment when—after many of our family members and friends had been killed, after we were thoroughly isolated, after all hope had disappeared and there was nothing left but desperation and determination to save a few individual lives—acts of resistance rippled throughout the ghettos, Będzin among them.

CHAPTER 4

Resistance

Y es, Jews resisted, futile as we knew our efforts were. But no matter, we had to fight to stay human. According to the history books, underground resistance efforts spread in an estimated 100 ghettos in Eastern Europe, including Poland, Lithuania, the Ukraine and Belorussia. The goals were similar—to organize uprisings, break out of the ghettos, and procure weapons in order to be able to join non-Jewish partisan units. We never considered that we could seriously undermine the enemy. Rather, we sought to save as many lives as was possible and to connect with armed resistance fighters who were hiding in the forests and mountains.

The meetings of our youth group evolved quite naturally and logically into discussions about resistance activities. I assume that most resistance groups developed similarly to ours based on the realizations that we needed to defend what was left of our communities, and at this point, there'd be little to lose. Our youth group leaders made contact with young people in neighboring Sosnowiec. Our ghettos were called Lower and Upper Środula respectively. The two ghettos were divided by green fields, which some of us dared to cross so that we could sustain communication with one another.

Although I was not clever enough to make a plan myself, I was ready and willing to do everything I was asked to do for the cause. Our group's strategists focused on the changed political geography under Nazi occupation. Western Poland, where we lived, had been incorporated into the Third Reich, while the central part of the country was run as an occupied area called by the Germans Generalgouvernement. We had heard that Poles were being sent to labor camps there to work and not to be killed. We determined to find a way to send some of our girls, who did not look Jewish, to work in those camps in order to save their lives. That idea turned into a daring plan.

First, contacts had to be made inside the Generalgouvernement. Lola Pomerancenblum and I were assigned to cross the border of the Upper Środula ghetto, walk to the train station in nearby Sosnowiec, and board a train for Trzebinia, the city closest to the Generalgouvernement. It would take us another two to three hours to walk through the village of Krzemionka, cross some fields and get in touch with our contact, a man who lived very close to the central border and smuggled food and alcohol to the other side at night. If he agreed to take three girls with him to the other side, we were to give him money and linen, which could not be found in any stores. The girls were Danusia Furstenberg, Mira Tencer, and the third one's name I can't remember.

To make this treacherous trip, we needed false Polish identity papers, which were called *palcówki* ("fingers") because they contained one's fingerprints as well as one's name, address, age and nationality. The instructors in our group used chemicals to erase the ink on these documents and then inserted our new Polish names and addresses. Mine was Janina Baran, and I lived on Wiejska Street in Sosnowiec, but some traces of my real name remained visible on my *palcówka*, which gave me new reason to be fearful.

On the morning that Lola and I prepared to leave, we crossed out of the Środula ghetto and hid our yellow "Jude" patches under some stones. This patch was supposed to be sewn onto our clothes, not pinned as was ours for easy removal; the penalty for pinning it was death. Suddenly, we saw a young German policeman with a dog approaching us. "What are you doing here, dirty Jews?" he shouted. "To the police station!" he pushed us with his rifle. We thought for sure we were going to be killed.

I tried to tell him in broken German that we were not Jewish, that we were visiting our family who lived in the village on the other side of the ghetto, and that we were guilty only of taking a shortcut through the ghetto to catch a train to Trzebinia. I begged him to have mercy on us. He examined our bags. We each had packed a nightgown, toothpaste and toothbrush, soap, two sheets and two pillowcases. He inspected our pockets. He ordered me to unbutton my jacket to check further. A yellow patch with the Star of David was pinned to my blouse. I had completely forgotten about it. At first I froze but then I started laughing hysterically, telling him that my cousin had advised me to pin it on, so that if someone stopped me in the ghetto I could pretend to be Jewish, because the penalty for a Pole to be inside the ghetto was death. Maybe the policeman believed me, I'm still not sure. He turned to Lola, pushed her with his rifle, and shouted that she was Jewish. I laughed again and said that I was not so stupid as to have a Jewish friend. We went to the same church, I insisted—he could ask the priest. "We will see," he said, "at the police station." The situation seemed hopeless.

At the station, police officers took our documents and interrogated us, demanding to know where we lived, our names, age, and such. One of the policemen said I looked familiar to him and that he had seen me before (Great!). He looked up the address on my document and said that I lived in his district. I didn't even know where the street was located in Sosnowiec. Then he stated, "A 15-mark fine for each of you, and now get lost!" We paid, and when we started walking down the dark, narrow staircase I whispered to Lola, "Now they will shoot us in the back." I could see our bodies rolling down the stairs. We made it out of there and walked to the train station to continue on our mission. Once accomplished, we returned safely to the ghetto. I even brought back two pounds of flour for my mother, which I had bought from the smuggler.

Lola and I decided not to tell anyone about our awful escapade because nobody would have believed us. It seemed impossible even to me that we had eluded the Gestapo, especially knowing that people were regularly executed for petty incidents or for no reason at all. One can ask, if it was so easy to get away with exploits such as ours, why did six million Jews perish? But what happened to me then, and later, was truly inexplicable and probably happened to only one person in a million.

On another mission, I was asked to take a train to the German city of Gleiwitz near Katowice and walk through the first five residential streets beyond the train station. My assignment was to drop about twenty letters addressed to German families into five public mailboxes. The letters were meant for Germans whose sons had been killed in the war. I hadn't read the letters and didn't know their exact contents, but I delivered them and returned safely, having mapped the mailboxes' locations so that future deliveries would be easier to make. For this assignment I posed as a Deutsche Bund girl and wore a swastika on my arm; my yellow patch was again hidden under a rock near the ghetto.

My next assignment was to help two friends steal weapons from the apartment of a German man who we knew was a hunter. This Mr. Braun was a manager of one of the confiscated factories where Jews were forced to work. I was to ring the doorbell at his house and verify with the maid through the intercom that he and his wife were out of town. I was then to meet Harry Blumenfrucht and Kuba Rosenberg in a nearby building on the corner of Saczewska and Kołątaja Streets, let them know if it was safe to proceed, and wait there for them to bring me a briefcase with the weapons, which I was to take back into the ghetto.

Waiting inside one of the building's two main doorways (one on each street), I was approached by my two friends, Harry and Kuba, who were dressed like Gestapo with Gestapo pins in their lapels and swastikas on their arms. They handed me the briefcase, I walked through the building, out the other main door, and through the *Judenrein* city back to my friend Pola's house in the ghetto. I can still see my friends' happy faces when they saw me, especially Pola's; her beautiful eyes were swollen from crying as she hugged me. Her parents and little brother had been captured the night before in one of the round-ups, put on a train and sent to their death. She was 18 years old and all alone in the world. Even her boyfriend was gone, and, three months later, she would be gone, too.

There were six guns and one watch in the briefcase. The boys had taken the watch so it would look like a robbery, and, indeed, the next day, the newspaper reported that two "robbers" had tied the maid to a chair and stuffed her mouth so she would not scream. I don't remember ever touching the guns. They probably moved them quickly out of Pola's apartment, and I must have run home to be with my parents. They worried non-stop about me whenever I went off on a mission. None of us knew how to use a gun, but since we had hopes of joining the Polish partisans, we knew we'd need to come in with weapons.

Most Jewish armed resistance took place in 1942 and 1943. Everywhere, it was a desperate response, as was ours. We lacked training and arms; we operated in hostile environs; and since most Jews did not look Aryan, my co-religionists were vulnerable to exposure. Germans rewarded Poles with food supplies for turning in Jews. One live Jew was worth one kilogram of sugar.

General resistance efforts by Poles, which began in the same time period as the Jewish resistance, faced relatively favorable conditions. For example, the local populations were sympathetic and did not turn them in to the Germans. In addition, they were not segregated behind ghetto walls and could more easily make connections and obtain armaments. That's why, for us, joining their fighting units became our last hope for survival. But to do so, we knew we'd need to acquire weapons.

My group was emboldened by our successful arms procurement mission. Our next assignment, however, did not turn out smoothly. The manager of another army clothing factory, Mr. Michatz, lived a little ways from the city. To get to his house from the ghetto, one had to walk illegally down the longest street in the city through the fields behind our former high school, across the bridge of the Przemsza River and still farther. The fields, once full of happy children picking flowers, making wreaths, bathing in the river with friends and family, looked empty and strange to me now.

This time, Harry, Kuba, and Olek Gutman were the heroes sent to steal the weapons. They knew when Mr. Michatz would be in the factory. My assignment was to wait in the fields in a designated place, receive the loot and take it back to the ghetto. After waiting a long time, I finally went back to the ghetto worried and empty-handed. Kuba and Olek came back separately, but Harry had been caught on the way back. He was arrested and, we heard, physically tortured for weeks. The Germans tried to force him to reveal the identities of his partners, but his lips remained sealed through all the beatings. Harry finally died hanging from a tree.

It turned out that Mrs. Michatz, whom we had not expected to be at home, ran out of the house screaming and scared away my friends. She told the police that she had seen three men. Thus, we hurried to find hiding places for Kuba and Olek—aware that Harry might talk under torture. In addition, we sought hideouts for their mothers, knowing that if their sons' identities were to be revealed, they, as next of kin, would be held responsible and punished in their stead. Neither Kuba nor Olek looked Jewish, and we hoped that with false papers identifying them as Poles, they and their mothers would pass as

Christians. And they did. Kuba and his mother rented a summer cottage in the village of Zwardon in the West Beskid Mountains. Olek and his mother also stayed high in the mountains, each in a separate cottage, pretending to be strangers.

Life in the ghetto was turning for the worse. By the time of our weapons thefts, the transports to Auschwitz were increasing. The Gestapo continued to take people from their homes at night, from work, and from the streets. No place was safe. We wanted to resist or at least not go meekly to the crematoria. Even committing suicide was preferable. We met illegally with older friends who said they would try to connect us with the Polish partisans camped clandestinely in the surrounding forests and mountains. But as we already knew, the Polish fighters would speak to us only if we had weapons.

Our next-door neighbors had prepared a bunker that was accessed by crawling through a kitchen cabinet. It could hold eight people but only for a short time. It reminded me of a small cellar, with no light or food, and very little air to breathe. Once, when we heard that the Germans were rounding up people to be sent away, our neighbors allowed me and my parents to hide in their bunker. There was no room for the three boys and Pauline, but after I pleaded and begged, they allowed me to take Pauline in. I had to cover her mouth every time she whispered, "Are the Germans going to kill us?" They must have heard her, because they spent a long time in the kitchen trying to determine where the noise was coming from. We were terrified. Fortunately for us, they didn't yet know about this type of hiding place and therefore didn't find us. Eventually they uncovered the bunkers and were able to find almost everyone.

We heard people screaming, crying, and running outside our hiding place, and it seemed that the end of everything had come. But it hadn't, and much worse was still ahead. When things quieted down, we crawled out and went back to our house. There was blood everywhere—on the floor, bed, doors, and walls. We had made a hiding place for the boys in the attic and told them not to move until the raid was over, but there was no sign of them, and we never saw them again. Then we learned that my middle sister, Hania, her husband, Otto, and son, Peter, were also missing from their home. As usual, everyone who had been captured was taken to the orphanage and from there, most were transported to

Auschwitz or to labor camps. A few came back home, including my sister Hania and her family, who returned the next day, but they did not stay for long.

In July of 1943 I was sent to rent some cottages in the Beskid Mountains. I traveled on the train with two friends from the ghetto, Arieh and Szmulik, both of whom had very Semitic features. We pretended not to know each other. I hid in the train's bathroom while the police checked identification documents. Afterward, I was surprised and relieved to see the two young men sitting unharmed in their compartment. They had passed inspection. I delivered them to the village of Węgierska Górka according to plan and continued on alone to Jelesnia to contact our group's leaders, Lola and Samek, who were now married. They gave me further instructions to locate the others, who were hiding in various places. Some were in shepherds' huts in the mountains, and others were in the villages. This was the last time I saw Lola and Samek. They were later turned over to the Germans by Polish peasants.

I climbed the mountains for hours and found Olek's place first. He had explained to his landlords that I was his fiancée and that we were planning our wedding. That way I was able to spend a night with a roof over my head and eat a meal. The cottage had two rooms. The landlords and their daughter with her boyfriend slept in two beds in one room, where the stove stood, and Olek and I slept in the other room in one bed, careful not to touch each other. This was important to us because we were still young and totally innocent. Later, after the war, Olek told me how hard it had been for him that night because he thought he was in love with me. For the peasants, sleeping together was customary. Their daughter slept with her boyfriend, and we did not want to behave differently. Since the doors between the rooms remained open for the night, neither of us could sleep on the floor. In our room, pictures of Christ and Mary and a cross hung on the walls. We made sure to kneel and say Christian prayers out loud before retiring.

The next day, I went on to see Olek's mother and two girls from the Środula ghetto outside Sosnowiec. I had not previously met these people, and I can't remember the content of the messages I delivered to them.

When I returned to Będzin, I stopped on the Aryan side of the ghetto to look for my yellow "Jude" patch under its rock. I felt an unusual stillness in the air; the ghetto was very quiet. From the Aryan side, I heard someone call "Panno

Jadziu!" (Miss Jadzia). The former owner of the house where we lived in the ghetto stood nearby watering her cabbage patch. She warned me not to enter the ghetto, saying there had been another series of round-ups and deportations. Begun the previous Saturday, the "actions," as people called them, lasted several days. Everyone had been sent on freight trains to Auschwitz. "The screaming and lamenting was terrible," she said. Now, soldiers with machine guns stood positioned on rooftops, waiting to catch whomever had survived, ready to kill the few Jews who might crawl out from their hiding places. "Go away immediately and don't come back," she urged. I was so choked up I could only gasp, "My mom and dad, too?"

I remember my father would constantly plead with me to put an end to my resistance activities. I used to disappear for days at a time, and when I'd return, he'd say, "Have mercy! Don't endanger the whole family!" But I couldn't stop my work because I sensed that, sooner or later, we would all be sent to the crematoria. I wanted to help rescue as many lives as possible. If only a few people could be saved, at least they could tell the world what had happened to us.

Both of my parents, my two sisters and their families, and Pauline, were sent to Auschwitz on August 3, 1943. It was only after the war's end that I learned my parents were cremated there. By some miracle, Hania and Helen survived. Their husbands and 12-year-old Peter, the son of Hania's husband from his first marriage, were killed by the Germans in Auschwitz. Peter's mother, a Polish woman, had died giving birth to him.

I headed to the old train station, mustering all my strength to wear a calm expression on my "Aryan" face to cover the terrible pain burning inside and breaking my heart. I took a train to Zwardon, the village where Kuba, now called Józek, and his mother were hiding. After I reported the news, Józek pointed out that people who had escaped the round-ups might come to the mountains to hide. If they did, they'd likely be recognized by their frightened and Semitic appearances. They would certainly not look like vacationers. Many Poles hated Jews and would be happy to hand them over to the Germans. Although nobody suspected that Józek and his mother were Jewish (he was even dating a Polish girl who wanted to marry him), the dangers had now escalated for everyone. It became crucial to find safe hiding places for the newest fugitives as well as for ourselves.

Józek conjured up a bold plan to get us out of Poland. He recalled that a young woman in the ghetto had once told him that her brother, a dentist, lived in Slovakia. The dentist, Dr. Friedler, lived on Hlinkova Street in Prešov, a city far from the mountainous Slovak-Polish border and close to the Hungarian border. I was chosen to journey to Slovakia, contact this man and find out if it would be safe for us to hide in Prešov or in other Slovak towns. I did not think that this escapade would succeed. But at this point, with nearly all my family and friends dead, I was totally indifferent about everything and did not care whether I lived or died.

Frank, the son of Józek's landlord, was a smuggler. One night a week, he would climb the mountain, cross the border to Slovakia and head to a Slovakian village to trade sugar, alcohol, and cigarettes. Frank agreed to take me across the border on a Saturday night. I knew that he was paid for his help though I didn't know where the money had come from. I, too, was given a little money to cover the cost of my assignment. For the most part, I slept in the fields and mountains and fed myself berries or stolen vegetables. Sometimes I didn't eat for days.

On a Saturday evening, Frank, a friend of his and I began our ascent to the border, which ran across the mountaintops, when we heard dogs and a patrol approaching us. We lay motionless under the trees. When it became quiet again, we moved on. Before dawn, we reached the Slovakian house where the trading took place. The Slovak peasants spoke Polish, and one of them was supposed to take me to the train station in the morning and help me buy a ticket to Prešov.

That same morning, Frank and his friend left to return to Poland. I rested in the hayloft of a barn where the Slovak, who was supposed to help me, entered and tried to take advantage of me. I fought him off and was able to bargain my way out by handing over a little gold bracelet that my parents had given me. On the way to the train station, which was supposed to be a three-hour walk, he insisted on taking my gold ring with a small diamond chip—the last object in my possession that had belonged to my parents. When I refused, he gave me the Slovakian money that Frank had provided for the train ticket and abandoned me in the middle of nowhere.

It was a sunny Sunday morning. The mountain landscape was green and peaceful. A stream ran on my left, an occasional horse and buggy passed by on the dirt road, as did several people on their way to church. They were dressed in peasant clothes and carried their shoes in their hands. After walking along this road for more than an hour, I took a chance and asked a woman in Polish, using hand gestures, how much further it was to the train station in the village of Oszczadnica. I was able to understand much of what she said, since both Polish and Slovakian are Slavic languages. Finally, I saw the small station on the other side of the river, but there was not a bridge in sight. After a while, a man in a small boat paddled over and took me across. The station had a ticket window where I asked for a *listek* to Prešov, using the word I read above the window.

Inside the train car with me, a peasant woman pulled out a loaf of white bread and a big chunk of smoked bacon, and she and her husband proceeded to eat their breakfast. I had not seen bread like this in four years and for the last few weeks had eaten only what I could find in the fields. My stomach was growling from hunger, but when the man offered me some of their food, I refused because I was loath to start a conversation.

In the city of Žilina, I was supposed to have a two-hour wait and change trains. I went outside and walked around, thinking it would be safer than sitting in the station. It was a sunny day. People were well dressed, the men mostly in uniform (not German) and looking handsome. Fresh cut flowers were sold on street corners. Fruit stands displayed beautiful plums and bananas. It looked like the world I had known before the war. I couldn't resist and bought six plums with the rest of my money. I ate them all at once and, on the train to Prešov, spent most of the time being sick in the bathroom.

CHAPTER 5

Slovakia

When I arrived in Prešov in the late afternoon, it was easy to find Hlinkova Street, which turned out to be the main boulevard. Many people were strolling along its wide sidewalks—couples, families with dogs, babies in their buggies. Everyone looked friendly and pleasant. Some people had Semitic features—dark eyes, dark hair, long noses, in contrast to the blond, blue-eyed, button-nosed Poles and Germans to whom I'd been accustomed. I wondered whether some of them were Jewish. Later on I found out that Prešov was located close to the Hungarian border, and many Hungarians lived there. It once belonged to the Austro-Hungarian Empire, then to Hungary; later it became part of Czechoslovakia, and then Slovakia. The few Jews who were left in Prešov were restricted to certain streets. I was probably the only Jew walking on Hlinkova Street that Sunday afternoon, although the offices of several Jewish doctors and dentists remained intact.

I found the building I was looking for. On two of the nameplates in the long entryway were the names of Dr. Friedler and Dr. Ilonka Meyer, each marked with a Star of David and the word "Žid" ("Jew"). There was no answer at Dr. Friedler's office door, but when I rang the bell of Dr. Meyer's apartment, an elderly woman cracked the door open and peered out. She was Ilonka's mother and speaking in German, she gave me Dr. Friedler's home address and directions to get there. The doctor was not at home. It was growing dark and, tired and hungry, I sat down on the steps of the staircase and fell asleep.

The sound of footsteps on the stairs awoke me. Dr. Friedler and his wife stood before me and listened as I introduced myself as having come from his sister's town in Poland. They invited me into their home, and I told them about the last deportation that had removed close to 30,000 people from the ghetto. If their sister was still alive and in hiding, I explained, she would probably seek out my band of friends in the mountains. I described my reason for coming to Prešov and asked them to help me send a letter back to my friends to let them know that I had made it, and that a route could be established by which the doctor's sister and others could be sent to Slovakia. The Friedlers gave me food and let me wash up and sleep on a blanket on the kitchen floor.

The next morning they introduced me to Dr. Ilonka Meyer and seemed relieved to leave me with her. Ilonka was middle-aged, had red hair, thick eyeglasses and a warm, sincere smile. She took me to a Christian woman's house and arranged a room for me in a clean garden apartment. I took a bath—the first one in ages. Food was brought in on a tray, and soon I felt like a human being again.

Ilonka described how Czechoslovakia had been dismembered by the Germans in 1938-1939, with the Sudetenland region annexed to Germany, Bohemia and Moravia run as a Protectorate, and Slovakia run by an ultra-nationalist Slovak government that was beholden to Germany. In 1942, 75 percent of the Jewish population had been deported from Prešov to Auschwitz and other death camps. Those remaining lived in a designated part of the city; their businesses had been taken away or were controlled by the Slovak government. Though it was a struggle to stay afloat under these circumstances, they were fortunate to have survived the deportations with limited freedoms intact in a city that still had a standing synagogue and a functioning Jewish Council.

Ilonka also told me about a group of Slovakian Jews who had organized an illegal route in order to receive refugees fleeing from the German General-gouvernement in Poland. These Polish Jews would be transported across the Slovakian border to Hungary and sent to camps for Polish refugees that were under the supervision of the International Red Cross. But Ilonka had not heard of anyone coming from the part of Poland that was annexed to the Reich. I was the first.

At the office of the Jewish Council, located close to the synagogue, I was introduced to five well-dressed, middle-aged men who listened to me describe the small group of young Polish Jews who were hiding in the mountains in fear of being caught. The possibility existed, I told the Jewish Council, that others who had escaped the recent deportations might also be in hiding. I asked them to help me contact my friends and let them know it was safe to come to Prešov.

Their first question was: Did my friends have money to pay their way? My heart sank. I doubted that anyone had money. They described the great risk involved in organizing a route and did not think it would be possible to do so. Instead, they promised to send me to Hungary with the next transport (on the existing route) and thus save my life. Tears welled in my eyes as I thanked them and explained that I had not come to save my life, but to try to save many lives. I asked them to help me return and share my fate with my friends in Poland. I also asked for a gun to be able to end my life in case I got caught.

To my surprise, one of the men interrupted to say that the situation might not be totally hopeless. This fellow, Imrich Schwartz, pledged to do everything in his power to help the brave young heroes trapped in Poland. He stressed that it would take time to find a way to contact my friends and that I'd need to wait patiently in Prešov. The same day I sent a letter with this encouraging news to Józek via Frank the smuggler. Later, I learned that either the letter never arrived, or it never reached Józek.

Several weeks passed before Imrich, or Izi for short, presented me with a false document. My name was now Maria Zivczakova and, accompanied by a Slovak police detective who had been bribed, I took a train back to the little village on the Polish-Slovakian border that I had passed on my way in. I had written a postcard which was supposed to be smuggled to the other side and delivered to my friends. It said something like this: "It is a paradise here! Come and send the old and the children, too. The road to Hungary is open." I was hoping, against all odds, that my parents and little Pauline might still be alive.

I befriended several wonderful families in Prešov who, through the Zionist movement, welcomed and aided whoever, like me, had crossed the border to the city of Žilina (where I had waited to change trains). I found out later that my friend Olek, his sister Tusia, Józek, and a few others were the first to arrive in Žilina. After a short time, they were sent to Hungary. Olek's mother, Mrs.

Gutman, Ruth Landau, Fredka Oxenhandler, Leon Blatt and his parents, the Fishers, their daughter, her husband and 8-year-old son Jurek, and others eventually came to Prešov. Jewish families in Prešov volunteered to take them in and give them food and shelter before they continued on to Hungary. I continued to hope that someone from my own family would also come, but no one did.

All the people I knew who traveled this route survived the war. Their actual number was very small, perhaps around fifty from our part of Poland and a few hundred from the central region. Izi Schwartz was responsible for organizing the entire transport. This brave man took tremendous risks. Police and other authorities had to be bribed. Guides had to be found to accompany Jews through the forests at night to the Hungarian border. Izi hired three young Jewish men and several non-Jewish Slovak men to serve as travel guides. They were paid well in money and jewelry for their services. The night crew of the train was bribed, so that some of the refugees who either could afford to pay or were too weak or too old to walk all night could go by train. Only three to five people went at one time.

During this period, I lived at Izi's apartment. Sometimes the smugglers and policemen would come there to be wined and dined. It was my job to prepare the food and clean up afterwards. I can remember that for an appetizer each person got a whole can of sardines! I had not seen or eaten sardines for four years. I learned the Slovak language quickly. Izi and I became fond of each other and a close relationship developed between us. I was 19 years old and Izi was in his early forties. He took care of me and I admired his courage and the work he did. I was very grateful to him for helping me save the lives of my friends, and I was ready to leave with them for Hungary. But Izi did not want me to go and made it impossible for me to leave by threatening that the group would not make it across the border if I went with them.

I felt I owed Izi a lot and that's why I stayed with him. He wanted to marry me. I heard that he had an eight-year-old daughter and an Aryan wife somewhere in Hungary, but he claimed they were not married. Because I lived illegally in Prešov on false documents, we could not get married through the official channels. Instead, in early 1944, a religious wedding took place with a rabbi officiating and a small circle of Izi's friends as witnesses. I don't remember feeling happy or excited; to the contrary, I felt detached, as if the ceremony was happening to someone else. And in a way, it was, for I was still Maria Zivczakova, according to my fake documents.

In the spring of 1944 news came that Germany would tighten its grip on Hungary and Slovakia, Jewish families began to panic, knowing that this might mean the end. One day, Izi told me to pack a knapsack and be ready to leave with him and others who were going into hiding. We traveled part of the way by horse and cart to Stara Lubovnia, and then we climbed by foot high up into the mountains to a small shepherd's hut. On the way, we passed a mineral bath resort that had no visitors at this time. We also passed a Hitler youth camp for boys. Through the chicken wire fence I could see teenage boys playing sports. To my amazement I recognized one of the boys at play. He was the son of Mr. Mann, one of the men traveling in our group, who had arranged for his Aryan-looking son, to attend the camp.

It was the end of summer, and the sheep and cattle were already back down on the farms in the villages. The beauty of the landscape was incredible. Blue skies, chains of mountaintops with pine forests down their sides, green meadows, and perfect weather. It was hard to believe the horrors that were taking place below.

There were ten of us: Izi and myself, Mr. Mann, five young men (three of whom were the smugglers), and two young women. Izi had sent food supplies in advance, including flour, sugar, rice, beans, onions, and potatoes. We knew the eastern front was approaching, and we hoped we would be able to remain in the mountains until the Russians took over. It was there, in early September, that I would unknowingly conceive a child.

One morning, only a few days after our arrival, I saw something moving on a mountain ridge across from us. I called Izi and through his binoculars we saw three men on horseback. Assuming the worst, we guessed we were being watched by Germans who were planning to capture us. Our entire group quickly left the hut to hide. I hid in a tree for what seemed like hours until a loud voice called out, "Come back, we are Russians! Don't be afraid." One by one, we slowly approached the three Russian soldiers, who seemed friendly. Knowing Polish and Slovakian, it was not hard to understand their Russian. We felt hopeful until I noticed an inscription on one soldier's belt buckle that read *Gott mit uns* ("God with us" in German). They left, promising to be back, and I worried that they were really fighting on the German side. At this point, none of us trusted them. We suspected a trap, but we didn't know what to do.

The next morning, close to 100 Russian partisans—the scouts of the Red Army—arrived. They started a fire on the kitchen stove and cooked a meal for everyone, using up the provisions we had offered to them. Some of them were so hungry that they ate raw potatoes and onions. That night they raided a farm and brought back 300 sheep and the next day cooked a stew for everyone. They were young and cheerful, played harmonicas and sang Russian songs, and we felt much safer.

A handsome, young officer named Alexander, who spoke both Polish and German, was particularly friendly and sympathetic. He showed great interest in our personal histories—what had happened to our families during the occupation, how we had survived, and how we had helped others to survive. He documented everything we said on paper. He also asked Izi for the names of his police contacts, of the good people who had helped, of the officials who were bad, and so on. We were glad to be able to tell him our stories.

After a few days, the Russians told us they had to move forward and that we could travel with them to be safe. Eight of us decided to go. Taking all of our provisions and the sheep, we started on what became a two-week journey into the Tatra Mountains, a mountain range on the border of Slovakia and Poland. The major part and all the highest peaks of the mountains are situated in Slovakia. Many of the soldiers rode horses and they offered to carry me, but the slopes were steep and covered with branches, and I had never ridden a horse before. So I walked. All day long the soldiers cursed in their obscure vocabulary. The sheep dragged along behind us, getting thinner every day. There were also fewer and fewer of them because they were cooked for our meals. Once a day everyone ate a bowl of soup with some meat in it, took a short rest in a meadow and then continued on our way.

While we were passing through a mountain village one night, we suddenly heard gunfire. Everything went wild—horses galloping, people running, everyone yelling and swearing. Burning shells flew through the air. As we fled along a paved road, a Russian soldier grabbed my bag and blanket and lifted me onto his horse. The shooting went on until just before dawn. The Russians had captured a young German soldier who had been wounded in the leg, and some of the officers took pleasure in beating and kicking him as they dragged him along. As much as I hated the Germans for what they did to my family and friends, and as much as I wanted revenge for all the Jews they killed, I felt sorry for this man and wondered why they didn't just shoot him.

Alexander arrived that day and told our group that we would soon be approaching the "liberated" city of Banská Bystrica. This was good news as we were tired and dirty after two weeks' travel with no ability to bathe or change our clothes. Banská Bystrica had been the first city in Slovakia to be liberated by the Soviets. It later [October 27, 1944] fell to the Germans but was again taken by the Red Army. The city looked like a ghost town. Not a soul walked the streets. We stayed in a village on the outskirts of the city, which was almost entirely abandoned of its residents. We found empty homes where we washed up, ate, and slept like kings and queens on real straw sacks! In the morning as I was fluffing up my "mattress," I lost my wedding ring inside the sack.

That day, a pretty Russian girl came to talk to me. We had no difficulty understanding each other's language. A nurse and the Captain's girlfriend, she offered help if I needed it. The only request I made was to have my shoes repaired, and she took them to a shoemaker who fixed them. We quickly became friends, and she suggested that we exchange personal mementos by which to remember one another. All I had, aside from my clothes and a nightgown, was the ring from my parents, with which I would not part, and a four-leaf clover pendant set in gold that Izi had given me. She had seen the pendant before and thought it was beautiful. This meant I had to part with it. In exchange, she gave me a ring with a small aquamarine stone.

The next morning Izi and the smugglers were invited to have breakfast with the Captain. Red Army officers, seated around a long table covered with platters of food, sang and drank vodka from water glasses. In a private meeting after breakfast, the Captain told Izi that he and the three young smugglers were to go to Moscow to be honored for their heroism in saving lives. Izi agreed to go. I was to stay with the partisans. But I didn't want to part with Izi and remain in a country that was still occupied by Germans. I didn't want to be without a "bodyguard" surrounded by hundreds of sexually hungry men. Hurt and disappointed, I cried for hours. Finally, I ran to the Captain's quarters and begged him to send me to Moscow with Izi. It wasn't difficult to convince him. "You did your part and deserve to be honored as well," he said.

Izi felt conflicted about either of us taking this trip. He was reluctant to go, but the offer had sounded like an order. When he pondered planning an escape, I tried to talk him out of it, because I worried that he could be shot. No one was supposed to leave the premises, and the bridge was patrolled. My main concern was to get as far away from the Germans as possible. Going to Moscow seemed like a good idea because surely it was far away. I knew very little about the Soviet system. I also didn't know that I was pregnant.

The Captain, his girlfriend, and Alexander hugged and kissed us farewell and wished us all the best in Moscow. It was my first experience of airplane travel. The plane was small with a bench on each side. Two wounded soldiers and a Yugoslavian officer sat on one side; the three smugglers, Izi and I sat on the other. During the flight, we heard shooting. It felt like bullets were hitting the plane. We were flying over the front in the middle of the night. At one point, the plane seemed to be going down fast. I put my head on Izi's shoulder, closed my eyes, and said, "Goodbye, this is the end." Suddenly, I felt the plane flying steadily again. I learned years later that the abrupt drop might have been a maneuver to escape the bullets.

CHAPTER 6

Trapped in the Soviet Union

We were greeted at the Moscow airport by two men dressed in black leather coats and leather boots. They seemed friendly and said they would take us to a place where people were expecting us. First, we were brought to a room where all of our belongings had to be inspected. In my knapsack were a change of clothes, underwear, a nightgown, towel, toothbrush and toothpaste, needle and thread, mirror, Izi's navy blue robe and gray pajamas, and his two pairs of binoculars. We were asked to empty out our pockets. Izi's pen, knife, and scissors were put aside. Finally, we were taken outside and put into a long, black van. I don't remember seeing the city, so I don't think the car had windows. Eventually, I heard the sound of gates opening, and when the car stopped, we stepped out and went through a door, along a hallway, and into a room where we were searched again. My two rings, the binoculars, needle and thread, and mirror were all recorded on paper, put into a small bag and taken away. A woman escorted me into a screened-off room and told me to take off my clothes and bend over. She looked into my rectum and vagina. After I dressed again, I was taken down a hallway and put into a windowless cubicle. I could not see or hear people in close proximity. I waited there for hours, horrified. I thought I heard Izi's "smoker's" cough. I called out his name and the names of the three smugglers who had come with us. No one answered. I would never see Izi again.

Hours later, I was taken away, led down another hallway, and locked up in a small solitary cell that had a heavy iron door with a peephole and a little window with grated bars just below ceiling level. At that moment, I realized I was in prison. I banged on the door and tried to tell the guard it was a terrible mistake. Mixing Polish and Russian words, I pleaded that I hadn't done anything wrong. I asked her to let me talk to someone who could help me. She didn't understand anything I was saying and just nodded, saying, "Yes, yes." I was held in this cell for three months with no explanation as to why I was there. It was Butyrki Prison in Moscow. I later learned that it was the same penal institution where the famous Soviet poet Mayakovsky and other political prisoners were jailed during Stalin's long reign of terror.

The cell had a narrow cot with a thin, tattered rug that served as a blanket. In one corner, a metal soup bowl, a wooden spoon, and a pot of water sat on a nightstand. In another corner stood a small, covered, metal garbage can, which was to be used as a toilet. The walls were painted shiny green. On one wall hung a framed copy of the prison rules and regulations printed in Russian, which I could not read. I paced back and forth, crying and trying to understand what was happening. I was young and totally ignorant about the USSR and its communist government. Before the war, when I was barely a teenager, I never read the newspapers—I was only interested in my immediate surroundings and relationships at school, in the neighborhood and in my family. Under German occupation, we did not have access to newspapers or libraries, and the only subject that dominated our thoughts was the Nazi horror going on around us. When we talked about the war, it was with the hope that the Russians would liberate us from our bondage. Instead, I wound up imprisoned in a Soviet jail.

Because I was not allowed to lie on the cot during the day, I would spend each day pacing from one end of the cell to the other, counting the steps, one to seven. At night, I slept with my clothes on. Each morning and evening, the door was opened and I was walked to a washroom to empty the toilet can. I never saw another prisoner. Breakfast consisted of a pot of boiling water and a hunk of bread, two-and-a-half inches thick, that looked like dark, wet clay. For the first six days I piled the bread on top of the nightstand until it got moldy. The guard asked if I was going to eat the bread, and when I said no, she asked if she could have the pieces and took them all. The main meal of the day was a small bowl of soup—dirty water with a few small fish bones, a piece of potato skin and a cabbage leaf. On the seventh day, I ate the bread.

I counted the days as they went by. It was the beginning of October 1944, and I knew I had missed my period, but I assumed it was due to the strain I was under and did not worry about it. Every day I was allowed to walk with my hands behind my back in a small, damp courtyard between the prison buildings. I tried to take in as much fresh air as possible during the fifteen minutes allotted for outdoor exercise. I never saw anyone except the same one guard. In the long corridors, the guards would signal each other by knocking their keys on the metal stair rails. Sometimes I heard a cough and was sure it was Izi. I worried about how he would survive on this horrible food and without cigarettes. On October 8th, the day of my 20th birthday, I became hysterical. I pounded the door, screamed, demanded that someone talk to me and explain why I was in jail. It was useless.

The cell was getting colder as the fall turned to winter. In the evenings, a uniformed inspector would come into my cell. I was ordered to stand at attention and listen to him. I understood very little of what he said, but, as time went on, I began to comprehend the language. He usually pointed to the rules and regulations that were hanging on the wall, underlining with his finger the NKVD (Soviet secret police) signature and saying it out loud. This was how I learned my first four Russian letters. I tried to tell him about my situation and ask him why no one did anything about it. There was no response. At night I tried to huddle under the old blanket, but the guard would look through the peephole and immediately wake me up, saying, "Prisoner! Hands out from under the blanket!" This happened every night.

When I missed my period a second month, I requested to see a doctor. I was examined and told that I was pregnant. Frightened, I asked the doctor to perform an abortion. I did not want to bear a child under these miserable conditions. How could I possibly have a healthy child in jail? I was terrified and wished I were dead. But the doctor said they would not perform an abortion. The doctor was an older, gentle-looking man, and seemed to understand what I was saying, but he couldn't help me. The prison wouldn't allow it.

I paced, cried and worried. I was always hungry and very cold. Even though the moisture that dripped down the walls had now turned to ice, I was still forced to sleep with my arms on top of the blanket. I was never called for questioning or given an explanation for my incarceration. One day, I received a small care package, which contained a can of food that had a salty, meaty taste. I ate the can's entire contents at once and it tasted good. Later I learned that it was lard. The package also held a few lumps of sugar, a handful of salty, dry fish the size of smelts (*kilka*), tobacco and a piece of brown paper to roll it in. I asked the guard to give this to my husband—I still imagined that I could hear Izi's cough—but he did not take it.

Weeks went by. The inspector looked in every day and recited each rule as he pointed to it. Gradually, I figured out what the words meant and learned a few more letters and sentences. I was not able to talk to anyone for three months, and no one talked to me. At times, I thought I was losing my mind.

Finally, in January 1945, I was awakened in the middle of the night and taken for questioning. My interrogator was a woman. She introduced herself as Barylo and spoke Yiddish. She told me that an arrest permit had finally been issued and now I was officially a prisoner at Lubianka Prison, the Moscow headquarters of the Soviet secret police. Lubianka was the notorious penitentiary for political prisoners that Aleksander Solzhenitsyn described in his writings. The charge against me was espionage! I understood Yiddish because my parents had spoken it, but I never learned to speak it myself. I could speak only broken Galician Yiddish (the Austro-Hungarian dialect) with German mixed in. The interrogator could not believe that a Jew from Poland could not speak fluent Yiddish, and at first she did not want to believe that I was Jewish. Indeed, she did not believe my story at all and accused Izi and me of having worked for the Germans. She warned me that I had better answer all her questions about Izi's political work truthfully because there were shelves full of documentation which could prove we were spies.

I went back to my cell, not wanting to believe what I had just heard. The Russians had been the only hope for the Jews in the ghetto, and here I was imprisoned by them and accused of working for the Germans. At this point I felt my life was over. I wept for my parents, my sisters, my friends, myself, and the baby I was carrying inside me. I wished that I had been sent to Auschwitz to be cremated with the rest of my family. I had completely lost the will to live.

I was transferred to another cell with five women—all "political prisoners." One was a former opera singer who, after fifteen years in labor camps, was to be interrogated again on completely new charges. Another woman had made a few critical remarks about the Communist Party, and a third had been turned in by an angry neighbor simply because she had been taking English lessons from a private tutor; as I learned, the English language and the hiring of a private tutor were considered bourgeois, anti-socialist offenses in Stalinist Russia. For all of these "crimes," my fellow inmates expected to be sent to labor camps in the north for at least ten years. I was the youngest among them, and these women seemed to understand me a little. They believed I was innocent, befriended me and provided moral support. When, for example, a few books were delivered to the prison, my cellmates helped me learn how to read them. This is how I very slowly learned the Russian language.

Every morning we prisoners were taken to the washroom to use the sink and clean out our metal toilet cans. Once a day we were taken for a 20-minute walk in the small courtyard. No talking was allowed and our hands had to be held behind our backs. Once a week we were taken to the bathhouse and given a piece of soap and a small wooden basin filled with water. First we soaped our hair and body, then splashed some of the soap off and finally poured the water over ourselves to rinse off completely. We were then given a towel and our clothes, which were still hot from being disinfected. After bathing we were taken back to our cells. We never saw other prisoners, but we regularly heard the clanking of keys knocking on metal.

I was interrogated more often now, always after being awakened in the middle of the night. I would sit across from Barylo, my stomach growling as she ate a big sandwich in front of me, and defend myself against her barrage of false and humiliating accusations. She insisted I came from a capitalist, bourgeois family. As evidence, she waved a photograph that showed me standing in front of a car in Prešov. The car belonged to me, she declared, when, in fact, the photo had been taken of me standing on a street in front of a parked car. I tried to convince her that my father was not a rich man, but she refused to believe me. I told her that my brother had read the biography of Leon Trotsky, one of the leaders of the 1917 Russian Revolution, and that he had taught me a poem by Mayakovsky. Little did I know that the writings of both men were banned in the Soviet Union at that time; mentioning their names did not help my cause.

At one point, two high-ranking officers in uniform took over the interrogation sessions and asked me endless questions about Izi. When I told them the little I knew—that Izi had helped transport Polish Jews from Slovakia to Hungary in order to save their lives—the officers accused me of lying and declared that they had the documentation to prove me wrong. Those nights were terrifying. I could hear people, mainly men, screaming and crying in the other interrogation rooms. It sounded as though they were being beaten. I worried about Izi. I also worried about my baby, who was now showing signs of life inside a body that was full of sorrow, pain, anger, and hunger. I wondered how a baby could possibly be healthy on such small portions of soggy bread and dirty, watery soup.

Eventually, I told Barylo that I would sign any document with any accusations against me that she wanted to put in it, because I wanted to die. I pictured myself standing in front of a wall, being shot, and that seemed preferable to going on like this and delivering a baby in prison. "No," she said, "you will work first for 25 years in labor camps and only then you will die if you don't tell us the truth now." But there was nothing to tell. I went back to my cell humiliated, heartbroken, tired, and hungry.

One evening in early May, when we had almost given up on getting our walk for the day, we were taken to a different courtyard. It was a very small yard on the roof with a concrete floor and tall concrete walls. We could see more of the sky from this place and feel more air. Suddenly we heard a gun salute. Later, some of the girls saw fireworks and someone said the war was over. I don't remember feeling any emotion at all. I was eight months pregnant and, for me, the whole world was so cruel that I did not care. I just wanted to die.

Shortly afterwards I was transferred back to Butyrki Prison and put in a cell with seven other pregnant women. Some were political prisoners and others were not. It was a large cell with two tiers of wooden boards on each wall, where we were to sleep. There were no mattresses or pillows. In my condition—skin and bones with a huge stomach—this was extremely uncomfortable. I also desperately needed something larger to wear. One day, one of the girls pulled a needle-shaped fishbone out of her soup. It even had a hole in it. I ripped apart my only pair of stockings to use as thread and, using another girl's contraband pair of scissors, we cut Izi's navy blue robe into pieces to make a maternity "sack" out of it. I used the fishbone as a needle and sewed the fabric together with loose stitches.

Every aspect of giving birth and caring for a newborn in a prison kept me awake at night. What would the baby eat? Where would it sleep? I felt a desperate need to have my own mother nearby to help me through the birth. When my first contractions began, I didn't know what to expect or what to do. I grabbed onto a post in the cell but slid down to the floor, crying in pain. I had to use the can often, and each time I was afraid that the baby would fall into it. After a few hours, the contractions came closer together and I suddenly felt fluid run down my legs. It wouldn't stop, and I screamed. The watchman came in, followed by two men with a stretcher. As they carried me down the hallway and up the stairs, I felt what I thought was the baby's head between my thighs. Worried that it would get squashed, I cried "Głowa!" (head) in Polish, but they did not respond. The word for head in Russian is "Golova," though I did not know that at the time. Or maybe they just didn't care. Anyway, it was the water bag I was feeling, not the baby's head.

Finally, they put me on a table, and I heard a doctor and a nurse telling me to push harder, push harder. The pain was excruciating without any anesthetic. Finally I heard a baby's weak cry. "It's a boy!" a nurse exclaimed and showed me a long, skinny infant with dark hair. He reminded me of Izi. She asked me what I would name him. I wanted to name my son after my father but I didn't, because according to the Jewish tradition, a baby cannot be named after a loved one who is still living. I had not seen my father die, and I did not want to give up hope that he might be alive. Casting about for a name that did not sound Jewish, in case another "cataclysm" would befall the Jewish people, I thought of Prince Edward and decided, quite spontaneously, to name my son Edward Szpigelman.

It was freezing cold in the room and when, after an hour, the placenta had not come out, the doctor forced it. He then gave me fourteen stitches with no anesthetic, which was so unbearable, I passed out. It was June 6, 1945, almost one month after Nazi Germany had surrendered to the Allies.

Eventually, the baby and I were taken to a cell specifically for mothers and children. Three other mothers were there, each with a child who had been born in the prison—Lili, just over a year old, ten-month-old Genia, and four-month-old Mali. Lili's mother was a beautiful woman who said her husband was a general fighting against the German army and that she had been imprisoned because her Latvian grandmother was of German descent. Mali's mother came from Estonia and had never been interrogated. Genia's mother was a Russian prosecutor and had been arrested for accepting a bribe. Later on, the number of mothers and babies in the cell increased.

Each of us was given a bed, a small crib and a nightstand. I also received ten thin muslin diapers and two dark, flannel baby blankets for my newborn. A nurse taught me how to diaper my baby. When she was through, my son looked like a miniature mummy wrapped tightly, hands and all, in his blanket. Once a day the dirty diapers were taken away, laundered and returned clean. Since I was supposed to breast-feed my baby, my daily food rations now included, in addition to the "soup," a cup of milk, two small lumps of sugar, a larger portion of a better quality bread, and a lot of boiled water. But I was unable to nurse because my nipples were too small for Eddie to grasp. He would cry and cry from hunger. Mali's mother brought her to me, hoping that a larger infant might be able to pull my nipple out, but Mali did not want to work so hard. I cried constantly too, knowing that my baby was hungry. After this problem was overcome, my nipples got infected, and every feeding became extremely painful. Then I developed boils on my breasts that had to be lanced and drained. Mali's mother was a good person; she had an abundance of milk and sometimes allowed Eddie to nurse. But my baby was not gaining weight.

Eddie developed a high fever, which the doctor said was pneumonia. The nurse who came every day to check on the children showed us compassion. She sponged Eddie down and applied mustard compresses to his chest. I tried to keep him comfortable by holding him in my arms and walking him back and forth in the cell throughout the day and night, singing the Russian lullabies I had learned.

Eventually, Eddie's health improved and I was able to persuade the nurse that he needed additional food. He gained weight and was becoming a beautiful baby. He resembled my mother, whom I missed deeply. Whenever my cellmates got letters and packages from their families, I was reminded that my baby and I were all alone in the world.

Supplementary food was brought in every morning for all the children— cooked farina with soybean milk and a spoonful of fish oil. There was never fruit, vegetables, juice, or meat. The farina would sometimes have a funny taste by the afternoon, since there was no refrigeration, but the hungry children ate it anyway. Each day I set aside one of my lumps of sugar and used a piece of thin string to cut a slice from my bread ration. I put these into two bags I had made out of diapers to set aside for a "rainy day."

At one point, I exchanged my blue nightgown for some t-shirts for Eddie, and the gown's recipient said she would wear it to a ball when she got out of jail. Since she was not a political prisoner (I had heard she was in jail for murder), she figured she would soon be freed in an amnesty for mothers with children. And so she was.

Eddie was about nine months old and I had been in prison for almost one-and-a-half years when my interrogator told me that, due to lack of evidence against me, the charge of espionage had been revised. The new, lesser charge was "SOE", which meant in Russian that I was considered a "socially dangerous element." My sentence was now five years, beginning from January 1945. My first three months in prison were not being counted as time served! I also learned that I would soon be sent to a labor camp.

By early May 1946, Eddie and I were boarding a train. The jail authorities had supplied food for our trip—small fish dried in salt (for a baby!), tobacco (I did not smoke), and stale bread. At each station, Russians came up to the train to sell milk and rolls. They could see my baby through the window, and I begged for milk in exchange for a few lumps of sugar. The "rainy day" supplies I had saved in prison were lifesavers now. I soaked the bread in milk and added a lump of sugar to feed my hungry baby. At night, I put him on the luggage rack to sleep. There were not enough diapers for the trip, so I would hold him over the toilet.

It was good to see trees, green grass, and the sky again. At small train stations, I saw men playing harmonicas or accordions and sometimes a few young people were dancing. But I harbored a terrible fear about a future in which Eddie and I might be separated.

We were taken off the train at Vologda halfway between Moscow and Kotlas and marched to an old, primitive jail, where Eddie and I were put in a small cell with several women. In the middle of the night, I was awakened by what felt like small animals jumping in the bed. Hungry rats had found the food package I had placed on the windowsill over the bed. Rats were jumping all over my baby! I scooped Eddie up and pounded on the door, begging the watchman to let us out. Not accustomed to seeing a baby in prison, he opened the door to let us stay in the hallway "for a short time only." Putting Eddie on the table to sleep, I tried to explain that I was terrified that the rats would bite him. Then Eddie woke up and smiled at the guard, which softened him up enough to allow us to stay in the hall until morning.

That morning, I heard someone call my name from behind a wooden cell door. It turned out to be Rudi, one of the three smugglers from Slovakia who had been arrested with me in Moscow. He had recognized my voice in the hallway the night before. All three smugglers were in the cell and were in desperate need of food and cigarettes. When the watchman was not looking, I pushed some of the bread, tobacco, and brown paper I had saved from my care package under their old warped wood door. I asked about Izi, and Rudi told me that while they were held together in a Moscow cell, Izi had found a piece of glass and slit his wrist, but he was saved and then transferred. None of them had heard anything about him since.

A few days later, Eddie and I were put on a train heading north toward "Corrective Labor Camp A-O," a transit camp from which prisoners were assigned to other camps. The trip took more than two weeks, going via Kotlas, a city in the northwestern province of Komi SSR, and Uchta, the last station before the camp.

Upon arrival, we were taken to a barrack that housed close to 100 people and assigned a wooden board to sleep on. The next day, I took Eddie outside to breathe the fresh air and heard two women speaking Polish. They were delighted to see the baby, and cooed and played with him. Among the thousands of prisoners in this camp, there were no other children. Eddie was the first and only child.

That is how I met Barbara and her friend Janka, registered nurses who worked in the camp infirmary. When Barbara found out we were Polish Jews, she immediately took us under her wing—bathed Eddie, cooked him gelatin from fresh berries, and advised me how to cope.

Barbara and her husband Zygmunt, a surgeon, had lived in Warsaw before the war. They joined the Polish underground army, later called the Home Army (AK), in 1939, after Poland was defeated, and fought against the Germans in the forests. When the Russians took over, they had been arrested and sent with many others like them to Russian labor camps. Zygmunt now worked in a hospital at Vitlasian, a nearby camp in the Komi SSR.

Barbara introduced me to some of the other "old timers," people who had good positions in the camp and could be useful in finding me a job. Living conditions were better in this camp than in others, so it would be advantageous to stay. But my future there would remain insecure, because I had no professional training. I got a job working for the camp seamstress, although I did not know how to sew. Fortunately, the seamstress was kind and covered for me.

Eddie took his first steps not long after we arrived, and everyone hugged and kissed him—the camp's only child had caught everyone's attention. The fresh air, better food, and affection were good for Eddie, and he was happy, but children were not permitted on the camp grounds, and the camp commander ordered me to place him in the children's home 45 minutes away. Now, I thought, they are taking my baby away from me! I had been with Eddie day and night for almost a year in the cell and suddenly I was going to be separated from my child, the only loved one I had left in this world. Mothers were allowed to visit their children on Sundays if the authorities permitted them to leave the camp. I was heartbroken, and I cried a lot.

Zenia Baczynska, the Polish head nurse at the children's home, was finishing her 15-year sentence that year. Her communist father had taken her to live in Russia when she was a little girl. He had died in a labor camp. Zenia was hoping to be reunited with her 8-year-old son and husband, a former prisoner at this camp, when she got out. Speaking Polish together was a source of comfort for me. Understanding my worries and misfortune, she promised to take special care of Eddie and assured me that after she left, Barbara would take her place and assume her responsibilities. Her reassurances helped me cope with the separation from my son.

Not long after our arrival, I was transferred to a nearby camp called San Gorodok, where I went to work in a tailor shop. Here, two former nuns mended clothing such as quilted jackets and pants for the prisoners and guards. For the more privileged people, they repaired fur or leather jackets and sheepskin coats. One of the camp administrators lived next to the tailor shop, and the nuns used to prepare special meals for him. I have no idea where he got the food, but it probably came from prisoners who tried to bribe him with items from the care packages they received from home. He invited me to share a meal with him—a delicious hot soup with rice in it, the first rice I had eaten in years—and told me I could continue to eat well and take some food to my baby if I would agree to inform on people in my barracks. He made it clear that I would also have to be "nice" to him. I refused and, after a struggle, was able to free myself and run back to my barracks.

He took revenge by assigning me to hard physical labor. The very next morning, I was assigned to join a group of laborers in cutting down trees. We marched in a line through the fields, the wind blowing in our faces, but there were no trees in sight. Finally we reached fields where some tall plants called *Ivanchai* (Ivan's tea) grew. We were ordered to cut and pile them in cords. Each prisoner had a daily quota to fill, and when I was lucky I would find a rock to pile the plants on, which made my harvest appear bigger. I learned this trick from the other prisoners, some of whom were helpful. Most were accustomed to the cruel life in Communist Russia and to oppressive work in the labor camps. Normal terms for political prisoners ranged from ten to twenty-five years, and it was not uncommon for a prisoner to spend most of his or her adult life in prison for no reason that was ever apparent to them. Thieves and murderers had a greater chance to be freed before the end of their sentence than did political prisoners, who never received an amnesty. Those who survived their long sentences were not allowed to return to their families upon release but had to live in exile in designated districts, often near the camps.

When autumn came and there were no more Ivanchai to cut, I was assigned to clean the barracks and supply the water and wood. Each large room contained more than 100 wooden bunks and a stove, and I had to wash the wooden floor every day on my hands and knees, using a bundle of twigs as a scrub brush. Eight or ten times a day I filled my two pails at the well down the hill and then carried them back up to the barrack on a yoke across my shoulders. I had to carry enough water to scrub the floor and fill the metal barrels used for drinking and washing up. Each prisoner was given a tin basin into which four inches of water was poured and used to wash up after work. I was also responsible for sawing and chopping the firewood. I could not manage the chopping, but there was always someone willing to help me.

After I finished a day's work, I'd request permission to visit my baby at the children's home. On the way, I'd trade my bread ration for a cup of milk from a former prisoner who lived in exile and kept a goat. It hadn't occurred to me that the goat's milk might not agree with a baby who had never had fresh milk before. Eddie was never able to tolerate the milk I brought him.

It took about an hour to walk from the children's home back to the camp, so I sometimes missed the main meal. When I did, my bunkmate, Sonia, took care of me. She was from the Ukraine and was serving her twenty-second year. She still didn't know why she had been sentenced, except that her parents had owned land before the revolution. She worked outside the camp, taking care of pigs, and was able to steal some sort of flour, from which she made edible patties. She would save one or two for me, and those kept me going. Sonia knew how to sew, and she made a dress for me out of Izi's pajamas that I had had in my knapsack when we were arrested. She knew that, because I was scrubbing in the barracks all day, I could reciprocate by guarding her hidden food and other belongings from prisoners who might steal them. Unfortunately, Sonia unknowingly brought in lice, which I found on my clothes and body.

Sonia introduced me to a young political prisoner, who told me there was a position open for a nurse at the camp infirmary. A "nurse" was someone who took temperatures, changed dressings, and kept the infirmary clean. I was promised this job and told that the doctor would teach me how to change dressings and what ointments to use, but when I met the doctor I realized I would have to exchange sex for this opportunity, and when I refused, somebody else got the job.

Nevertheless, I continued to enjoy the company of the political prisoner, who read to me from the works of poets who had been censored by the Communist regime. Not yet knowing how to write Russian, I used the pink paper and purple ink he gave me to copy the poems letter by letter. I have kept these now-faded poems ever since. One of them, by the Russian poet Yesenin, the most popular poet of the early revolution who later committed suicide, dared to say in retrospect, "such a short way we went and how many mistakes we made." It felt good to spend time with this nice, cultured, and intelligent man who seemed sad and worried even though he was very close to the end of his sentence.

Winter was approaching and it was getting very cold. Each prisoner was supplied with a quilted jacket, a pair of pants, mittens, hat, felt boots called

Valonki and rags to wrap their feet in to keep them from freezing. We were also issued a thin, washed-out blanket and a precious wooden spoon which, if lost, would not be replaced. Prisoners often stole spoons and other belongings. The safest place to keep small valuables was in one's boots in the daytime and under one's head at night. I slept wearing most of my clothes because it was very cold and also because I didn't think I'd otherwise find them in the morning. There were no pillows or bed sheets. My mattress was a two-inch thick sack filled with sawdust.

I received a daily ration of a three-inch thick, soggy piece of bread, which seemed to consist of water more than grain. We were also given a ladle of very thin, watery soup, with, if one was lucky, a fishbone or a piece of potato skin in it. With the soup, we got a two by two-inch square of gruel, made of unrecognizable ingredients. We ate this meal in a dining barrack near the kitchen.

We often had to work seven days a week, because we were told to volunteer on Sundays, and nobody dared to disobey. When I heard that a new nursing course was to be taught on Sundays at a site outside the camp premises, I jumped at the chance, because it would allow me to see my child on the way back and would also excuse me from working on Sundays. I signed up and was accepted. I still didn't know how to write Russian, but I tried very hard to learn as much as possible. The woman doctor who taught the course took us to a nearby hospital, which was only for free citizens. Many of the patients had gangrenous feet, a common occurrence in the Soviet Union, where the temperature could drop to -40°C and quickly freeze toes, fingers and noses.

The stench from the gangrene was terrible, but I did as instructed and took off the old dressings, cleaned the feet, and put on new dressings. It was not the gangrene, however, but the sight and smell of the blood I saw while watching a doctor perform a D & C (dilatation and curettage) on a woman which, combined with my weakness, made me faint. As a result, I could not visit Eddie that day, which made me feel both guilty and sad.

Soon our teacher grew seriously ill from abdominal cancer, stopped teaching and died a short time later. That was the end of our class, so I was very surprised when, several months later, I received a diploma stating that I had completed a seven-month nursing course with high marks and could be considered a practical nurse. I don't think that I attended more than seven class hours, and had learned very little. The diploma became invaluable in ways that I could not have imagined.

Eddie got very sick and vomited so much that he lost 13 pounds and could not walk, sit, or even hold his head up. He was taken to the hospital, where most of the personnel, including the doctors, were freed prisoners and qualified prisoners. However, I, as a prisoner, was not allowed inside the hospital. A nurse would bring Eddie to me in a small lobby for a short time, and I felt so frightened and helpless watching my dear little baby slowly dying. I cried, pleaded, and begged the nurse to take good care of him.

My friend Barbara, now the nurse in the children's home, intervened for me. She wrote about Eddie to her surgeon husband, Zygmunt, and when she learned that he would be attending a doctors' meeting at this same hospital, she advised me to get a pass to meet with him there. I planned to ask him to examine Eddie and call his case to the attention of the other doctors, but Zygmunt's meeting finished early, and when he called my camp to request an earlier pass for me, my pass was cancelled altogether. The authorities suspected me of having arranged a date with a man outside the camp. Zygmunt, whom I had never met, waited and did not understand why I never showed up, but he must have examined Eddie and talked with the staff about him, because the change in my son's care was noticeable. Eddie started to regain his strength and eventually got well.

Near the hospital, a large pharmacy distributed medications to many other pharmacies, hospitals and labor camps in Komi SSR and to the correctional camp in Varkuta in the Arctic Circle. Some of the medications were prepared at the pharmacy, others were shipped in and kept in large storage magazines. The operation was headed by a pharmacist who had finished serving his 25-year political sentence. He was a tall, handsome man with white hair, who, one could guess, had come from Russian Jewish aristocracy. I can only remember his first name, Lev, and I met him after I found out that there was a position open in the pharmacy office.

In applying for the job, I had an advantage over prisoners who knew only Russian because I knew the Latin alphabet, in which the names of medications were written. I also knew the names of many common medications because, before the war, my brother, Poldek, used to get a lot of medication samples in the mail, and I used to help sort them.

I relayed my experience to the head of the pharmacy and got the job, which turned out to be a huge success beyond my hopes. By working outside the camp in an office with free people, I could visit my child without getting a special pass, which was always difficult to obtain.

My job was to write invoices for the medications that were shipped out, noting the unit price and using the abacus to figure out the cost. I already knew how to figure it out in my head as well as on paper, but the orders were to use the abacus, so I learned how. I also learned to write Russian because the final sum had to be written both in numbers and words.

My work was double-checked by a young accountant and then signed by the head accountant. My co-worker (and later a good friend) was a man named Walter whose parents had moved from Germany to Russia when he was a little boy. Walter was serving his fifteenth and final year in the prison camp. He was around 40 years old and had worked in the pharmacy for many years. Like most of us, he also was a political prisoner, though he was allowed to live outside the camp in a one-room hut with a three-square-foot entrance room where he could wash up and keep the cat's litter box. The main room, smaller than my cell in the Butyrki Prison in Moscow, contained a cot, a tiny table and a wood-burning stove. In front of his hut, Walter had planted a small garden where he grew vegetables and potatoes. He taught me to write Russian, instructed me at work, and sometimes checked my invoices before they were sent to the accounting office.

Walter and his lady friend, an ex-prisoner whom he planned to marry the following year, went fishing together on Sundays, and they often shared some of the smelt they caught with me, frying them up so I could give them to Eddie on my way to or from work. Eddie, now eighteen months old, was back at the home, where Barbara took care of him, feeding him the small fish and playing with him. Sometimes I would get some mashed potatoes from Walter and feed Eddie myself, but this was against the rules and I didn't want to get Barbara in trouble. The children did not get a varied diet. They ate only soy milk with farina. I didn't know much about children's nutritional needs, but I knew that what they were getting was insufficient, and that worried me.

In winter, it was so bitterly cold, I was sometimes afraid I would not make it on my trips to visit Eddie. It took an hour to walk from my place to the children's home. The temperature could go down to minus 40°C. The strong wind would bite at my face, which was wrapped up to my eyes with a rag in order to prevent frostbite. Many times my fingers and toes were so numb that I thought I had lost all feeling in them.

Walter always knew how to help me. I was most grateful to him whenever the big boss, usually under some false pretext, called me into the warehouse when nobody else was around. Walter always managed to show up and disturb any planned scenario. He was indeed risking his job by doing this. Under the circumstances, had he lost, it would have ruined both his future and his life.

Walter once gave me a photograph, on the back of which he had written: "One who can act like a human under these circumstances is a real human." He was a man who inspired loyalty. One day in spring, his sister and her nine-year-old daughter got permission to come from far away in Russia to visit him. He had not seen his sister for fifteen years, and didn't know his niece. It was almost impossible to get such a permit, and people were generally afraid to ask for one anyway or simply to be in contact with political prisoners. Thus, his sister was a brave lady.

Since I worked in the pharmacy and now knew some free and influential people, I was able to stay away from camp after work for a longer period, so the four of us took walks in the forest, where, even in that cold climate, some beautiful wildflowers were blooming. Some reminded me of miniature orchids.

One day we went to see my son. Eddie liked Walter's niece and wanted to stay close to her. He was almost two years old then and had never seen a little person like her. She played with him gently, and I know I saw him smile. I don't think he had regular opportunities to play; for instance, I don't remember seeing any toys in the children's home. Certainly he hadn't had toys in jail. As usual, it was heartbreaking to say goodbye to Eddie, but I knew I was supposed to be grateful that I could see, hug and kiss him even once in a while.

The young accountant who checked my invoices invited me on a few dates, but each time, I turned him down because I did not like or trust him. Besides, I was not interested in dating and I told him so. Angry with me, the man got nasty and began to find mistakes in my invoices. I suspected he was putting them there. I complained to the main accountant, who talked to the younger man about it, but the latter must have wanted to take revenge on me, because he lied to the camp authorities about me and my behavior. Soon, the camp commander called me in and told me I was being sent to a punishment camp in Varkuta in the Arctic Circle. My child was to stay behind at the children's home and I would probably never see him again, for I knew that few people survived Varkuta. It felt like someone had hit me on the head, but what had I done to be hit so many times?!

It took a lot of crying, begging, and persuasion to make the commander believe me and change his decision to send me away. Maybe someone free who knew me put in a good word for me. I do not know what or who influenced him, but I stayed on.

One day, the pharmacy boss introduced us to an old man who had just transferred to our camp and was supposed to start working in our pharmacy. As the result of a stroke, the man dragged one leg and his speech was slurred, so it was difficult to understand him. A brilliant man with a lot of pharmaceutical knowledge, he had spent about twenty years in labor camps. We learned from him later that he had been one of the czar's advisers before the revolution and had a wife and two sons in Moscow who had not communicated with him for all those years in fear of losing their freedom.

Walter told me that, after her visit to the camp, his sister had written a letter to this old man's wife and told her about him. It must have been a moving letter, for a few months later the wife came to visit her husband. Seeing him again was a big shock, and she was unhappy. Needing someone to talk to, she picked me, and I listened. The woman told me that she felt only pity for her husband, they had nothing in common and their sons did not care about their father.

It probably was like that with many families under the communist regime. The sons wanted to be free, to study in the universities and make a place for themselves in life. My own experience had taught me how easy it was to be falsely accused and lose one's freedom. The woman gave me her address in Moscow, and I promised to write her if something happened to her husband.

Time went on. My "big sister" and friend Barbara was transferred to another camp in Vietlasian. She was scheduled to work there as a surgical nurse in the same hospital where her husband Zygmunt had his surgical practice. What a break for them! Not long after her transfer, Zygmunt was pardoned and repatriated back to Poland. Barbara stayed on, pregnant, until she was transferred back to her old position as head nurse in the children's home. I was relieved, knowing that my baby would again have special care and love.

In the fall of 1947, an amnesty was issued for mothers with children, if they were not politically accused. The paragraph that I was sentenced under was divided into "politically dangerous to society" and just "dangerous to society". Both were under paragraph SOE, socially dangerous elements, though I don't remember the number. I had not been called to the office and was not notified, so I assumed I was not on the amnesty list. I almost lost my mind seeing other mothers leave with their children. Again and again I went to see the commander and demanded my rights, demanded that he double-check my file. Maybe a mistake had been made, I said. After all, I was a mother with a child and had not been sentenced under the spy paragraph. Finally, after a week of anguish and three years of unjust imprisonment, I was notified that I was free to take my baby and go back to the world, where everyone that I once knew and loved had been murdered.

The camp authorities issued me a train ticket to Moscow and a document stating that I had been freed from the corrective camp and had permission to travel. Without such a document, one could not board a train or travel by any other means in Russia. I also received some food and a small amount of money to buy milk for the baby.

Barbara gave me courage and sensible advice. Twice my age and very clever, she was already a married woman and a mother when the war broke out. She and her husband Zygmunt were partisans who could provide medical treatment. Their nine-year-old daughter, hiding with them in the forests, was killed by a bullet. Her heartbroken parents grieved their loss for years.

Barbara showed me a photograph of Zygmunt and told me to get his address from the Polish embassy in Moscow. She gave me the name of her cousin, who worked at the embassy, and said she was sure Zygmunt was in touch with him and trying to intervene in her case. Zygmunt did not know about her pregnancy or his newborn son, and she wanted me to inform her cousin of her condition.

It was now the fall of 1947, more than two years after the war had ended. I was a 23-year-old woman and my child was almost two-and-a-half years old. Eight years had gone by, none of them good for me.

We said goodbye to our friends and, with the baby in my arms and my knapsack on my back, started our long journey to freedom. A potty for the baby was tied to the knapsack. As irreplaceable as the wooden spoon, I guarded it carefully. I don't remember much about this trip, only that it took ten days, that I bought milk for Eddie from the people who brought it to the window whenever the train stopped, and that I fed Eddie food that Walter had packed for him.

In Moscow, we went straight to the Polish embassy, where we were given food, money and a place to stay in the suburbs. We relaxed, washed, and slept in a regular bed. Several other "ex-criminals" like me were also staying in this house waiting for documents and other formalities in order to return to Poland.

My first step was to return to the embassy to make sure they would help me repatriate. Although no one was waiting for us in Poland, I knew I did not want to stay in the Soviet Union, and Poland was the only country where we had a chance to go.

I quickly learned how hard it was to be on time for appointments when you have to care for a baby. If I missed the morning train, I'd miss my appointment at the embassy, but I could not leave without first feeding my child and waiting until he used the bathroom. If Eddie spilled milk or wet himself, we'd have to wait until his clothes dried because he only had one set of clothing.

The winter was approaching, it was already very cold, and the distance to and from the train station was unbearably long. Carrying a two-year-old clad in his long, heavy, quilted coat from camp was more than I could easily bear. I had to stop often to rest on the road.

Finally, I was able to meet Barbara's cousin at the embassy and after listening to my description of her situation, he promised to do everything possible to get her out. He also informed me that the repatriation to Poland had ended several months earlier. Nevertheless, he said that small groups of Polish people would still be able to return home. In the meantime, we were to remain in Moscow until they could send us to a repatriation camp at Grodno, a city near the Polish border, where we were to wait for further instructions.

Because the house in the suburbs was no longer available, we had no alternative but to live on the streets of Moscow in the bitter cold. The embassy had given me a little money, but all the shops had only empty shelves, no goods to buy. If bread was available, people stood in line for it half the night, and it sold out early in the morning. During the day, the only food available to buy was ice cream. I walked in the streets of Moscow on those winter days, Eddie in my arms, and slowly licked ice cream cones to appease my hunger. Sometimes we were able to get hot soup in a soup kitchen. Once I told a friendly young woman who stopped to admire Eddie that we were spending our nights on a bench at the train station, and she took us to her parents' home for a few nights and fed us.

In Russia in those days one could not move freely without one's identification documents and a travel permit; not having them was grounds for arrest. People carried their documents in safe inner pockets, because they were often stolen, although at the time, I did not know this. One day, while getting on a streetcar, I felt a tug on my bag and looked back to see a diaper, my underwear and toothbrush (it had survived all those years) on the ground. When I put them back into the bag, I noticed that my papers were gone. On days like that in Moscow, I wished I had never left the labor camp, where I did not have to struggle to find food and shelter as I did in the so-called free world.

We went back to the embassy, where I learned that I needed to get a document, which stated that I had lost my documents. Not long after this incident, I was issued a ticket to Grodno, a travel permit, and money.

The train to Grodno was to leave in the late afternoon, but we waited for it almost the entire night. The train station was crowded with people, some slept on the floor, others sat eating or drinking, all were waiting for the same train. The Russians were used to such situations and did not complain, though I never saw a single smile. Eddie slept on a bench, and I asked a man to watch him while I went to ask for some information. When I got back, Eddie was still asleep, but the precious, irreplaceable potty was missing. This created a huge problem for us, for there were no public bathrooms anywhere. But at this point, I thought, what was one more problem?

When the train finally came, everyone pushed to get in, only to stand for endless hours until we finally got to Grodno, where we were told that the repatriation camp was still seven kilometers away. The eight passengers who were headed there would have to walk. I had to carry Eddie because he did not have boots for that kind of weather. He felt so heavy in his quilted coat that I was afraid I would drop him. "Eddie, sit light!" I said, and he knew that meant he should cling closer. Someone helped me with my knapsack, and another carried Eddie for a while, but the road seemed endless and there was nothing to see but acres of snow-covered fields.

Little did I know that, in order to get repatriated, I would walk that road eight more times in the near future, each time asking myself, "Is it worth it?" I was trying with all my strength to go back to a country where Jews were not welcome, where I had lost my family and friends, and where I no longer knew anyone. I had been a 14-year-old girl when the war began; now I was 23 and felt years older. Those eight years are normally the best in a person's life, and I am sure they would have been for me under normal circumstances. But I lived them in misery and knew I would never be young again. My only certainty was that I did not want to stay in the USSR.

The huge repatriation camp was now nearly empty. A few people greeted us as we entered a barrack that could easily accommodate 200. There was no running water or toilet inside, and the outhouse, a crucial facility when one has a child, was not nearby. We took a place on the upper sleeping board with the others and slept in all our clothes, trying to keep warm in the freezing cold. Eddie used to wake me in the middle of the night to use the toilet. Since there was no container nearby, the two of us would have to climb down from the bunk and go out into the aching cold. I had to urge him—sometimes with anger I confess—to hurry so his behind would not freeze.

I was the only woman, and Eddie was the only child. He soon became everyone's buddy and received much love and affection. But weeks went by and there was no mail for us. Some of the inmates were sent to Poland; new people arrived and were also sent. I was losing hope. My fellow inmates offered some material help, so I decided to go back to Moscow. I carried Eddie and walked the seven kilometers back to Grodno and again waited several hours for the train. Grodno, once known as a center of Jewish culture, looked is if it had suffered a pogrom—the streets were desolate, the shop windows were shattered and their doors busted in. The stores had once belonged to Jewish merchants, there had been thousands of scholars, all happy and wealthy people before the war, before the Germans killed and liquidated everything. Walking the streets while waiting for the train, I met a young Jewish couple, one of the very few that survived. They were very hospitable and made a meal for us though it meant having little for themselves.

At the Polish embassy in Moscow, I received money and a promise to look into my case, but no shelter. I sought out the woman who had visited her elderly husband at the camp, hoping that she would not turn us away. She took us in and provided me with the first bath in a bathtub that I'd had in seven years. It felt wonderful! She made potato pancakes for supper, two for each of us, and introduced me to her two sons who hardly lifted their heads from their books. I did not care because it was so good to feel clean and warm and know that we would have a roof over our heads for the night.

The family lived in a three-room apartment—a kitchen and two rooms. The sons occupied one and the other was divided by a heavy curtain. A young couple with a one-year-old baby occupied half, and my benefactor the other. Eddie and I slept on the floor beside her bed, but this time we had a blanket and pillow.

We spent a few days in Moscow, going by subway to the embassy where we received a sandwich and moral support. The Moscow subway stations were lavish and impressive, but the commuters always looked sad and angry. We were advised to go back to Grodno with the encouraging promise that we would soon be sent to Poland. Before leaving Moscow, we passed a store that had just received a food delivery. We got in line and were lucky enough to get a bag of sugar and another of flour. These came in very handy later. We also found a place to get hot soup, which kept us warm and alive.

We endured another long wait at the railway station. Luckily, Eddie was already used to sleeping on the bench, but first he amused himself by running around the big pine tree that had been decorated with glitter and shiny balls to celebrate the New Year. (Christmas was not observed in an atheist society.) He was a good-looking boy who caught people's attention and they stopped to talk and give him a hug.

We got back to Grodno full of hope. I carried Eddie to the camp, where conditions were terrible. Everyone slept huddled together on the top bunk to keep from freezing, but some people were ill, there was no medical help, and Eddie and I were exposed to sickness. Eddie caught a terrible skin infection from a young man who had played with him.

Every day, we waited for the mailman, but there was never news for us. So, once again, we returned to Moscow. There was no telephone communication available, and my only recourse was to go the embassy and plead. This time I spoke to a top official and got his solemn promise to help us. So we went back, hoping that in a few days we would be arriving in Poland.

The good news came soon. We got ourselves together and climbed onto the open truck that was to take us to the train that went to Poland. The truck started moving and we were waving goodbye when the mailman ran up with a telegram. The truck stopped, the driver read the message and told me to take my baby and walk back to the camp. I must have been a very dangerous person in the eyes of the Soviet government.

I am not really able to describe how heartbroken and disappointed I felt. But I did not give up. I decided to go back to Moscow, knock on doors of some Russian (not Polish) officials and make sure that I got out of the country once and for all. I realized that to do this I could not have a child in my arms who would delay everything. This, I believed, was my last chance. I walked with Eddie to Grodno where I met a young Jewish lady who had two little children. I gave her the bag of flour and some sugar that I had saved and begged her to take care of my son for a few days. When she agreed, I waited for the train to Moscow.

This time I was able to meet with Barbara's cousin. He was very disturbed when he heard what had happened to us and told me to meet a friend of his, an important Russian official. I arrived on time, though he was late. He apologized when he finally came in and then patiently listened to me. When I finished, he asked me to wait in his office and disappeared for more than hour. He came back smiling, shook my hand, and said that everything would be different for me from now on. His promise lifted my spirits and gave me hope. When I asked him if he knew anything about Izi, he replied, "Don't inquire about him again because he is not alive." I had to believe him.

Returning to Grodno, I picked up Eddie, gave the woman some money I had gotten at the embassy, and walked through the seven kilometers of snow again. Only four people were left at the camp. The rest were back in Poland. I waited, slowly losing hope and my mind as well, or so I thought. A man in camp told me about a Polish doctor named Ptaszek who lived in the city of Lwów and was very involved in helping Polish people repatriate.

I decided to give it one more try, though I was very discouraged and growing weak and sick. Eddie and I again trudged to the station, and I bought a ticket to

Lwów. (Ironically, both Grodno and Lwów belonged to Poland before the war.) We arrived in the late afternoon only to learn that the doctor was out of town and would not be returning soon. The doctor's wife gave me the address of a Jewish family who she knew would put us up for the night. I was tired and hungry and felt that nothing good would ever happen to me again. I was simply tired of living. We came to the railroad tracks, and I walked slowly along the rails, holding my son, whom I loved so much, very close to me, and waited for a train to come and end my misery. Then I felt my baby's little hand wiping away the tears that were running down my face. "Mommy, don't cry," he said. "I love you so much." Then he started to cry, too, and hugged me tight. I got off the tracks and went about finding a place to sleep.

We were received well by the Jewish family. We bathed, ate, and slept in a bed. We were invited to stay for a few days, and so we waited for the doctor to return from his trip. It was no use; he did not come. With the help of the Jewish man, and using the rest of my money, I bought a train ticket and we went back to the repatriation camp. A few days later, an order arrived to deliver Eddie and me to the Polish border. We boarded a freight train and sat on a big pile of black coal in a boxcar. I was not really sure where we might end up.

It was the end of January 1948. The train crossed the border into Poland. In the little border town where we landed, I contacted the "city" hall and was told we would find some Jewish survivors in the city of Bialystok. So we went there, and the Jewish committee provided us with a room, board, and some clothing that had been sent by the Jewish organizations of the world. Oh, they took very good care of us.

I wrote a letter to Zygmunt, Barbara's husband, and he sent a telegram back saying come to Łódź with the baby at once. He would gladly meet us at the train station, help us in any way he could and take care of us. In the meantime, I had learned through an agency in Warsaw that my brother was alive in Jerusalem and was looking for members of his family. The agency provided his address and I wrote immediately.

The day I received his answer was the best day of my life, for I learned from him that my two sisters, Helen and Hania, were also alive. They had survived Auschwitz and Bergen-Belsen and were living in Germany and Czechoslovakia, respectively. That same day I received a telegram from each of them, and it was like a miracle from heaven.

EPILOGUE

We stayed in Łódź for three years. Zygmunt (Dr. Podlipski) used his influence to help me get a job as a practical nurse in a large government hospital. Because of a shortage of medical help, I performed the tasks of an RN. Later, I worked as director of a childcare center, where working mothers brought their babies from 7am until 5pm. Eddie attended a pre-kindergarten in the same building.

I missed my family. In the fall of 1950, Eddie and I emigrated to Israel to reunite with my brother, his wife and children, and my sister, Hania. A short time later, I met my future husband, Richard Lipski. We married in April of 1951 and lived in Ramat Gan. Eddie quickly learned to speak Hebrew, attended school, played soccer and made many friends. Three years later, we were blessed with a baby daughter, Miriam. The hot, humid climate and the difficult life in Israel did not agree with me. In March of 1958, we emigrated to the United States, where we reunited with my oldest sister, Helen and her family in Chicago.

Richard worked as a professional engineer and I held several jobs until I found my niche in a North Side hospital where I was employed for 21 years. We retired in 1983 and have been living in Tucson, Arizona, ever since. As the living patriarchs of our family, we most enjoy visiting with the younger generation, which has grown to 33, including our nieces and nephews and their wonderful spouses and children.

In the spring of 2003, Eddie passed away after a valiant fight with esophageal cancer which later spread to his bones. He left three wonderful sons—David, an attorney married to Robin, a doctor of osteopathy; Mark, a website designer and talented musician, who is married to Heidi, a graphic artist; and Tobias (Tobie), a recent law school graduate, currently studying for his MBA, and engaged to Katherine, who also is a student of the law. David and Robin have given us two delightful great-grandchildren, Justin and Elliot, who have fond memories of their "Papa Ed".

Our daughter, Miriam, is an interior designer and is married to Richard Glabman, a business executive. Their daughter Lindsay, our only granddaughter, is currently a student at Columbia University in New York; she is a gifted writer and an aspiring actress. Alex, our youngest grandson, is a very bright high school student and talented athlete. We look forward to sharing in their future successes.

Isabelle Choko

Chess champion, France, 1956

RES | **Isabelle CHOKO** (26 ans) est la nouvelle championne de France des échecs

Chess champion, France, 1956

One year old, Łódź

Isabelle Choko's parents on the eve of the war, Hersz Mottl and Yenta (née Galewska)

Isabelle Choko with her cousin, Edith
Sztrauch, Poland, 1933

Łódź ghetto school, ca. 7th grade. Known Survivors: Danusia Liebrach
(fourth row, 3rd from right); Isabelle Choko-Sztrauch (third row, 3rd from right);
Malwinka Gerson (third row, 2nd from right); Marysia Mazur (second row, 3rd from right);
Tusia Cygielberg (second row, 2nd from right); Jurek Halperin (front row, second from
right); Jozio Nadel (third row, 4th from right); Rutka Berlinska (second row, 2nd from left).
The photographer, Roman Freund, also survived

Room 11.   BED 18.

RECORD OF DRUGS ADMINISTERED.		
DRUG	DOSE	TIME AND DATE GIVEN
A.T. Serum		
A.T. Serum		
MORPHIA		
MORPHIA		

MALARIA TREATMENT.				
Date				
Atebrin (grms.)				
Quinine (grains)				
Other Drugs. Date and dosage				

MALARIA:— B.T. ☐   M.T. ☐   Q. ☐   Clinical ☐

DYSENTERY:—B.Ex. ☐   E. Hyst. ☐   Indef. Ex. ☐

SULPHONAMIDES:—If drugs of the sulphonamide group are given, A.F. W3211 "Sulphanilamide label" must be used to record dosages.

No further entries will be made on this form when A.F.1 1220 is taken into use.

(52-6417) J. Spender 150 rue du Bac Paris 7e

Army Form W3118.   R.A.F. Form 3118.   Naval Form M304.

FIELD MEDICAL CARD.

*Army No.................... Rank............... Service....................

Surname {BLOCK LETTERS} STRAUCH Initials Isabella
Nationality Polish   Sex F.
Unit................ Religion R.C. Age 16

*In the case of P's.O.W., write Serial No. allotted by A.F. W3000.

Insert X in square alongside CORRECT answer. DO NOT CROSS OUT.

Battle casualty ☐   Battle accident ☐   Injury ☐   Sick ☐

R.A.P. Unit................................   Date first seen 21. v. 45

Date of wound or onset of illness....................

Diagnosis of Unit M.O.:—
Mild Starvation Oedema.
....
....

Transferred to..........................

Date.................... M.O.'s Signature....................

Admitted to No.	Diagnosis:—		Date:—
..........Fd. Amb.			
..............F.D.S.			

CLINICAL NOTES AND TREATMENT.	(Dates and Units in which treated must be stated.)

P.H.   About 5/52 in Belsen.
H.P.I.   Diarrhoea bad and often. Vomiting o. Oedema of feet. Cough slight. Appetite - fair.
O.E.   Anaemia +. Skin dry. Sores on arms and legs and on buttocks.
E.   Tongue pale, smooth. Gums ✓.

21.v.45.   Plasma (conc) O j.   Diet I
Nicotinic acid 300 mgs daily.
22.v.45.   Diarrhoea a little better.
23.v.45.   Diarrhoea gone. Oedema almost gone. Off nicotinic acid.
Comp. vit. tabs ij bd.
24.v.45.   Tongue ulcerated. Now on Diet II.
Sores dressed with ung. anaesth. + prontosil powder.
29-8-45.   Zones de circulation inférieure aux ... TRAIT: Prontosil et Cugment 8g
3-VI-45   Modifie ac silence de 5 travers de doigt a la base ...
Souffle au dessus   Température le soir   Transpiration

10/6/45. Screen Lungs

15-6-45 L'état general bon   ... in plus de Température

18-6-45 La malade s'est un peu levé (sanctus)   pas de température
....   TRAIT: vit B

This card must NOT be destroyed. It must accompany the patient if he is evacuated to U.K. together with all temperature charts, additional clinical notes, etc., attached to the patient.

Medical report by British military physicians, Bergen Belsen

IDENTITETSKORT

Pièce d'Identité — Identitätskarte — Karta tożsamości

Denna talong tjänar såsom legitimation under den första tiden för Eder vistelse i Sverige. Den skall företes för gränskontrollmyndigheten och transportledaren och bör därför förvaras lätt tillgänglig.

Samma nummer, som Ni tilldelats i Lübeck, skall anbringas å allt Edert bagage.

Ce talon sert de pièce d' identité pendant le premier temps de votre séjour en Suède. Elle doit être produite au contrôle des passeports et à l'officier de transport et pour cela doit constamment être à la portée. Vous devez marquer tous vos bagages avec le même numéro, que vous avez reçu à Lübeck.

Dieser Abschnitt dient als Legitimation während der ersten Zeit Ihres Aufenthaltes in Schweden und soll stets zum Vorzeigen bereit-gehalten werden um die Kontrolle durch Grenzbehörden und Transportleiter zu erleichtern. Dieselbe Nummer, die Ihnen in Lübeck zugeteilt wurde, sollen Sie an jedem Ihrer Gepäckstücke anbringen.

Talon niniejszy służy jako tymczasowa legitymacja na pierwszy okres pobytu Pana(i) w Szwecji. Ze względu na konieczność legitymowania sie w podróży należy talon ten mieć stale przy sobie.

Przydzielonym w Lubece numerem należy oznaczyć również wszystkie należące do Pana(i) pakunki.

		Ser. L N:o *960*
Tillnamn Nom de famille Familienname Nazwisko	*STRAUCH*	**Vid registrering i Lübeck tilldelat nummer.** Le numéro de registration, que vous avez reçu à Lübeck.
Samtliga förnamn Tous les prénoms Sämtliche Vornamen Imiona	*IZABELLA*	Die Registrierungsnummer, die Ihnen in Lübeck zugeteilt wurde. Numer rejestracyjny, przydzielony Panu(i) w Lubece.

Födelsedatum		**Nationalitet**	
Né(e) le Geboren am Data urodzenia	*18 19 1930*	Nationalité **Staatsangehörigkeit** Narodowość	*POLEN*

Hemort Domicile Heimatort Stale miejsce zamieszkania	*LODZ*

Egenhändig namnteckning:
Signature de l'étranger:
Eigenhändige Unterschrift:
Własnoręczny podpis: *Strauch Izabela*

Passkontrollens noteringar — Place reservée — Reservierter Platz — Miejsce zarezerwowane

Inreseortens datumstämpel:

D
8 JULI 1945
POLISEN I NORRKÖPING
INRESAN

T
JULI 1945
Inresan Trelleborg

Hörd i Löystabruk 25.9.45. Statspolisen, Stockholm. S.M.

A. E. ANDERSSONS BOKTR. MALMÖ

Isabelle Choko's ID card issued in Sweden

In hospital before going to convalescent home, Late Aug./Sept. 1945, Sweden; Isabelle Choko (left) and another young girl (right) were the youngest of the group sent to Sweden

During convalescence in Sweden, November 1945; Far right Hanka Sercarz, Isabelle Choko's cousin

Altunaslad den 12/10 1945

Kappa 1 st, Klänning 1 st, Huvudbonad 1 st
Vantar 1 par, Halsduk 1 st, Underklänning 1 st
Korsett 1 st, Bysthållare 1 st, Kofta 1 st, Benkl 1 par
Strumpor 2 par, Skor 2 par,

Lövsta bruk 12/10 45
B. Brovall

List with contents of Isabelle Choko's "luggage" that she brought to France.

Arrival in France, February 1946

Isabelle Choko with uncle Zygmunt Sztrauch, aunt Toni Sztrauch and cousin
Georges Sztrauch, Paris, 1946

Frances Irwin

Frances Irwin with number tattooed on her arm upon arrival in Auschwitz

Bais Yaacov class. Frances Irwin's oldest sister is the second person from the right in the top row

Frances and Reuben Irwin on their wedding day. The couple standing beside them and who gave them away were unfamiliar

Frances Irwin and her husband, Reuben, in DP camp, Austria

Frances Irwin (second from right) and her husband, Reuben
(back), at "The Golden Doors," Germany, where they stayed
until their emigration to the U.S.A.

Frances Irwin standing at memorial stone for the four women who
smuggled ammunition into Auschwitz-Birkenau

Frances Irwin standing at Końskie memorial stone in Treblinka

Frances Irwin at cornerstone ceremony of
the United States Holocaust Memorial
Museum in Washington

בית חכנסת העתיק בקונסק

Old synagogue in Końskie burnt down by the Germans three days
after conquering the town

Lotti Kahana-Aufleger

Lotti Gottesman
Editor's note: Captions on the photos have been entered by the author.

Solomon Gottesman in WWI, Austrian army (leaning on a bicycle)

The Shaiovitz family (Lotti's grandparents' family)

Solomon, Adela and Lotti Gottesman

Siegfried and Lotti's wedding

Gitta on her way to Romania as an "orphan"

Lotti and Gitta Aufleger (september 1945)

Siegfried asking for a loving care of
Gitta as an "orphan"

Siegfried asking for loving care of Gitta as an "orphan"

Простянец с/совет.   Справка.

Простянецкого р-на   Видана настоящая гр.

Вінніцкой области   Ауфлейгер Зигфрид Давідовіч

№ 61 Апреля 1944 р.   в том, что он проживал в

с. Простянець.   Еврейском лагере на Простян-

нецком совхозе до освобож-

дения Красной Армией 13 го Марта

1944 года. Справка видана для

переезда на родину в г. Черновцы.

О чем Простянецкой с/совет

свідчить.

Председатель с/совета

Секретар-

Подписи пред. С/совета и секретаря

РИК простянець.

Отв. Секр.

7/IV-44г.

Siefried's permit to leave Trostinetz
camp liberated by the soviet army

Siegfried's permit to leave the Trostinetz camp, following its liberation by the Soviet army

Тростянец с/совет   Справка

Тростянец. р-на   Видана настоящая

Винн. области   гр. Боттеснан Саломон

№3. 1 Апреля 1944г.   Мейрович жена

м. Тростянец.   Адела Юдовна и дочка

          Лотие Соломоновна

в том что они проживали

в Еврейском Лагере на Тростянец

Ком совхозе до освобождения

Красной Армии 13 го Марта 1944г

Справка видана для переезда на

родину в гор. Черновицы О чем

Тростянецкой с/совет свидетельству

Пред с/совета (подпись)

Секретарь. (подпись)

(неразборчивая подпись)

Solomon, Adela and Lotti's permit to
leave Trostinetz camp (issued by the
Soviet authorities)

Soviet permit for Solomon, Adela, and Lotti to leave the Trostinetz camp

The Aufleger family home, Siebenburgerstrasse, Czernowitz

The Jewish school on Siebenburgerstrasse, Czernowitz

Lotti Kahana-Aufleger (1984)

Margit Raab Kalina

Margit Raab Kalina, 1937

The Raab family (from left to right): Ignac, Rosa, Margit, Leopold (Poldi), 1938

Margit Raab Kalina with brother Poldi (left)
and cousin Poldi Weitzner (right), 1933

Margit Raab Kalina, 1947

Jane Lipski

YADZIA SZPIGELMAN 11 y.old

11 years old, 1935

Jane Lipski (bottom) with her father, Mayer Josef Szpigelman; uncle, Mayloch Szpigelman; two great aunts, Sara Szpigelman and Rozia Hamburger, 1937

Jane Lipski's cousins, Szmulek and Szulim Szpigelman, 1939

Jane Lipski (middle front row), May 1940   Jane Lipski's friend Pola, 1942

Jane Lipski's sister, Hania

Jane Lipski, 1948

Jane Lipski and Eddie, January 1948, Łódź

Jane Lipski, Poland, 1948

СССР

Министерство
Внутренних Дел

УПРАВЛЕНИЕ
Исправительно-трудового
ЛАГЕРЯ

„А О"

20 Ноября 1947г.
№ 1835

СВИДЕТЕЛЬСТВО

Выдано тов. _Шпигельман Янине_

Иосифовне род. в _1924_ год

в том, что он_а_ закончил_а_ _12_ _ноября_ м-ц

1947 г. _семь месяцев_ курс_ов_ _Медицинских сестер_

и усвоил_а_ проходимые дисциплины на _____

а) специальные: _Внутренние болезни._ _____ 1

Хирургия 1

Основы сан. службы РККА. 1

Лекарствоведение, рецептура и эл. лат грам. 1

Анатомия и Физиология человека. 1

Гигиена. 1

Инфекционные болезни. 1

б) общеобразовательные: _МПВО_ 1

Глазные болезни 1

Болезни уха, горла и носа 1

Физиотерапия и Массаж 1

а также выполнил_а_ установленные практические работы: _____

При центральном Сангородке.

и выпущен_а_ с квалификацией _Медицинской сестры._

ОСНОВАНИЕ: Приказ по Управлению ИТЛ АО МЕД за № _607/л_

от _20 II.47._ и протокол экзамен. — квалификационной

комиссии от _12.11.47г_ № _____ и курсовых экзаменов

за №№ _____

Зам. Нач. Управления
ИТЛ АО МВД

Нач. Сектора
подготовки кадров

Начальник курсов _Мушкарский_

Jane Lipski's medical nursing certificate, 1947 (in Russian)

S S S R
M I N I S T R Y
OF THE INTERIOR

A D M I N I S T R A T I O N
OF THE CORRECTIVE - LABOR
C A M P
"A - O"
The 20th of November 1947
No. 1825

C E R T I F I C A T E

Issued to Miss SZPIGELMAN Janina daughter

of Joseph, born in the year 1924 certifying,

that she completed on the 12th of November

1947 a s e v e n m o n t h s course of m e d i c a l n u r s e s

and acquired passable training in:

a) SPECIALITY: Internal diseases 4

Surgery 4

Principles of sanitary service RKKA 4

Pharmacology, formulation of prescriptions & dosage . 4

Anatomy and physiology of the human body 4

Hygiene 4

Contagious diseases 4

b) Medical Training For Air Defense 4

Diseases of the eye 4

Diseases of ear, nose and throat 4

Physical therapy and massage 4

and also carried out the prescribed practical assignments at the Cent-

ral Sanitary Establishment and was graduated as a qualified Medical

Nurse. ---

B A S I S: Government Decree on Administration of CLC AO MVD
No.607/1 of 11.20.47 and protocol of the Board of
Examiners of 11.12.47 and course exams.

ROUND SEAL WITH NATIONAL EMBLEM: MINISTRY OF THE INTERIOR SSSR ADMINIS-
TRATION OF THE CORRECTIVE LABOR CAMP "A-O".

Deputy Chief of the Administration of CLC AO MVD: Signature illegible
Chief of Personnel Training Sector: Signature illegible
Chief in charge of the courses: Signature illegible

I, Adam Wilk of Chicago, ILLINOIS, Translator & Notary Public
in and for the County of Cook, State of Illinois, do hereby
certify that, having adequate knowledge of the Russian and English languages, I have made the aforegoing translation from the
Russian original and that it is a true and accurate English re-
production of the Russian document.

My Commission Expires Aug. 4, 1968

T R A N S L A T O R
& NOTARY PUBLIC * *

Translation of Russian medical nursing certificate

Walter, the pharmacist she befriended at hospital near Komi SSR

Dr. Zygmunt Podlipski

Eddie, 13 years old, 1957

Jane Lipski (right) with Poldek, Hela and Hania, 1980